MODERN WEAPONS

COMPARED AND CONTRASTED
MODERN WEAPONS

TOP SPEED · ARMAMENT · CALIBER · RATE OF FIRE

MARTIN J. DOUGHERTY

CHARTWELL
BOOKS, INC.

This edition published in 2012 by

CHARTWELL BOOKS, INC.
A division of
BOOK SALES, INC.
276 Fifth Avenue Suite 206
New York, New York 10001
USA

ISBN: 978-0-7858-2924-9

Project Editor: Michael Spilling
Design: Colin Hawes/Brian Rust
Picture Research: Terry Forshaw

Printed in China

Contents

Introduction

Modern weapons systems are fearsomely effective, but the question of which is the most effective is a difficult one. The criteria for judging a sniper rifle differ from those relevant to a submachine gun; an interceptor and a ground-attack aircraft require very different characteristics to properly fulfil their role.

Modern weapons systems are fearsomely effective, but the question of which is the most effective is a difficult one. The criteria for judging a sniper rifle differ from those relevant to a submachine gun; an interceptor and a ground-attack aircraft require very different characteristics to properly fulfil their role. We will thus make no attempt to compare hugely different weapons systems; each has a role to play in modern warfare and would flounder hopelessly if pushed into a different niche. However, within each general type it is possible to make a comparison using the characteristics that make a weapon effective for that purpose.

Comparing Like for Like

On the front lines of mobile warfare, armoured vehicles need to be fast, capable of crossing obstacles, well protected and armed with effective weapons. Their range dictates the distance over which operations can be conducted, and of course those that carry personnel need to be able to carry enough to get the job done. Not all of these factors are relevant to all armoured vehicles of course. For armoured fighting vehicles (tanks) the primary concerns are firepower and armour protection, whereas a reconnaissance vehicle could not be expected to carry such a heavy weapon but needs a long range and high speed.

Aircraft are normally optimized for either air-to-air combat or attacking ground targets. Range and speed are always important factors, but these are relative – an interceptor designed to prevent enemy bombers from entering friendly airspace needs to be faster than the bombers themselves, but does not need anything like the range of an intercontinental bomber as interceptors are by definition defensive aircraft. Armament is another critical factor for aircraft, and again is mission-dependent. A handful of air-to-air missiles will normally suffice, but a strike platform may need to carry large numbers of bombs in order to make its hazardous mission worthwhile.

For artillery and missile systems, the ability to hit a distant target with a payload large enough to disable it is the critical factor. Gun systems fire a relatively cheap shell compared with a long-range missile, but can put a large quantity of explosives into a target area for the same cost, giving good 'bang for buck' but at a shorter distance. For missiles, range and precision are important, along with the size of the warhead. Rate of fire and range are also important to both gun and rocket systems. Rockets are ideal for saturating a target in a short time, whereas gun systems can maintain a bombardment more or less indefinitely.

Relevant Criteria

The different types of small arms also fall into distinct niches. There is little point in comparing sniper rifles with assault rifles; they do very different jobs and both have their place. Yet the same characteristics can be used to compare weapons within a general type. The weight and size of the weapon is important in close combat or when moving in and out of vehicles. Rate of fire and magazine capacity are more important than accuracy in most situations, but when combat takes place at longer ranges it is the

Feature 1
Compares a similar aspect of weapons' capabilities (in this case, rate of climb).

Feature 2
Compares a relevant aspect of weapons' capability (here, maximum altitude).

Weapons Type
Features a number of similar weapons types to compare relevant data.

Mirage 2000 Rate of Climb
285m/sec
(935ft/sec)

Rate of Climb
Rate of climb is primarily determined by the power-to-weight ratio of the interceptor. Some designs gain an additional advantage by the use of a rocket booster, which greatly increases the power output of the interceptor for a short time.

F-22 Raptor Rate of Climb
254m/sec
(833ft/sec)

MiG-25 Rate of Climb
208m/sec
(682ft/sec)

MiG-31 Rate of Climb
208m/sec
(682ft/sec)

Tornado ADV Rate of Climb
76.7m/sec
(252ft/sec)

MiG-25 Altitude
20,700m
(67,913ft)

MiG-31 Altitude
20,600m
(67,585ft)

F-22 Raptor Altitude
19,812m
(65,000ft)

Mirage 2000 Altitude
17,060m
(55,971ft)

Tornado ADV Altitude
15,240m
(50,000ft)

Maximum Altitude
Speed is of little use if hostile aircraft can simply fly past above the interceptor's ceiling. However, it is not necessary to reach the same altitude as an intruder; only to get high enough to bring it within missile range.

Interceptors 1
Rate of Climb and Maximum Altitude

▶ **Mikoyan-Gurevich MiG-25**
▶ **Mikoyan-Gurevich MiG-31**
▶ **Lockheed Martin**
   F-22 Raptor
▶ **Dassault Mirage 2000**
▶ **Panavia Tornado ADV**

As the name suggests, an interceptor is a defensive fighter aircraft whose primary role is to prevent hostile and unknown aircraft from penetrating friendly airspace. This may be a fairly benign interception, where an unidentified aircraft is 'eyeballed' to determine its nature and escorted out of restricted airspace or, if in distress, led to a safe landing. However, it may also be necessary to prevent bombers or strike aircraft from reaching their targets, ideally by intercepting them as far out as possible.

A multi-role aircraft or an air-superiority fighter can make a good interceptor so long as it meets two crucial needs: an interceptor must be able to climb to a high altitude, and do it quickly. Many bombers can fly very high and very fast, creating a need for a specialist aircraft that can reach the necessary altitude before the bomber formation is past and out of range. Straight-line speed, climb rate and maximum altitude are more important than agility; many specialist interceptors are poor dogfighters but possess tremendously powerful engines.

A good interceptor force can be a powerful deterrent to a potential aggressor. Historically, many nations have tested the resolve as well as the capabilities of others by probing at their airspace. This is sometimes under the guise of a 'navigational error' and sometimes a blatant violation. An interception can be a tense moment, but if successfully carried out it is a clear demonstration of both the means and the will to preserve sovereignty over local airspace.

OPPOSITE: A Dassault Mirage 2000 fires a Matra Super 530 air-to-air missile. The Mirage 2000 is also armed with two DEFA 554 30mm (1.2in) cannon with 125 rounds per gun, packing a heavy punch. More recently, the Mirage has taken on many of the features designed for the new Dassault Rafale.

18   Compare and Contrast

Compare and Contrast   19

Specifications
Includes specifications for precise comparison of data.

Analysis
Includes concise analysis to provide context for comparison.

precision of the weapon that makes all the difference.

Thus within each category of weapons we have chosen relevant criteria for comparison. There is still no clear or simple answer to vague questions like 'What is the best sniper rifle?' but it is possible to choose the one best suited to the task at hand by comparing its performance in the relevant area. There may be no 'best

rocket-artillery system' as such, but it will become clear that some are much more effective than others at certain ranges, or can deliver a much greater payload in a single salvo. The trick is to ask the right questions: 'What is the best armoured vehicle?' is meaningless. 'Which reconnaissance vehicle gives the best balance of speed and firepower?' is a valid question that can be answered with hard data.

Air Power

Powered flight is a little over a century old, and has been an indispensable part of military strategy for most of that time. Ultimately, what happens in the air is of no consequence unless it affects the course of operations on the ground or at sea. Even an unarmed aircraft can provide reconnaissance information or transport a small quantity of critical supplies, and therefore affect the strategic situation. Lightly armed, crudely converted civilian aircraft have been fielded in various conflicts; any air power is better than no air power. However, for true effectiveness, specialist aircraft are required.

Combat aircraft tend to specialize in one area: air-to-air, ground attack or close support of friendly troops, and strike. There is room for significant variation within each general role: for example, an air-superiority fighter will have different characteristics to an interceptor, even though both exist to shoot down enemy aircraft.

LEFT: A Soviet-built MiG-29 'Fulcrum' from Germany's Fighter Wing 73 'Steinhoff' fires a radar-guided AA-10 'Alamo' short-burn air-to-air missile, 2003. Once adversaries for NATO fighter pilots, MiG-29s are now flown by the German Air Force as part of NATO.

Air-superiority Fighters 1

Combat Radius and Ferry Range

▶ **McDonnell Douglas F-15C Eagle**
▶ **Chengdu J-10A**
▶ **Sukhoi Su-30**
▶ **Lockheed Martin F-22 Raptor**
▶ **Eurofighter Typhoon**

Air-superiority fighters, as their name suggests, exist mainly to contest control of the skies with enemy fighters, and to shoot down bombers, attack and reconnaissance aircraft. To this end, they must be fast and agile as well as able to carry a reasonable warload. Ideally, attacks are made at medium range with radar-homing missiles, which requires relatively little manoeuvring, but a fighter may become involved in a close-range fight using short-range missiles and possibly its gun.

'Dogfighting' in the traditional sense is avoided wherever possible by fighter pilots, who prefer, if they can, to make a fast pass, shoot and dash clear of any retaliation. If necessary, the fighter can come around and make another pass. Although this is less fuel intensive than a 'turning fight' – i.e. a dogfight – the rapid acceleration required for a gun pass eats into the fighter's fuel reserves. Thus combat radius tends to be much less than the aircraft's maximum range.

When flying a long distance, for example when ferrying itself between bases, a fighter cruises at an economical throttle setting and optimum height. If, for any reason, the pilot is forced to use a lot of throttle – for example, to avoid an attack whilst en route – then he may run short of fuel and not be able to reach his destination. Tanker aircraft can be used to allow a fighter to cruise to a distant combat area before conducting an in-flight refuelling. The aircraft's full combat radius is then available during the active part of the mission.

TOP RIGHT: A Russian Sukhoi Su-27 'Flanker' fires an R-73 (AA-11 'Archer') air-to-air missile. Highly rated, the Su-27 is one of the most exported aircraft of the post-Cold War period. It has recently been superseded by the Su-30, the latest member of the 'Flanker' family.

Combat Radius

A fighter's combat radius is at best an estimate, based on the assumption that the pilot will make considerable use of high-throttle settings during combat. Aircraft with afterburners eat through their fuel at an alarming rate.

J-10A Radius
1600km
(994 miles)

F-15C Eagle Radius
1967km
(1222 miles)

F-15C Eagle Ferry Range
5550km
(3449 miles)

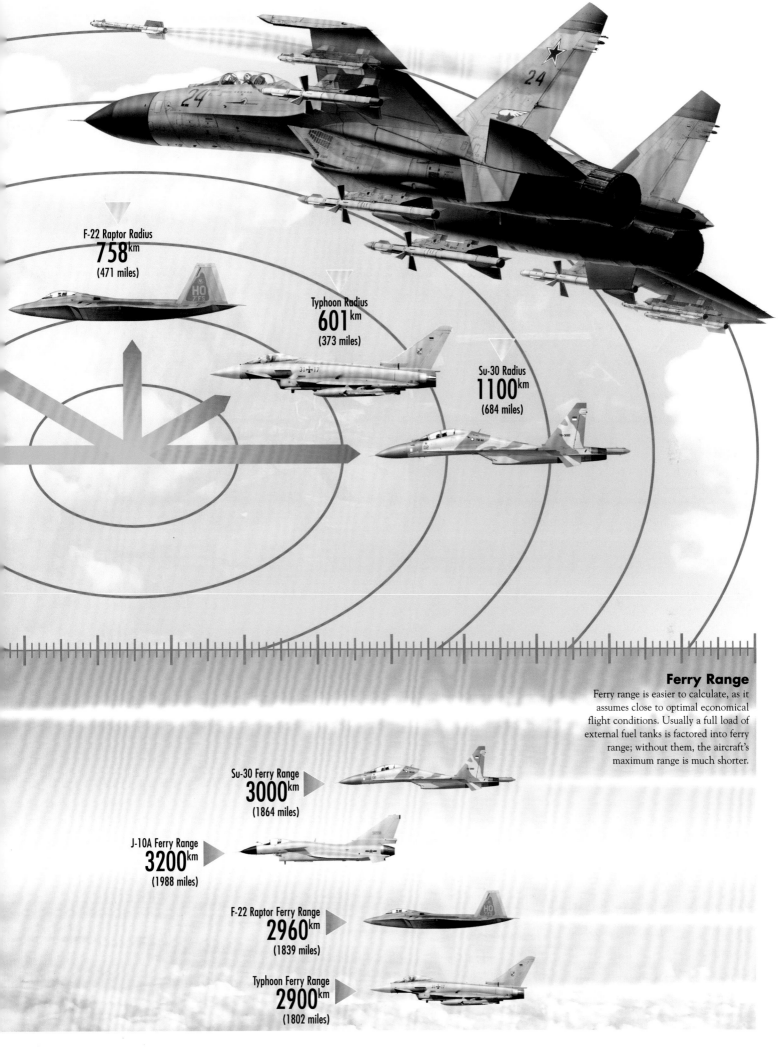

F-22 Raptor Radius
758km
(471 miles)

Typhoon Radius
601km
(373 miles)

Su-30 Radius
1100km
(684 miles)

Ferry Range

Ferry range is easier to calculate, as it assumes close to optimal economical flight conditions. Usually a full load of external fuel tanks is factored into ferry range; without them, the aircraft's maximum range is much shorter.

Su-30 Ferry Range
3000km
(1864 miles)

J-10A Ferry Range
3200km
(1988 miles)

F-22 Raptor Ferry Range
2960km
(1839 miles)

Typhoon Ferry Range
2900km
(1802 miles)

F-15C Eagle Speed
Mach **2.5**

Su-35 Speed
Mach **2.25**

Air-superiority Fighters 2

Maximum Speed

▶ **McDonnell Douglas F-15C Eagle**
▶ **Chengdu J-10A**
▶ **Sukhoi Su-35**
▶ **Lockheed Martin F-22 Raptor**
▶ **Eurofighter Typhoon**

Speed is of critical importance to a fighter aircraft for several reasons. A fighter must be able to get into range to fire or launch its weapons. If a hostile aircraft is faster, the fighter may be able to simply flee, or at least prolong a 'stern-chase' situation until the enemy runs short of fuel. Height is an advantage here, allowing the fighter to use gravity in a dive to gain extra speed, but much depends on the power of its engines and its aerodynamic design.

Speed is also important in combat. A fast fighter can make a pass and then escape before the enemy can react; the longer it is in range, the more likely it becomes that the enemy will be able to launch a missile in pursuit. A fast aircraft can also come around for another attack, or head for a different target, in a shorter time frame. Speed usually correlates with acceleration, so a fast fighter is usually also one that can regain its speed soon after 'scrubbing off' speed in a tight turn or a climb.

Afterburners, which put additional fuel into the hot jet exhaust to generate additional thrust, use a huge amount of fuel for the extra speed they provide. They are thus used when the plane needs to 'sprint' or to accelerate rapidly, such as during take-off or combat. The new generation of fighters tends to use 'supercruise' engines, which give many of the benefits of afterburners without the immense fuel expenditure.

OPPOSITE: A US Air Force Lockheed Martin F/A-22 Raptor (left) and a McDonnell Douglas F-15C Eagle (right) fly in formation. The two paired up after an historic fly-by by the F/A-22 at the First Flight Centennial Celebration at the Wright Brothers National Memorial in Kill Devil Hills, North Carolina, in 2003.

Maximum Speed

Top speed is measured in Mach numbers, which are a multiple of the speed of sound at a given altitude. The aircraft's actual velocity may change with altitude; as a rule, greater height equates to greater speed.

F-22 Raptor Speed
Mach **2.25**

J-10A Speed
Mach **2.2**

Typhoon Speed
Mach **2.0**

Gun Armament

The choice of gun armament for a fighter is problematical. Some designers favour a 20mm (0.79in) gun with an enormous rate of fire, while others use 27mm (1.06in) or larger cannon firing more slowly and therefore requiring less ammunition to be carried.

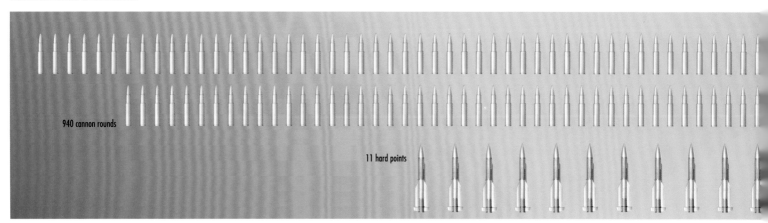

940 cannon rounds

11 hard points

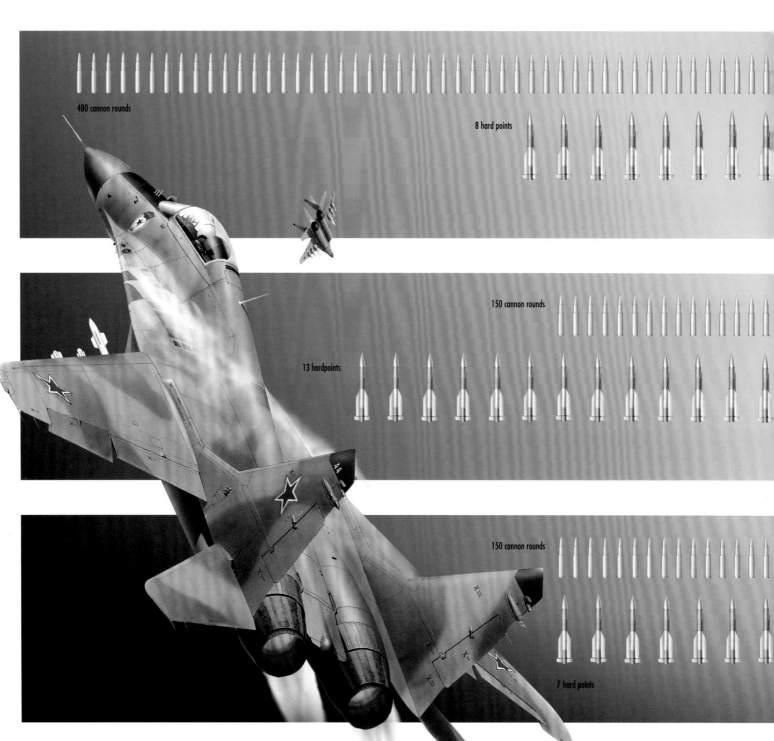

480 cannon rounds

8 hard points

150 cannon rounds

13 hardpoints

150 cannon rounds

7 hard points

McDonnell Douglas F-15C Eagle
Armed with one 20mm (0.79in) M61A1 Vulcan cannon.

Lockheed Martin F-22 Raptor
Armed with one 20mm (0.79in) M61A2 Vulcan cannon.

Eurofighter Typhoon
Armed with one 27mm (1.06in) Mauser BK-27 cannon.

Mikoyan-Gurevich MiG-29
Armed with one 30mm (1.2in) GSh-30 cannon.

Air-superiority Fighters 3

Number of Cannon Rounds and Hard Points

▶ **McDonnell Douglas F-15C Eagle**
▶ **Lockheed Martin F-22 Raptor**
▶ **Eurofighter Typhoon**
▶ **Mikoyan-Gurevich MiG-29**

Most combat aircraft carry a gun of some kind. Often this is a rapid-fire rotary cannon, though sometimes more conventional cannon are carried instead. Lighter weapons such as machine guns are incapable of damaging most modern combat aircraft even if they have the range to achieve a hit. Cannon ammunition is heavy, and a high rate of fire is necessary to give a reasonable chance of a hit on a fleeting target. Although the numbers of rounds carried can be very high, this ammunition supply often equates to just a few seconds of continuous firing.

Other weapons, such as bombs and missiles, are carried on 'hard points', which can often also carry fuel tanks or equipment such as radar jammers or reconnaissance pods. A large number of hard points equates to a powerful and/or highly flexible warload, but not all hard points can carry all weapons. Big and heavy weapons such as large long-range missiles can only be carried on hard points under the fuselage or close to it on the wings. Outer-wing hard points and wingtip rails can carry lighter weapons.

Some smaller weapons can be carried in multiples on a hard point, further complicating decisions about how to arm an aircraft. A mix of extra fuel tanks, large medium-range radar-guided missiles and smaller short-range infrared-guided missiles gives the fighter a flexible capability. There is often a standard air-superiority loadout for any given aircraft, or several for use in well-defined circumstances. However, armament must be balanced against overall weight – more weapons means more fuel used to fly the same distance at the same speed.

OPPOSITE: With a design that emphasized manoeuvrability, the MiG-29 'Fulcrum' was one of the few Soviet-era fighters to remain in service after the break-up of the Soviet Union.

Multi-role Aircraft

Payload

- ▶ **Lockheed Martin F-35 Lightning II**
- ▶ **Sukhoi Su-30MK2**
- ▶ **Eurofighter Typhoon**
- ▶ **Saab JAS 39 Gripen C**
- ▶ **Mikoyan-Gurevich MiG-35**

Modern multi-role aircraft can carry a very significant payload, but there are always trade-offs to be made. Long-range or powerful weapons are of necessity large and heavy, which limits the weight and space available for other weapons or fuel tanks. Aircraft such as the Eurofighter Typhoon have numerous hard points on the fuselage and wings, allowing a highly variable loadout, but this is only part of the story; they must also have the necessary electronics to use a wide range of weapons systems.

Multi-role aircraft are less efficient in any particular role than specialist designs, but their flexibility goes a long way towards offsetting any weakness. Once air superiority is won, aircraft that were serving as fighters can be retasked to ground attack or other roles, effectively increasing the number of platforms available for any given mission for the same amount of budget pounds. Ground-attack platforms can be switched to an air-superiority role if the enemy air force resurges. This is particularly useful for carrier-borne forces using aircraft such as the F-35 Lightning II; fewer different classes of aircraft aboard a carrier means a simpler supply and maintenance situation.

Recently, air forces have become interested in the 'swing-role' concept, whereby aircraft set out from base with a mixed armament and switch between roles during the mission as necessary. This permits part of the force to act as cover against enemy fighters while other aircraft make their attack, then to switch to the ground-attack role while the 'fighter' role is taken over by those whose ground-attack munitions have been expended.

Payload

A large theoretical maximum payload allows a highly flexible loadout, but it is not always possible to take full advantage of an aircraft's capacity. Heavy loading increases the required length of runway, and it may be beyond the capacity of an aircraft carrier's catapult to get a fully laden aircraft off the deck.

F-35 Lightning II
8.1 tonnes
(8 tons)

Su-30MK2
8 tonnes
(7.9 tons)

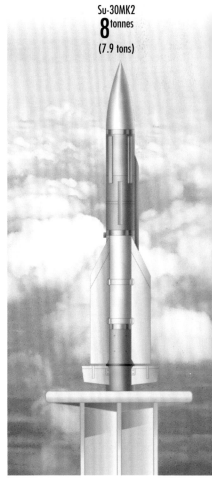

tonnes
8.1

tonnes
8.0

Lockheed Martin F-35 Lightning II

Sukhoi Su-30MK2

A Saab JAS 39 Gripen C fighter fires an MBDA Meteor beyond-visual-range air-to-air missile.

MiG-35 Payload
5tonnes
(4.9 tons)

Typhoon
7.5tonnes
(7.4 tons)

JAS 39 Gripen C
6.5tonnes
(6.4 tons)

tonnes
7.5

tonnes
6.5

tonnes
5.0

Eurofighter Typhoon

Saab JAS 39 Gripen C

Mikoyan-Gurevich MiG-35

Mirage 2000 Rate of Climb
285m/sec
(935ft/sec)

Rate of Climb

Rate of climb is primarily determined by the power-to-weight ratio of the interceptor. Some designs gain an additional advantage by the use of a rocket booster, which greatly increases the power output of the interceptor for a short time.

F-22 Raptor Rate of Climb
254m/sec
(833ft/sec)

MiG-25 Rate of Climb
208m/sec
(682ft/sec)

MiG-31 Rate of Climb
208m/sec
(682ft/sec)

Tornado ADV Rate of Climb
76.7m/sec
(252ft/sec)

MiG-25 Altitude
20,700m
(67,913ft)

MiG-31 Altitude
20,600m
(67,585ft)

F-22 Raptor Altitude
19,812m
(65,000ft)

Mirage 2000
Altitude
17,060m
(55,971ft)

Tornado ADV
Altitude
15,240m
(50,000ft)

Maximum Altitude

Speed is of little use if hostile aircraft can simply fly past above the interceptor's ceiling. However, it is not necessary to reach the same altitude as an intruder; only to get high enough to bring it within missile range.

Interceptors 1

Rate of Climb and Maximum Altitude

▶ **Mikoyan-Gurevich MiG-25**
▶ **Mikoyan-Gurevich MiG-31**
▶ **Lockheed Martin**
  F-22 Raptor
▶ **Dassault Mirage 2000**
▶ **Panavia Tornado ADV**

As the name suggests, an interceptor is a defensive fighter aircraft whose primary role is to prevent hostile and unknown aircraft from penetrating friendly airspace. This may be a fairly benign interception, where an unidentified aircraft is 'eyeballed' to determine its nature and escorted out of restricted airspace or, if in distress, led to a safe landing. However, it may also be necessary to prevent bombers or strike aircraft from reaching their targets, ideally by intercepting them as far out as possible.

A multi-role aircraft or an air-superiority fighter can make a good interceptor so long as it meets two crucial needs: an interceptor must be able to climb to a high altitude, and do it quickly. Many bombers can fly very high and very fast, creating a need for a specialist aircraft that can reach the necessary altitude before the bomber formation is past and out of range. Straight-line speed, climb rate and maximum altitude are more important than agility; many specialist interceptors are poor dogfighters but possess tremendously powerful engines.

A good interceptor force can be a powerful deterrent to a potential aggressor. Historically, many nations have tested the resolve as well as the capabilities of others by probing at their airspace. This is sometimes under the guise of a 'navigational error' and sometimes a blatant violation. An interception can be a tense moment, but if successfully carried out, it is a clear demonstration of both the means and the will to preserve sovereignty over local airspace.

OPPOSITE: A Dassault Mirage 2000 fires a Matra Super 530 air-to-air missile. The Mirage 2000 is also armed with two DEFA 554 30mm (1.2in) cannon with 125 rounds per gun, packing a heavy punch. More recently, the Mirage has taken on many of the feaures designed for the new Dassault Rafale.

Air-to-Air Weapons

A wartime interception mission may be a technical exercise rather than a tactical one. The pilot may reach a suitable launching point for his missiles, use radar to lock them onto a target, launch and track his weapons and then return to base without ever coming into visual range of his opponents.

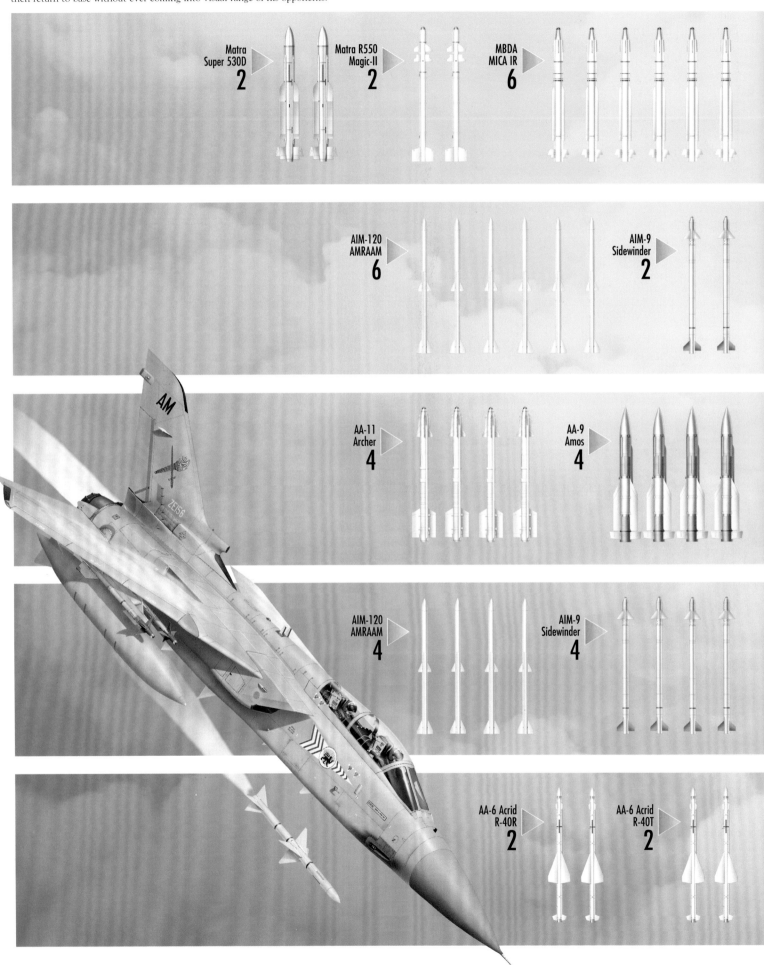

Matra
Super 530D
2

Matra R550
Magic-II
2

MBDA
MICA IR
6

AIM-120
AMRAAM
6

AIM-9
Sidewinder
2

AA-11
Archer
4

AA-9
Amos
4

AIM-120
AMRAAM
4

AIM-9
Sidewinder
4

AA-6 Acrid
R-40R
2

AA-6 Acrid
R-40T
2

Mirage 2000

F-22 Raptor

MiG-31

Tornado ADV

MiG-25P

Interceptors 2
Air-to-Air Weapons

▶ **Dassault Mirage 2000**
▶ **Lockheed Martin F-22 Raptor**
▶ **Mikoyan-Gurevich MiG-31**
▶ **Panavia Tornado ADV**
▶ **Mikoyan-Gurevich MiG-25P**

Most interceptors are primarily missile platforms. Some dispense with a gun entirely in order to save weight, and many lack the agility necessary to make effective use of a cannon. Similarly, missile armament may include short-range 'dogfight' missiles, but long-range radar-guided weapons can be more useful for the interception role. To use longer-range weapons, the interceptor only need get within launching distance rather than having to jockey for a firing position against a wildly evading aircraft.

Long-range missiles greatly increase the area an interceptor can cover. The MiG-31 can launch the Mach 4.5 AA-9 Amos missile, with a range of 160km (99.4 miles). This missile was developed to engage even the extremely fast, high-altitude SR-71 Blackbird reconnaissance aircraft; it can tackle anything else that comes into range. Other missiles are more modest, but with engagement ranges of 30–50km (18.6–31 miles) or more, they permit the interceptor to function as a mobile missile battery, engaging multiple targets without approaching closely.

Interceptors generally operate fairly close to friendly airspace and need be less concerned with enemy fighters than less defensively orientated aircraft. However, it is possible that an interceptor might become involved in close-range combat against an agile fighter-bomber or fighter escorts sent along with a strike package. In such a situation, a pure missile-platform-type interceptor, optimized for rate of climb and straight-line speed, would be at a disadvantage. Aircraft such as the F-22 Raptor, primarily an air-superiority fighter but capable of undertaking the interceptor role, are better suited to such circumstances.

OPPOSITE: Some interceptors are specialist designs, others like the Tornado Air Defence Variant (shown here firing an AIM-9L Sidewinder air-to-air missile) are adaptations of multi-role aircraft.

Ground-attack Aircraft 1

Warload

- ▶ **Fairchild Republic A-10A Thunderbolt**
- ▶ **Sukhoi Su-25TM**
- ▶ **Hawker Harrier GR3**
- ▶ **North American Rockwell OV-10D Bronco**
- ▶ **Embraer Super Tucano**

Ground-attack aircraft tend to be somewhat slower than fighters, and may not be as agile. Their primary role is to accurately put bombs, rockets and missiles down on a ground target, and they often operate at very low level to do so. This exposes the aircraft to hazards ranging from specialist anti-aircraft weapons to optimistic small-arms fire. While some aircraft, notably the A-10 Thunderbolt, are heavily armoured against ground fire, the best defence is to come in low and fast, make an attack pass and then leave the area at speed. When flying at low level, ground-attack aircraft can benefit from ground cover, effectively hiding behind hills and forests.

The A-10 and Su-25 are powerful platforms carrying a large warload. They are capable of striking multiple targets during a mission and can inflict serious damage on an enemy force. For precision targets such as bridges and bunkers, they can use guided missiles or bombs, though these are not always necessary. Great precision is possible, even with unguided ordnance, when flying relatively slowly at low altitude.

However, such capabilities come at a price that many air forces cannot afford. Aircraft such as the Bronco and Super Tucano may look dated, but they can be very effective in the close-support or light strike role. These simple, cheap, easy-to-maintain aircraft are most effective against insurgent forces that lack anti-aircraft capability, and for this reason are often referred to as COIN (counter-insurgency) aircraft.

Warload

The A-10 Thunderbolt carries a massive warload that almost equals those of the other three aircraft combined. However, it lacks the range and low-level capabilities of the Super Tucano or Bronco, and costs a great deal more to operate.

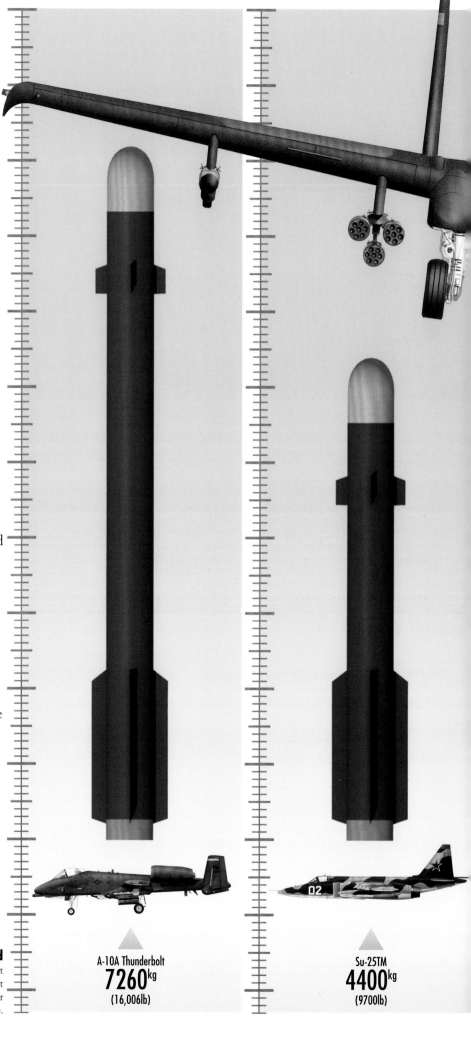

A-10A Thunderbolt
7260 kg
(16,006lb)

Su-25TM
4400 kg
(9700lb)

LEFT: The A-10A Thunderbolt is a pure ground-attack aircraft, heavily armoured and equipped with an immensely powerful 30mm (1.2in) cannon capable of destroying tanks. In addition, it can carry a wide range of guided and unguided weapons and can even launch short-range heat-seeking air-to-air missiles. These are primarily used against enemy helicopters.

Harrier GR3
2268kg
(5000lb)

OV-10D Bronco
1633kg
(3600lb)

Super Tucano
1550kg
(3417lb)

Ground-attack Aircraft 2

Endurance and Combat Radius

▶ **Fairchild Republic A-10A Thunderbolt**

▶ **Sukhoi Su-25TM**

▶ **McDonnell Douglas AV-8B Harrier II**

▶ **North American Rockwell OV-10D Bronco**

▶ **Embraer Super Tucano**

Endurance and combat radius are somewhat related for a ground-attack aircraft. However, much depends upon the aircraft's speed – a fast jet can go a lot further in an hour than a light piston-engine aircraft. For an aircraft intended to take off, fly to the vicinity of a high-value target and attack it before returning to base, speed and radius of action are more important than endurance as such. Fast strike aircraft are sometimes called upon to loiter whilst awaiting a call for support from ground troops, but their speed is such that often they can go straight from the runway to the strike area.

Endurance is important for aircraft that might have to search for targets or remain on call in a combat area for an extended period before making an attack. High-endurance, light strike aircraft are excellent COIN platforms for this reason; they can loiter or search for targets for several hours, and hunt down minor enemy assets such as small groups of armed insurgents on which it might not be worth 'wasting' a fast jet strike.

Light aircraft such as the OV-10D Bronco have also at times been used as a forward-air-control platform, from which an officer can direct the actions of faster and more capable strike aircraft. Their primary value, however, is in their low cost. A light strike platform, equipped with low-cost bombs and cannon, still represents a significant strike capability and can be available in sufficient numbers to cover a wide area, with at least one aircraft constantly on call for ground support.

OPPOSITE: The Su-25TM has 11 underwing and under-fuselage hard points, allowing it to carry up to 4400kg (9700lb) of disposable weaponry. Hard points include rails for two AA-8 Aphid (R-60), or other, air-to-air missiles.

Super Tucano Endurance
8.67 hours

OV-10D Bronco Endurance
5.5 hours

A-10A Thunderbolt Endurance
2 hours

Su-25TM Endurance
2 hours

AV-8B Harrier II Endurance
1.5 hours

Endurance
The enormous endurance of aircraft like the Super Tucano must be balanced against their relatively low performance – a significant proportion of their flight time is spent transiting to and from the combat area. A lower-endurance but faster jet can be there and back before the light strike platform has reached its target.

Combat Radius

A short-ranged strike platform must be based close to the battle area, or it will not be able to reach its targets. This necessitates operating from improvised air bases much of the time, and requires a robust and easily maintained aircraft.

OV-10D Bronco Radius
1380km
(857 miles)

Super Tucano Radius
1325km
(823 miles)

A-10A Thunderbolt Radius
460km
(286 miles)

Su-25TM Radius
400km
(249 miles)

AV-8B Harrier II Radius
370km
(230 miles)

Maximum Speed
High-performance strike platforms come at a price, but the ability to sprint into a target area, deliver an attack and then retire just as quickly greatly enhances survivability when operating in hostile or contested airspace.

F-111 Speed
Mach **2.5**

F-15E Strike Eagle Speed
Mach **2.5**

Su-24MK Speed
Mach **2.0**

F-35A Speed
Mach **1.6**

F-117 Nighthawk Speed
Mach **0.92**

Loaded Weight
The F-117, which trades speed for stealth, was used during the Gulf War to attack heavily defended targets that other aircraft could not reach, and to eliminate air defences and open a path for less stealthy platforms.

Strike Aircraft 1

Maximum Speed and Loaded Weight

▶ **General Dynamics F-111**
▶ **McDonnell Douglas F-15E Strike Eagle**
▶ **Sukhoi Su-24MK**
▶ **Lockheed Martin F-35A**
▶ **Lockheed F-117 Nighthawk**

F-111 Loaded Weight
37,600kg
(82,894lb)

Su-24MK Loaded Weight
38,040kg
(83,864lb)

F-15E Strike Eagle Loaded Weight
36,700kg
(80,910lb)

F-117 Nighthawk Loaded Weight
23,800kg
(52,470lb)

F-35A Loaded Weight
22,470kg
(49,538lb)

Strike is a role rather than a precise aircraft type; some strike platforms are derived from fighter designs, whilst others are effectively light bombers. Speed is important to a strike platform, enabling it to make its attack and then escape before retaliation can be brought to bear, and to get quickly to and from the target area. The longer the aircraft is aloft, the greater the risk it runs.

Most strike aircraft can carry a large warload, but some that are capable of carrying out the strike role, along with various other tasks, are more limited. The small warload of the F-35 is offset by its other capabilities; it is stealthy and, in some variants, can make a vertical take-off and landing from an air base so damaged by enemy attacks as to be unusable by conventional aircraft.

BELOW: Stores are carried externally on fuselage and wing hard points, as shown on the underside this Su-24 'Fencer' (below). Although some strike aircraft also have an internal weapons bay, this cannot rival the enormous capacity of a strategic bomber.

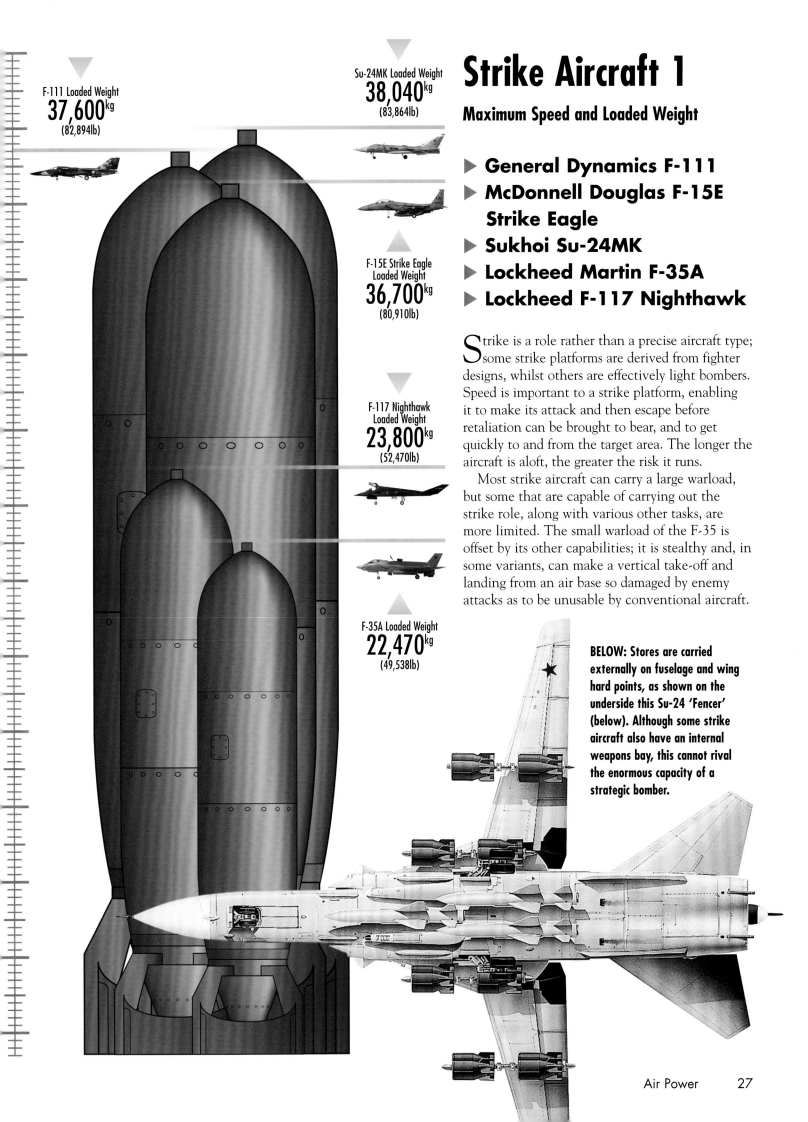

Strike Aircraft 2

Combat Radius

▶ **General Dynamics F-111**
▶ **McDonnell Douglas F-15E Strike Eagle**
▶ **Lockheed Martin F-35A**
▶ **Sukhoi Su-30MK**
▶ **Sukhoi Su-24MK**

Strike aircraft occupy a niche between dedicated close-support ground-attack platforms and strategic bombers, and can usually fulfil the roles of both of these types to some degree. They can usually deliver guided and unguided bombs, rockets, missiles and specialist ordnance such as runway-cratering munitions. Some carry air-to-air missiles and can be reasonably effective in the air-to-air role, though only those derived from fighter designs stand much chance against a pure air-superiority aircraft.

Strike platforms need to be able to cruise a long distance whilst carrying a potent warload, but cannot match the long-range performance of strategic bombers. However, they are extremely versatile, and can attack from a range of altitudes against various targets. Many are equally adept in the anti-ship role, which requires specialist munitions and the ability to locate distant targets in a wide expanse of ocean. Range is a significant asset in this role, not least because enemy shipping is rarely encountered close to friendly air bases.

Strike aircraft may be called upon to assist ground forces by attacking enemy armoured vehicles in close proximity, or to penetrate deep into enemy territory to destroy a strategic bridge, power station or supply dump. Their warload can be tailored to the mission at hand, or sometimes more diverse weaponry is carried. A mixed loadout enables the aircraft to respond to requests for assistance from ground forces or to be retasked to attack targets of opportunity. Using a large laser-guided bomb against a single tank may be overkill, but it is certainly effective. In the Gulf War this practice became known as 'tank plinking'.

OPPOSITE: The F-15E Strike Eagle was developed from the F-15 Eagle, a high-altitude fighter designed under the maxim 'not a pound for air-to-ground'. Like the somewhat similar Russian Su-30, the F-15E proved to be a formidable strike platform.

Combat Radius

The diagram shows the strike aircraft's combat radius from a fixed point, the French capital city, Paris. The shortest-ranged strike platforms are capable of flying halfway across Europe and back in a single sortie. Those with 'longer legs' can achieve much greater distances, enabling the aircraft to attack from bases located well back from the combat area.

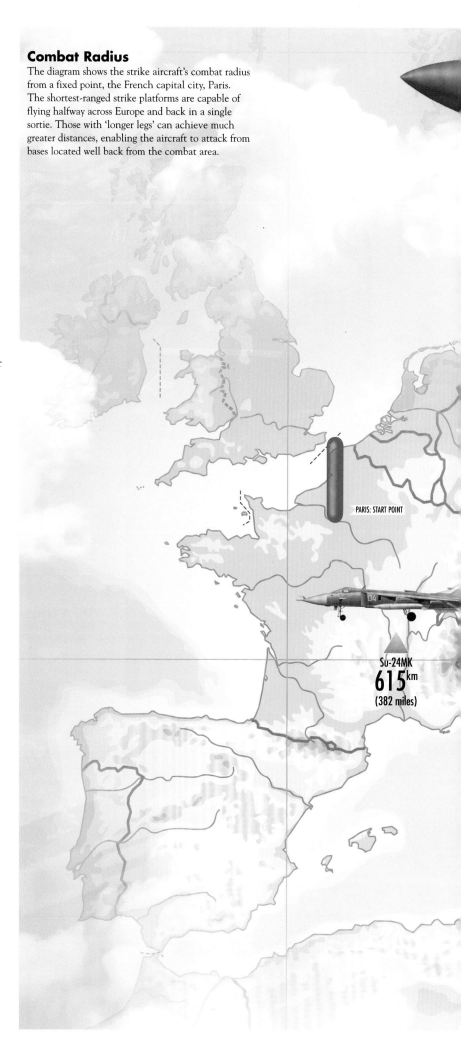

PARIS: START POINT

Su-24MK
615 km
(382 miles)

Su-30MK
1010km
(628 miles)

Vienna

Milan

Budapest

F-15E Strike Eagle
1271km
(790 miles)

Rome

F-35A
1090km
(677 miles)

Athens

F-111
2140km
(1330 miles)

Bombers 1

Warload

▶ **Rockwell B-1 Lancer**
▶ **Tupolev Tu-160**
▶ **Boeing B-52 Stratofortress**
▶ **Northrop Grumman
  B-2 Spirit**
▶ **Tupolev Tu-95MS**

Strategic bombers were, until recently, dedicated to deep-penetration attacks on targets of strategic importance such as industrial areas or cities. Originally this was carried out with highly inaccurate 'dumb' bombs, necessitating the dropping of huge amounts of ordnance to hit a given target. Even with good aim, a torrent of unguided bombs will scatter considerably, causing widespread rather than concentrated damage.

The invention of nuclear weapons created a much greater probability of totally destroying the target, and for many years the strategic-bomber force remained on alert as part of a policy of nuclear deterrence. The probability of having to deliver nuclear weapons was always, fortunately, rather low, and even at the height of the Cold War the bomber force retained its conventional capabilities. These were augmented by the ability to launch missiles, enabling the bomber to launch an attack from well short of the target and greatly enhancing survivability.

The creation of affordable guided bombs has improved the effectiveness of bomber attacks using conventional munitions, vastly reducing the number of bombs that must be dropped to obtain a reasonable chance of a hit. In addition, GPS-guided bombs have enabled heavy bombers to move into the close-support role.

Today's ground forces can call for a precision strike from a B-52 Stratofortress that may have entered service half a century or more ago. With a huge bombload aboard, a B-52 can deliver a single weapon or multiple bombs to within a few metres of the aim point … and keep on doing it.

RIGHT: More recent bombers such as the B-1 and Tu-160 are faster than earlier types, and the B-2 is almost infinitely more stealthy, but the venerable B-52 (top right) and Tu-95 continue to serve as 'bomb trucks' capable of delivering a cost-effective but heavy strike.

Warload

Precision weaponry has made an enormous bombload less necessary to achieve results. For aircraft that have a large weapon capacity this translates into the ability to carry a great number of more potent weapons and to do more with the number of weapons that can be carried than the original designers would ever have dreamed possible.

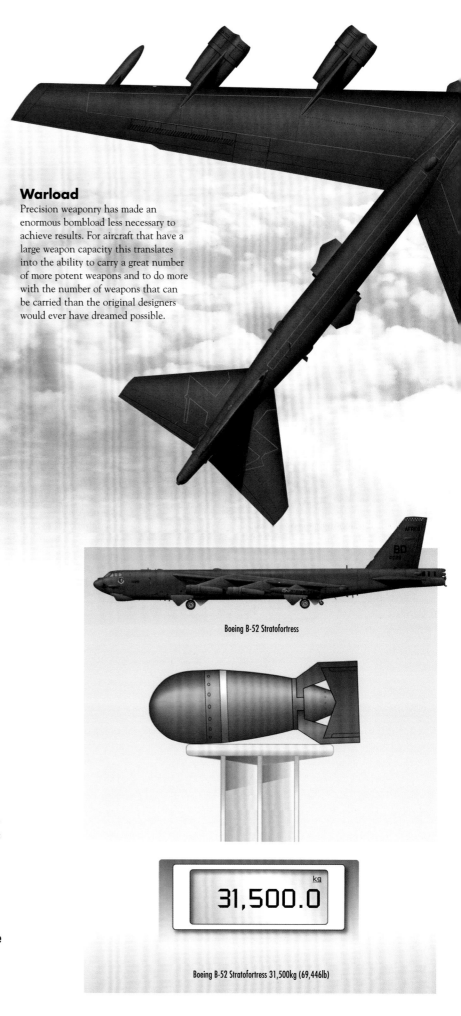

Boeing B-52 Stratofortress

31,500.0 kg

Boeing B-52 Stratofortress 31,500kg (69,446lb)

Rockwell B-1 Lancer

Rockwell B-1 Lancer 56,700kg (125,002lb)

56,700.0 kg

Northrop Grumman B-2 Spirit

Northrop Grumman B-2 Spirit 23,000kg (50,706lb)

23,000.0 kg

Tupolev Tu-160

Tupolev Tu-160 40,000kg (88,185lb)

40,000.0 kg

Tupolev Tu-95MS

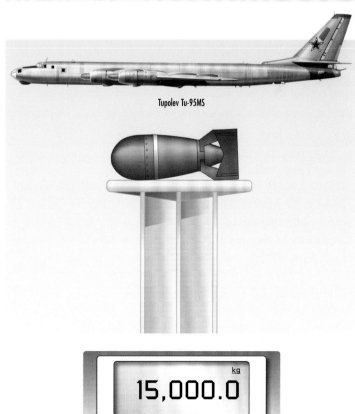

Tupolev Tu-95MS 15,000kg (33,069lb)

15,000.0 kg

Bombers 2

Operational Range

▶ **Rockwell B-1 Lancer**
▶ **Tupolev Tu-160**
▶ **Boeing B-52 Stratofortress**
▶ **Northrop Grumman B-2 Spirit**
▶ **Tupolev Tu-95MS**

Long-range bombers give their operators the capability to strike at distant targets, which may be located on another continent or deep within enemy territory. This can necessitate a very long mission, but it does bring almost any location within range of attack.

During the war in Iraq, US bombers were able to strike enemy targets without deploying forward from their bases in Hawaii. The logistical benefits of this capability are considerable – bombers need a lot of support to keep them flying, and any redeployment means moving the entire support and maintenance apparatus to a new location.

Penetration of enemy airspace is always hazardous. Traditionally, flying very high was a reliable method of avoiding enemy defences, but this prompted the deployment of very high-altitude missiles and interceptors. High-flying aircraft are also easy to detect, making interception or missile attack more likely. A low-level 'sprint' penetration offers a better chance to avoid detection or to get through the areas where defences are thickest before a response can materialize. Aircraft such as the B-1 and Tu-160 were designed for this kind of penetration.

More recently still, low-observable ('stealth') technology has made high-level penetration feasible once again. This has the advantage of extending the combat range of the aircraft – low-level, high-speed sprints eat fuel at a prodigious rate, whereas high-altitude cruising is highly economical. Advances in engine technology and aerodynamics also allow an aircraft to travel further on the same amount of fuel.

TOP RIGHT: The intercontinental bomber, such as the B-2 Spirit shown here, was a creation of the Cold War but remains relevant to today's complex military–political situation. The ability to strike targets anywhere in the world is a powerful tool in both warfighting and diplomacy.

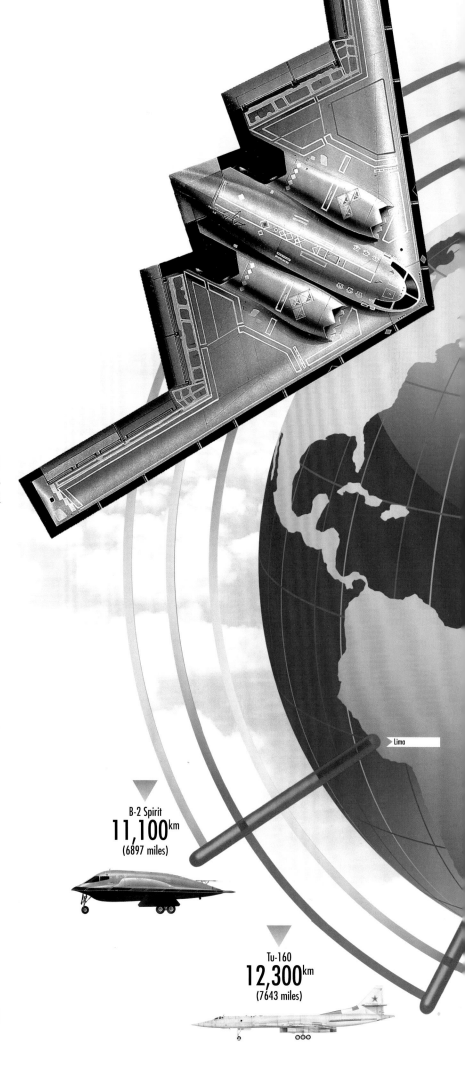

Lima

B-2 Spirit
11,100km
(6897 miles)

Tu-160
12,300km
(7643 miles)

Operational Range

This diagram shows the operational ranges of long-range bombers from the North Pole. Few aircraft can match the endurance of the piston-engined Tu-95 'Bear', which was designed for long-duration patrols over the ocean. Cruising at high altitude and modest speed, this venerable workhorse can go almost anywhere ... but not quickly.

NORTH POLE

Dubai

Harare

Rio de Janeiro

Falkland Islands

B-52 Stratofortress
7210km
(4480 miles)

B-1 Lancer
11,998km
(7455 miles)

Tu-95MS
15,000km
(9321 miles)

Combat Radius

The ocean is a big place, and one of the best defences a carrier group has is uncertainty about its location. If the range of its aircraft is known, the rough position of the carrier can be extrapolated. Longer-range aircraft translate to greater ambiguity regarding their point of origin.

MiG-29K
1000km
(621 miles)

Su-33D
1000km
(621 miles)

Naval Aircraft

Combat Radius

▶ **Dassault Rafale M**
▶ **BAE Sea Harrier FRS Mk 51**
▶ **Mikoyan-Gurevich MiG-29K**
▶ **Sukhoi Su-33D**
▶ **McDonnell Douglas F/A-18C Hornet**

Sea Harrier FRS Mk 51
1000km
(621 miles)

Dassault Rafale M
1852km
(1151 miles)

F/A-18C Hornet
740km
(460 miles)

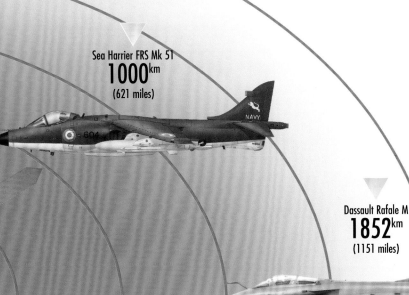

1 Combat radius can be extended by carrying fuel tanks on some hard points instead of weapons. This was particularly necessary on early-model Hornets, which had a limited internal capacity. The redesigned F/A-18E/F model, or 'Super Hornet', remedied this deficiency.

2 Hook-arrested carrier landings take their toll on airframes. The longer the CAP can stay airborne, the less landings have to be made on a given deployment, which improves serviceability rates significantly.

Naval aircraft usually have two engines, giving improved 'get-home' capability in case of malfunction or combat damage. This is necessary because these planes operate over long distances, usually with nothing but water beneath. Carrier-borne aircraft may have no alternative landing area to divert to in the event of a problem, so the ability to limp home on one engine can make the difference between a major repair job and a total loss.

Combat radius is important to naval aviation for several reasons. The whole point of naval air power is to extend the range of the fleet, so it makes sense to extend that range as much as possible. Short-range aircraft require that the carrier must come close inshore or launch its strikes from a point relatively close to an enemy force. This makes the carrier group vulnerable to counter-attack and negates much of the advantage conferred by air power over surface-action warships.

A large combat radius is also important defensively. It translates to the ability to make extended patrols, reducing the number of take-offs and landings needed to maintain a credible combat air patrol (CAP) each day, and allows defensive fighters to intercept incoming hostiles as far as possible from the carrier group. Enemy aircraft may be armed with long-range missiles, and must be intercepted before they can reach a firing position. This requires not only long range but a high fuel capacity to permit rapid or repeated interceptions, in the event that separated groups of aircraft are approaching.

OPPOSITE: The Sea Harrier is one of the few aircraft capable of making a vertical take-off or vertical landing. This consumes a great deal of fuel, however, and reduces the warload that can be carried, so Harriers normally operate much like other naval aircraft, making a rolling take-off.

Head to Head:
F/A-18 vs MiG-29

Maximum Clean Speed (at 11,000m/ 36,089ft) and Rate of Climb

▶ **McDonnell Douglas Boeing F/A-18F Super Hornet**
▶ **Mikoyan-Gurevich MiG-29**

There are many similarities between the F/A-18 and the MiG-29. Both are relatively light twin-engined aircraft capable of undertaking a variety of roles, but whereas the MiG-29 was developed primarily as an air-superiority fighter with some additional capabilities, the F/A-18 was always intended as a multi-role platform. Its 'F/A' designation indicates that it is both a fighter and an attack aircraft. The F/A-18 was a naval aircraft from the outset, while the MiG-29 was land-based, although a navalized variant did later appear. The MiG-29 came from a project intended to counter new high-capability Western fighters such as the F-15. This programme diverged into the light MiG-29 and the heavier Su-27.

Both top speed and rate of climb are significant to the performance of a modern combat aircraft.

Either can be an advantage that permits the pilot to dictate the terms of an engagement. If things are not going well, an F/A-18 pilot can climb away from his opponent and come around for another pass or simply break off. A MiG-29 pilot can outpace an F/A-18 in a straight line, enabling a successful stern-chase pursuit or a timely disengagement by entering a shallow dive and exiting the combat at high speed.

RIGHT: The MiG-29 became the standard Soviet front-line fighter, and was 'inherited' by many nations at the break-up of the Soviet Union. Some are now serving in the air forces of NATO members, which the designers surely cannot ever have foreseen.

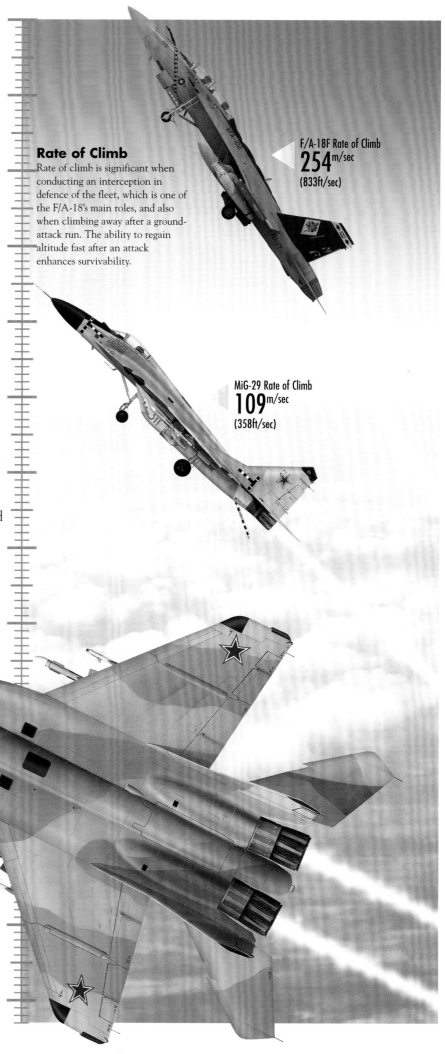

Rate of Climb
Rate of climb is significant when conducting an interception in defence of the fleet, which is one of the F/A-18's main roles, and also when climbing away after a ground-attack run. The ability to regain altitude fast after an attack enhances survivability.

◀ **F/A-18F Rate of Climb**
254m/sec
(833ft/sec)

◀ **MiG-29 Rate of Climb**
109m/sec
(358ft/sec)

Speed is always an asset in a combat aircraft, though flying straight and level at any speed is hazardous at best during combat. High straight-line speed is most useful when pursuing an enemy or attempting to make an interception.

MiG-29 Speed
2445 km/h
(1519mph)

F/A-18F Speed
1915 km/h
(1190mph)

F/A-18F Super Hornet
The E and F models are known as the 'Super Hornet' and are significantly heavier than the A–D variants. Significantly, they carry far more fuel and are capable of longer-range missions.

MiG-29
Since its inception, the MiG-29 has grown, becoming heavier and more capable, and it is today a true multi-role platform.

Head to Head:
F-15E v Su-30MK2

Operational Range

▶ **Sukhoi Su-30MK2**
▶ **F-15E Strike Eagle**

The emergence of (then) advanced Western fighters such as the F-15 and F-16 prompted designers in the Soviet Union to begin work on an aircraft to counter them. This project split into the MiG-29 and Su-27 aircraft, each with a different role. The Su-27 'Flanker' was developed further, eventually giving rise to the Su-30. Various versions of this aircraft have been built, including the Su-30MK. This variant was the basis for export versions sold to China, Indonesia and Vietnam. Where some other variants of the Su-30 had forward canards to enhance manoeuvrability for air-to-air combat, the Su-30MK2 bought by China was optimized as a strike platform and was modified to carry anti-ship missiles.

The F-15, originally developed as a specialized air-superiority fighter, was extremely effective in that role and enjoyed considerable export success. Although its designers had absolutely no intention of compromising and creating a multi-role platform, the F-15E variant, or 'Strike Eagle', was eventually created. This also proved to be a major success. One of the modifications from the original F-15 was the conformal fuel tanks that lay along the engine intakes and extended the Strike Eagle's range.

Chinese Su-30MK2s serve primarily in the maritime-strike role, for which a long operational range is necessary. F-15E Strike Eagles are more commonly deployed against land targets, and have successfully operated on close-support and long-range-strike missions against heavily defended targets, as well as in precision strikes against individual enemy tanks.

Both aircraft retain a very significant air-to-air capability.

F-15E Radius
4445km
(2762 miles)

RIGHT: The Su-30MK family has achieved considerable export success. Versions created for different customer nations are designated by a letter, thus MKI for India, MKM for Malaysia. The MK2 is based on the MKK version created for China, and has been bought by several other nations.

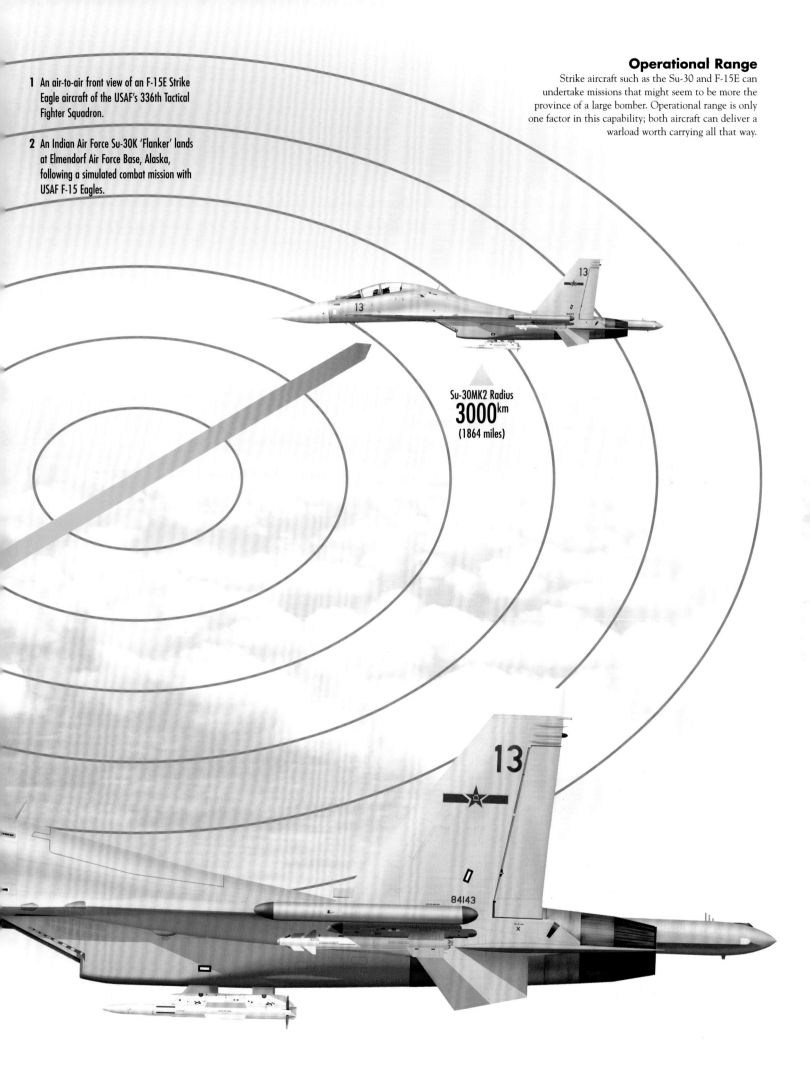

1 An air-to-air front view of an F-15E Strike Eagle aircraft of the USAF's 336th Tactical Fighter Squadron.

2 An Indian Air Force Su-30K 'Flanker' lands at Elmendorf Air Force Base, Alaska, following a simulated combat mission with USAF F-15 Eagles.

Operational Range

Strike aircraft such as the Su-30 and F-15E can undertake missions that might seem to be more the province of a large bomber. Operational range is only one factor in this capability; both aircraft can deliver a warload worth carrying all that way.

Su-30MK2 Radius
3000km
(1864 miles)

Harriers Compared

Maximum Take-off Weight and Rate of Climb

▶ **McDonnell Douglas AV-8B Harrier II**

▶ **BAE Harrier II GR7**

Maximum Take-off Weight

In order to make a vertical take-off, a Harrier must be lightly loaded. A rolling take-off is necessary in order to carry a full warload.

The Harrier was developed in the 1960s to meet a need for a lightweight multi-role combat aircraft that could operate from the most primitive of facilities. This permitted NATO air forces to be dispersed and thus better able to survive the opening strikes if the Cold War ever became an all-out conflict. The initial aircraft, named Kestrel, was developed over the next decades into a number of distinct models, all optimized for different roles.

Different users took modified versions of the Harrier and, later, the Harrier II into service. Some renamed their aircraft – the Harrier in service with the Spanish Navy is called the Matador. The Royal Navy used a version named Sea Harrier which was configured for air-to-air combat, while the RAF took a ground-attack version initially designated GR1. The US Marine Corps variant was initially designated AV-8A and, like Harriers in service elsewhere, progressed through upgrades and new model numbers.

The AV-8B was extensively redesigned by McDonnell Douglas from the earlier AV-8A/C Harrier. It has a new wing, an elevated cockpit and a redesigned fuselage. The re-designed cockpit shape is particularly noticeable. The AV-8B has a 'bubble' design which improves all-round visibility for air-to-air combat.

Performance does vary somewhat between models, as a result of changes to the engines and other components, or an increase in weight caused by additional electronic equipment.

McDonnell Douglas AV-8B Harrier II Weight 9415kg (20,757lb)

BAE Harrier II GR7 Weight 8595kg (18,949lb)

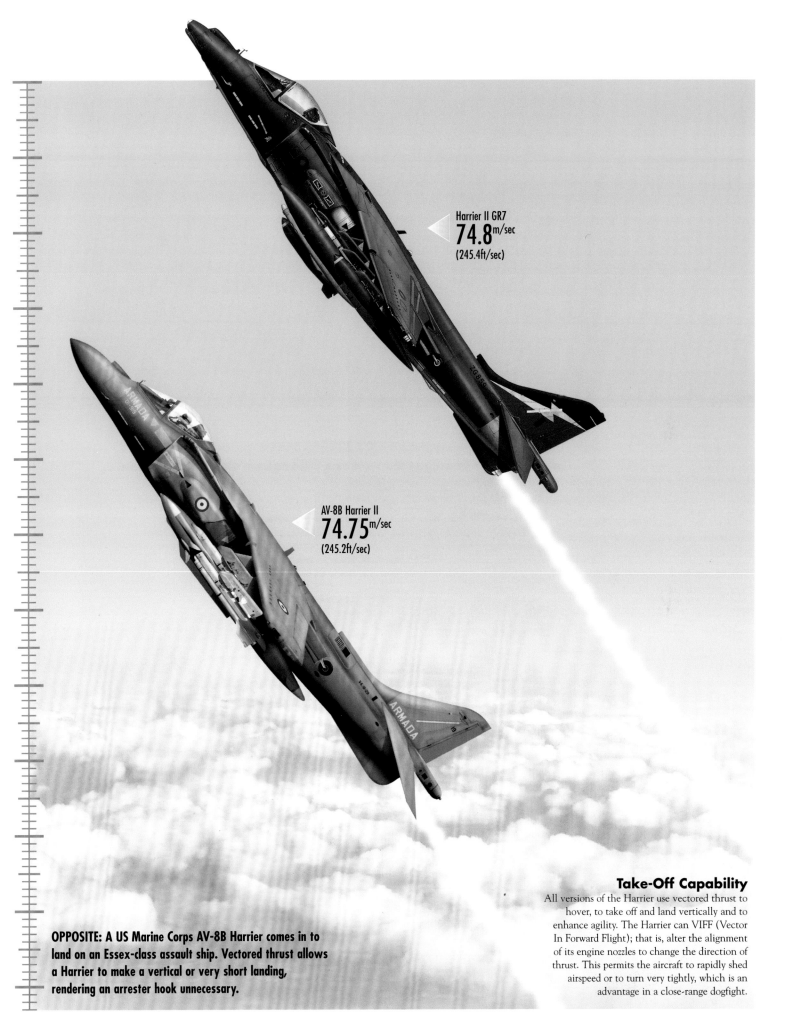

Harrier II GR7
74.8m/sec
(245.4ft/sec)

AV-8B Harrier II
74.75m/sec
(245.2ft/sec)

Take-Off Capability

All versions of the Harrier use vectored thrust to hover, to take off and land vertically and to enhance agility. The Harrier can VIFF (Vector In Forward Flight); that is, alter the alignment of its engine nozzles to change the direction of thrust. This permits the aircraft to rapidly shed airspeed or to turn very tightly, which is an advantage in a close-range dogfight.

OPPOSITE: A US Marine Corps AV-8B Harrier comes in to land on an Essex-class assault ship. Vectored thrust allows a Harrier to make a vertical or very short landing, rendering an arrester hook unnecessary.

F-35B Lightning II
18,000ᵐ
(59,055ft)

Harrier AV-8B
15,000ᵐ
(49,213ft)

Service Ceiling

The Harrier was subject to a number of compromises in order to squeeze vectored-thrust capability into an airframe. It was primarily intended as a low-level ground-attack platform; high-altitude air combat was not a design priority.

USAF VTOL Capability

Service Ceiling

▶ **McDonnell Douglas AV-8B**
▶ **Lockheed Martin F-35B Lightning II**

1 An AV-8B+ Harrier II from Marine Attack Squadron VMA-311 lands near Marine Corps Air Station (MCAS) Yuma, Arizona. The station has a simulated aircraft deck for the AV-8B Harrier pilots to practise their landings and take-offs.

For many years the Harrier was the only viable vertical-take-off-and-landing-capable aircraft available. Other attempts, such as the underpowered Yak-38, were not successful and fell by the wayside. The Yak-38 suffered from an extremely short operational range and very limited warload, and while the Harrier did compromise in some areas in order to obtain vertical/short-take-off-and-landing (V/STOL) capability, it proved effective enough to appeal to a range of operators.

The Harrier is a remarkable success story that has given good service for half a century. It is due for replacement by the Lockheed Martin F-35 Lightning II, which is designed to offer the same capabilities in a more advanced package. There are three variants of the F-35, of which the A model and the carrier-capable C model are not able to make vertical landings. The F-35B has been selected by the US Marine Corps, which operates its aircraft from relatively small aviation ships and crude forward air bases. The B model's short-field capability makes it an obvious choice to take over from the Harrier in the light fighter and strike role.

The F-35B offers a number of improvements over the Harrier, not least in terms of performance at altitude and the capabilities of its internal electronic systems. The F-35 is also far more 'stealthy' than its predecessor, which makes it more survivable in the modern combat environment. When the Harrier was designed, guided air-to-air and surface-to-air missiles were rather basic. Today, both types are highly capable and widely used by air forces throughout the world.

LEFT: Originally a British design, the AV-8B has become a symbol of US Marine Corps aviation. US designers were heavily involved with the creation of the improved Harrier II.

Transport Helicopters

Troop Capacity and Operational Range

▶ **Mil Mi-26**
▶ **Boeing CH-47D Chinook**
▶ **Boeing RH-53D Sea Stallion**
▶ **Mil Mi-17-1V**
▶ **Sikorsky UH-60 Black Hawk**

Mil Mi-26

Boeing CH-47D Chinook

Boeing RH-53D Sea Stallion

Mil Mi-17-1V

Sikorsky UH-60 Black Hawk

Mi-26 Range
1920km
(1193 miles)

Transporting personnel or cargo by helicopter is not as efficient as using a fixed-wing aircraft in terms of speed, fuel economy and capacity. However, helicopters have the advantage that they can operate from a rough field, and can get their cargo into a confined space that no fixed-wing aircraft could enter. Most transport helicopters are relatively modest in size, not least due to the enormous power required to vertically lift the weight of a large cargo. Smaller helicopters are also easier to operate from ships and restricted landing areas. Conversely, a transport helicopter needs to be big enough to carry useful amounts of cargo or numbers of personnel.

Thus the majority of military transport helicopters are roughly the same size, and can undertake a range of roles from troop transport to logistics, carrying moderately sized items of no great individual weight. For large loads, in terms of size or number of personnel, much larger helicopters such as the CH-47 Chinook are used. The Chinook dates from the 1960s but is so effective in the heavy-lift role that it has never been replaced in service. It can carry an artillery piece slung underneath, enabling fast deployment into terrain where even self-propelled guns cannot venture.

The Russian Mi-26 'Halo' is so large that it can be used to recover a downed Chinook, a feat beyond the capacity of the CH-47 itself. This immense helicopter was developed to transport armoured vehicles, but can also be used to deploy large numbers of personnel or an equivalent load of military supplies.

Operational Range
Rotary-wing aircraft are not as fuel efficient as fixed-wing equivalents, and require powerful engines to make a vertical take-off. The fuel required to make a long flight is heavy, and reduces the lift capacity available for personnel or cargo.

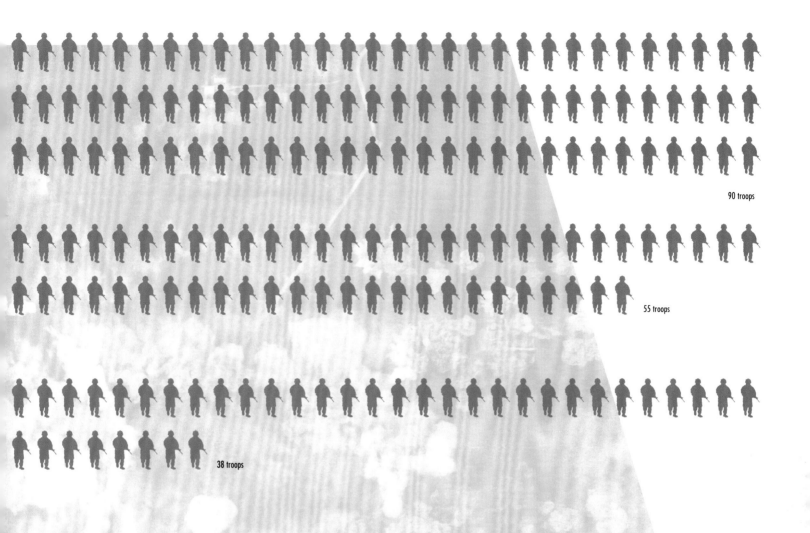

90 troops

55 troops

38 troops

30 troops

14 troops

Troop Capacity

Helicopter-transported infantry can deploy rapidly into a combat area, bypassing terrain and enemy-held areas that would impose delay on a ground force. Such forces must then be supported and resupplied, often by the same helicopters that deployed them.

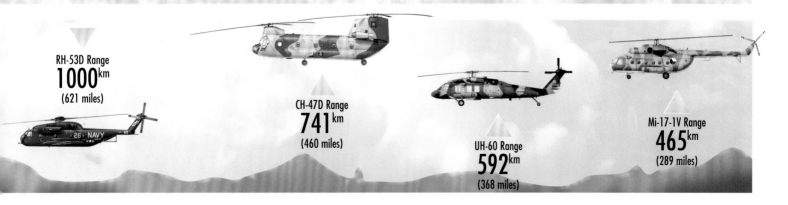

RH-53D Range
1000km
(621 miles)

CH-47D Range
741km
(460 miles)

UH-60 Range
592km
(368 miles)

Mi-17-1V Range
465km
(289 miles)

Eurocopter Tiger

F-ZWWW

Mil Mi-28

022

Kamov Ka-52

KA·50

H317

021

Bell AH-1W SuperCobra

242

Boeing AH-64 Apache

UNITED STATES ARMY

23259

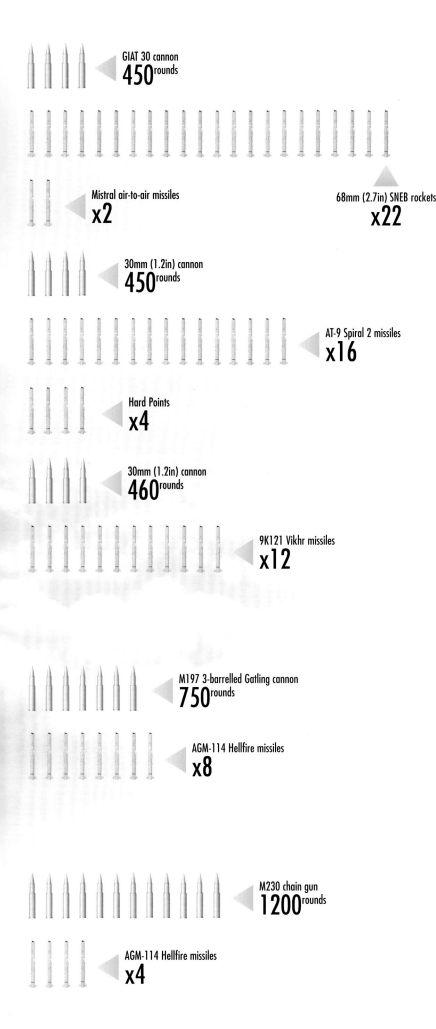

GIAT 30 cannon
450rounds

Mistral air-to-air missiles
x2

68mm (2.7in) SNEB rockets
x22

30mm (1.2in) cannon
450rounds

AT-9 Spiral 2 missiles
x16

Hard Points
x4

30mm (1.2in) cannon
460rounds

9K121 Vikhr missiles
x12

M197 3-barrelled Gatling cannon
750rounds

AGM-114 Hellfire missiles
x8

M230 chain gun
1200rounds

AGM-114 Hellfire missiles
x4

Ground Attack Helicopters 1

Weapons

▶ **Eurocopter Tiger**
▶ **Mil Mi-28**
▶ **Kamov Ka-52**
▶ **Bell AH-1W SuperCobra**
▶ **Boeing AH-64 Apache**

The attack-helicopter concept dates from the 1960s. The first examples were simply armed versions of transport helicopters; those with weapons were nicknamed 'gunships' and those without, 'slicks'. The rockets and machine guns carried by these early models were useful enough to prove that the concept was viable, but there was only so much that could be done with an armed transport. Dedicated attack-helicopter designs did away with any cargo capacity, using the helicopter's entire power output for speed and mobility, and to carry a large weapons load.

Many modern attack helicopters carry a turreted cannon, in addition to which a flexible armament of rockets, missiles and gun pods can be carried on stub wings. Unguided rockets are mainly used against relatively 'soft' targets such as infantry positions, while guided missiles are more effective against armoured vehicles. Attack helicopters often fly with a mixed armament to engage targets of opportunity, but it is not uncommon to use an all-missile loadout, turning the helicopter into a flying tank-hunter. Some attack helicopters can carry short-range air-to-air missiles for use against other helicopters, but this is not an ideal role. Where previous generations of attack helicopter used fixed guns aimed by pointing the aircraft, attack helicopters like the AH-64 Apache can engage targets to either side using a cannon aimed by simply looking at the target. Cued to a sensor on the gunner's helmet and fired with a conventional trigger, weapons of this sort enhance lethality by allowing fast engagement even of fleeting targets.

Weapons

A two-seat design allows the pilot to concentrate on flying when necessary and to use fixed weapons such as strafing rocket pods, which are aimed where the helicopter's nose is pointed. The weapons operator undertakes more technical tasks such as using missiles and the turret, and sometimes navigation as well.

Ground Attack Helicopters 2

Maximum Speed and Combat Range

▶ **Eurocopter Tiger**
▶ **Mil Mi-28**
▶ **Bell AH-1W SuperCobra**
▶ **Boeing AH-64 Apache**

Most attack helicopters are fairly well armoured, but their best defence is not to be hit. Staying low and making good use of terrain can prevent many hostiles from getting a clear shot or even realizing that the gunship is there at all, but when 'in the open' a helicopter must rely on the fact that it is not a large target and will be moving quickly.

High speed enables the gunship to make a fast pass through the target area, press home an attack and get out of range or behind cover before too much fire comes its way. Of course, high speed can also make targeting difficult, but guided weapons and advanced targeting systems go a long way towards offsetting this.

When a helicopter is travelling fast near the ground there is always the danger of a collision with terrain or buildings, or with the ground itself due to air turbulence if the aircraft is very low. High speed can also be a hazard to the helicopter itself; at high enough speed the rotor tips can break the sound barrier, causing severe instability as the rotors' aerodynamic conditions change.

Traditionally, attack helicopters had a fairly short operational range and were based close to the combat area. The new generation of gunships have longer legs. This is necessary if the helicopter is to operate at sea or from ships; transits to and from the target area can be lengthy. A long operational range also translates to an ability to loiter in the target area, waiting for an opportunity to strike.

Combat Range

A helicopter's radius of action is reduced if it must carry bulky ordnance that imposes a great deal of drag, especially when attempting to fly at high speeds with such a load. Atmospheric conditions such as air pressure and temperature can also affect combat radius.

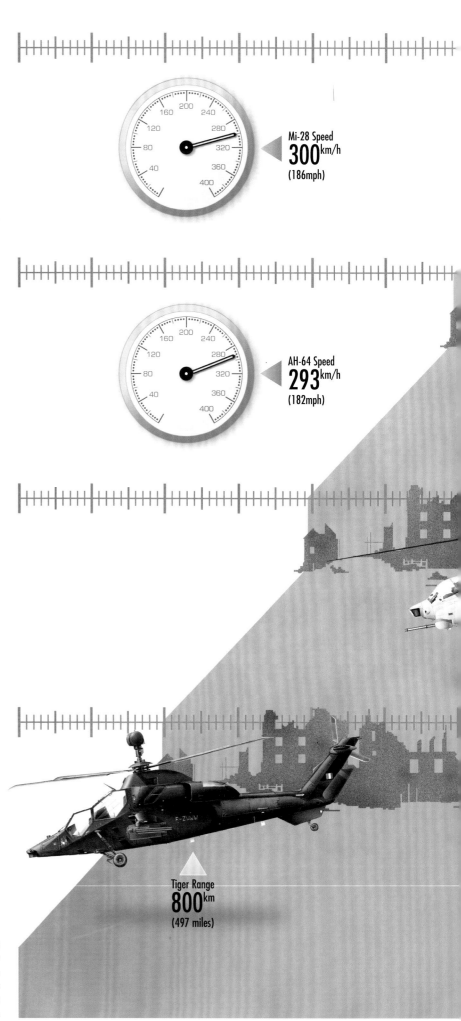

Mi-28 Speed
300km/h
(186mph)

AH-64 Speed
293km/h
(182mph)

Tiger Range
800km
(497 miles)

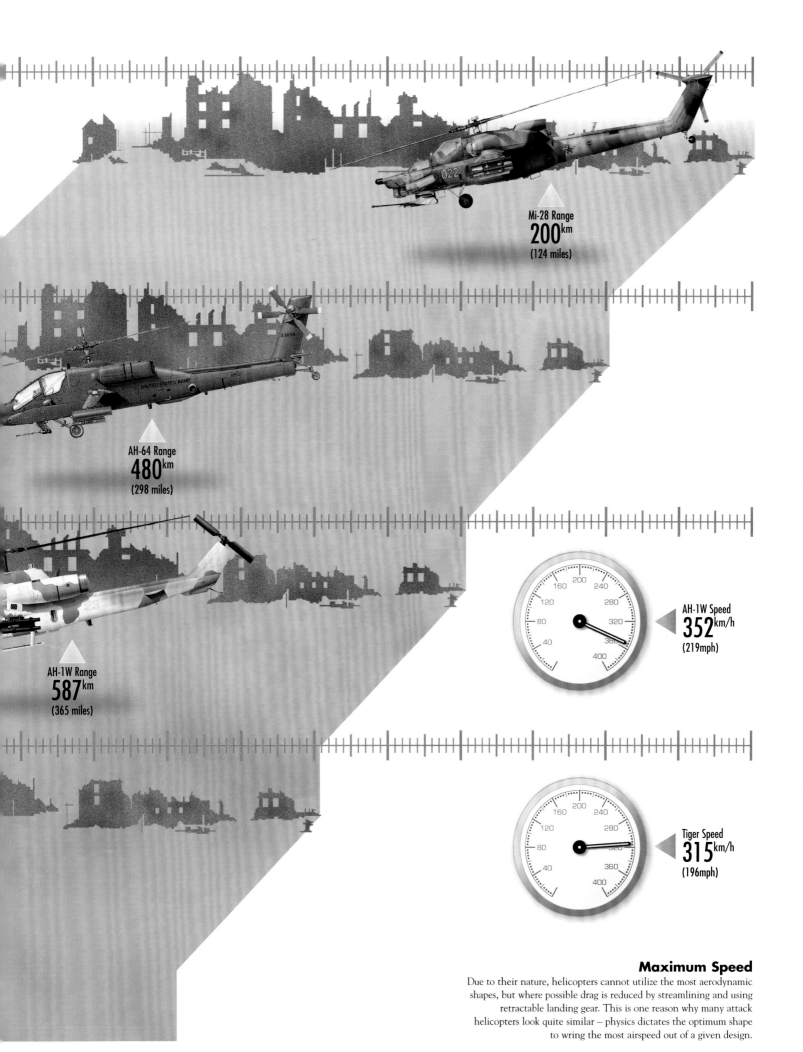

Mi-28 Range
200km
(124 miles)

AH-64 Range
480km
(298 miles)

AH-1W Range
587km
(365 miles)

AH-1W Speed
352km/h
(219mph)

Tiger Speed
315km/h
(196mph)

Maximum Speed

Due to their nature, helicopters cannot utilize the most aerodynamic shapes, but where possible drag is reduced by streamlining and using retractable landing gear. This is one reason why many attack helicopters look quite similar – physics dictates the optimum shape to wring the most airspeed out of a given design.

Armoured Fighting Vehicles

Combat vehicles primarily exist to provide mobility and protection to a weapons system or to a group of troops. They have revolutionized warfare, making it possible to launch high-speed breakthrough-and-exploitation attacks and to counter them. Where previously the battle front moved at the speed of a marching man, today's mechanized forces are capable of dominating a huge area, often surprising opposing forces by appearing where they are least expected.

New designs of armoured vehicle have appeared to fill an ever-increasing number of niches. Armoured Fighting Vehicles (tanks) directly engage the enemy with powerful guns, while Infantry Fighting Vehicles carry and support infantry forces. These expensive, top-end assets are supported by lighter reconnaissance, transport and specialist vehicles. Striking the right balance between capability and affordability is a tricky business; sometimes it is necessary to accept a lower level of capability in order to afford enough vehicles to fully equip a nation's armed forces.

LEFT: A German Leopard 2 main battle tank splashes through water during exercises. The Leopard 2 is in service with a number of European countries, including Denmark and Austria.

Gulf War 1991: Main Battle Tanks 1

Armour Protection: Turret and Hull

▶ **T-55**
▶ **T-72A**
▶ **M1A1 Abrams**
▶ **AMX-30**

The armoured fighting vehicles (AFVs) of the 1991 Gulf War were the product of a long contest between weapons and protection. Each advance in armour technology was inevitably matched by a weapon that could defeat it. Armouring tanks in ever-thicker steel worked for a time, but there is a limit to how much weight a tank can carry. Greater efficiency was necessary, and this came from two sources – improved materials and better shaping.

Sloped or curved armour creates a chance that an incoming round will glance off, and increases the effective thickness of the armour, even if the round does punch in. A round that arrives at a 90-degree angle to the armour will have to penetrate a much shorter distance than one that comes in at an acute angle. Composite armour uses layers of different materials to increase the overall effectiveness of the armour. It is hard to cast composite armour in anything but flat slabs, but it is still sloped for increased protection.

It is simply not possible to make a tank invulnerable from all angles, so designers attempt to maximize protection against the most likely threats. In a conventional tank-vs-tank action, most incoming fire will strike the hull front and the turret. However, experience has shown that a threat can come from anywhere, especially when tanks are operating in close urban terrain. Tank armour is often a compromise between reasonable all-round protection and the ability to defeat a top-end armour-piercing warhead from at least some angles.

Armour Protection

Due to intervening obstacles, the turret is often the only part of a tank that can be hit, especially at long range. Not surprisingly, it is often the most heavily armoured part of the vehicle, but this cannot be taken to extremes. Tanks likely to be engaged at short range need a well-armoured hull if they are to survive the encounter. Armour is only one aspect of a tank's protection; mobility is another. A tank that is so heavily weighed down by its armour that it cannot move quickly may actually be more vulnerable than a much lighter vehicle.

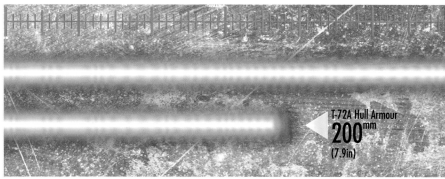

T-72A Hull Armour
200mm
(7.9in)

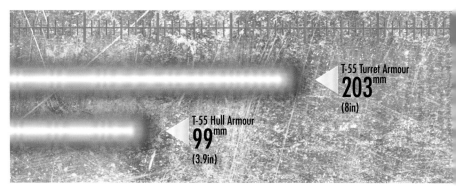

T-55 Turret Armour
203mm
(8in)

T-55 Hull Armour
99mm
(3.9in)

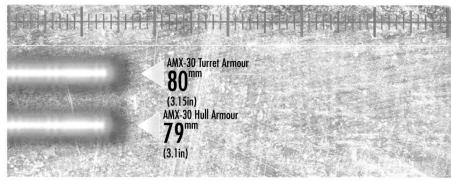

AMX-30 Turret Armour
80mm
(3.15in)

AMX-30 Hull Armour
79mm
(3.1in)

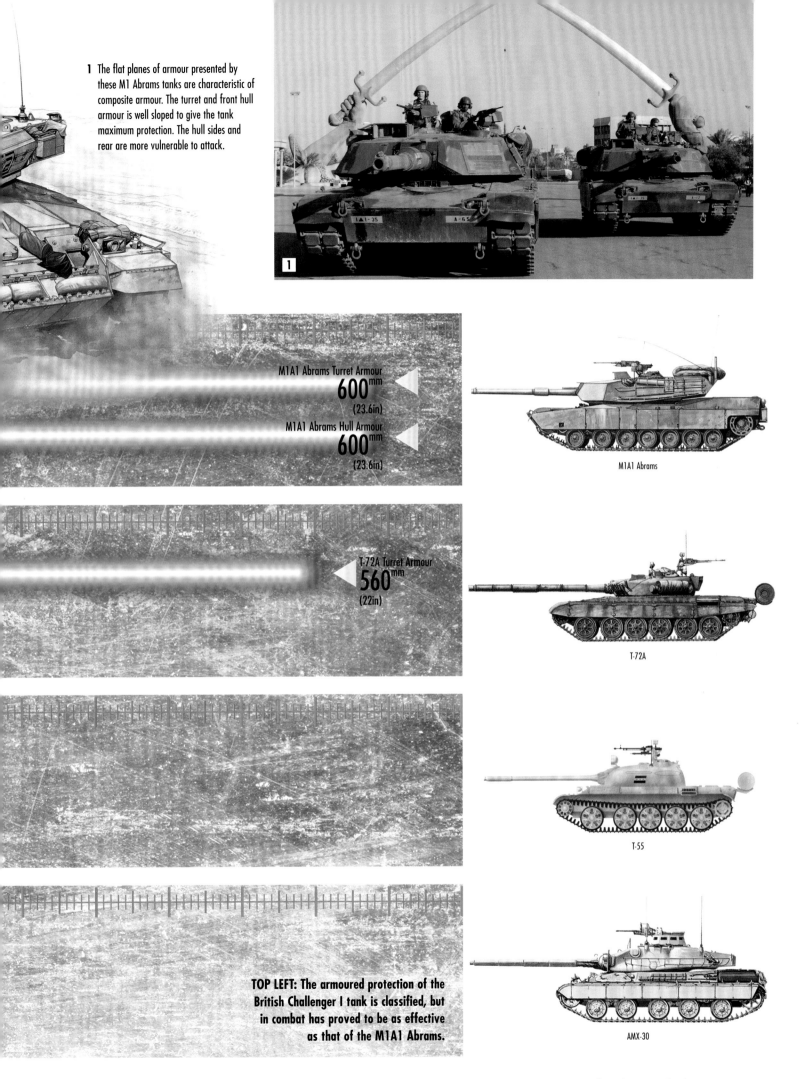

1 The flat planes of armour presented by these M1 Abrams tanks are characteristic of composite armour. The turret and front hull armour is well sloped to give the tank maximum protection. The hull sides and rear are more vulnerable to attack.

M1A1 Abrams Turret Armour
600mm
(23.6in)

M1A1 Abrams Hull Armour
600mm
(23.6in)

M1A1 Abrams

T-72A Turret Armour
560mm
(22in)

T-72A

T-55

TOP LEFT: The armoured protection of the British Challenger I tank is classified, but in combat has proved to be as effective as that of the M1A1 Abrams.

AMX-30

Gulf War 1991: Main Battle Tanks 2

Main Gun Range and Calibre

▶ **T-55**
▶ **T-72A**
▶ **M1A1 Abrams**
▶ **Challenger 1**
▶ **AMX-30**

The ability to hit the target at a great distance grants a tank both offensive and defensive advantages. Offensively, a long-range weapon enables the tank to dominate a larger part of the battle area and to hit targets it cannot approach. Defensively, it improves survivability – if a tank force can engage beyond its enemies' effective range, then the battle can be very one-sided. A tank's gun has to be powerful enough to penetrate the armour of a rival main battle tank (MBT) and to destroy any other target it is turned against. This requires a large, powerful shell. However, big shells take up a lot of space, which limits the number that can be carried. A lighter gun with more ammunition might seem like a good trade-off. Up to a point it might be, but a gun that is too light to penetrate an enemy tank is useless. Modern MBTs are rarely armed with weapons under 100mm (3.9in) in calibre; with anything lighter it may not matter whether or not a hit is scored.

T-72A — T-72A Gun Calibre **125**mm (4.9in)

M1A1 Abrams — M1A1 Abrams Gun Calibre **120**mm (4.7in)

Challenger 1 — Challenger 1 Gun Calibre **120**mm (4.7in)

AMX-30 — AMX-30 Gun Calibre **105**mm (4.1in)

T-55 — T-55 Gun Calibre **100**mm (3.9in)

Main Gun Calibre
Tank gun calibres have remained standardized in the 100–125mm (3.9–4.9in) range for several decades. These guns offer an excellent compromise between range, hitting power and ammunition capacity.

ABOVE: A main battle tank's gun is to a great extent its reason for existing. As shown in this illustration of the M1A1, it is a large and complex piece of equipment which must be loaded, aimed and stabilized from within the turret. The gun's breech takes up much of the front of the turret, with ammunition stowed in the rear. The crew and all other systems must fit into whatever space is left over.

Effective Main Gun Range
A gun's effective range depends on the velocity of its projectile and also how well it is aimed. It is not difficult to get a shell to travel several thousand metres. The trick is to hit a moving target at that range, from a firing platform that may be bumping across rough terrain at high speed. Long-range fire requires excellent targeting electronics to make best use of the weapon's capabilities, and there are additional advantages to having a highly accurate weapon. A tank that achieves a high proportion of hits to shots fired needs to carry less ammunition, which in turn means that a larger and more powerful gun becomes a viable option.

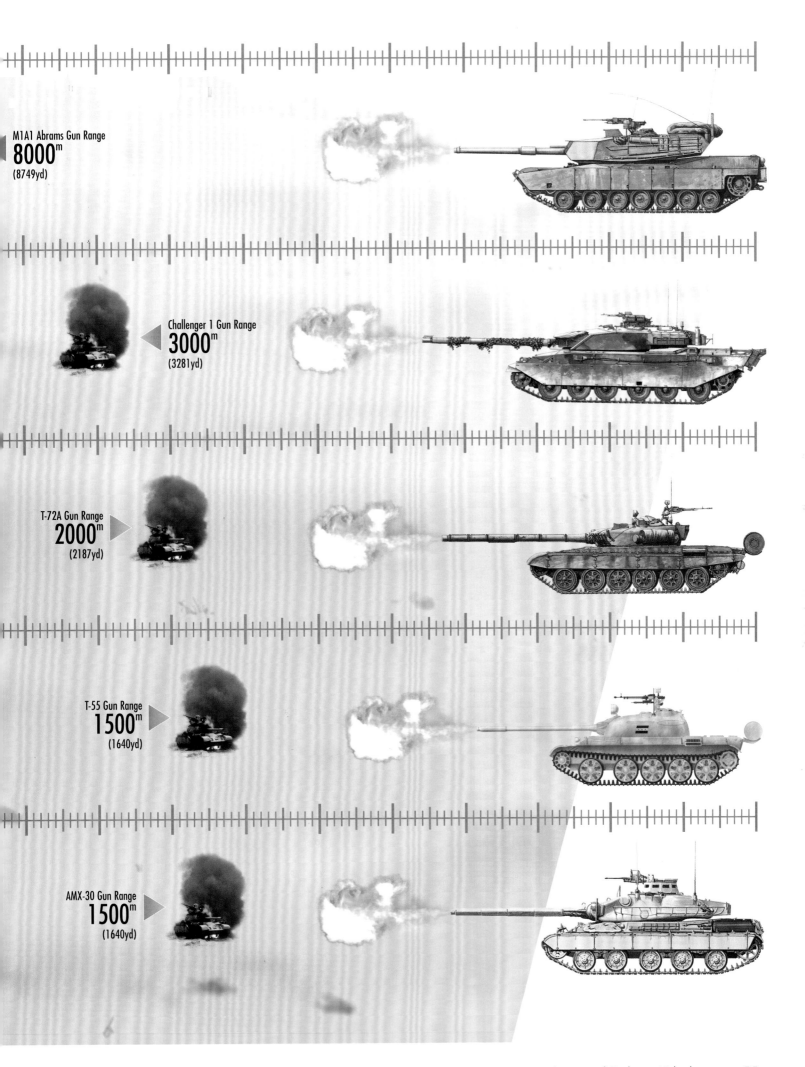

M1A1 Abrams Gun Range
8000ᵐ
(8749yd)

Challenger 1 Gun Range
3000ᵐ
(3281yd)

T-72A Gun Range
2000ᵐ
(2187yd)

T-55 Gun Range
1500ᵐ
(1640yd)

AMX-30 Gun Range
1500ᵐ
(1640yd)

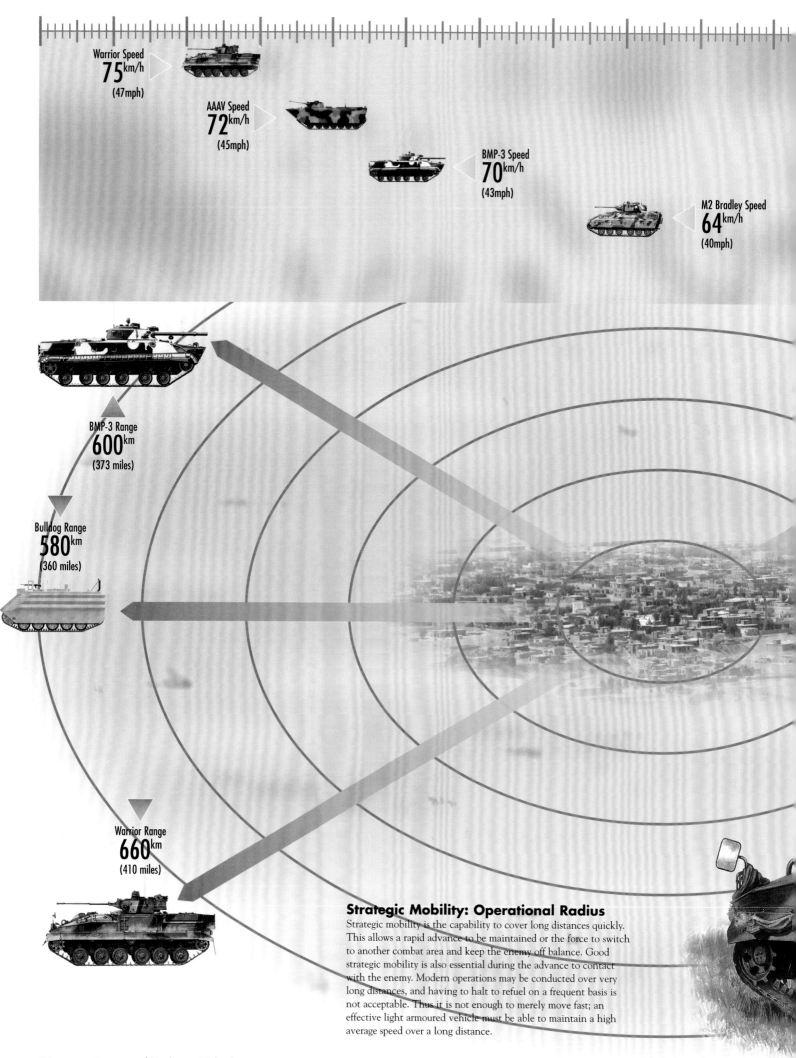

Warrior Speed
75km/h
(47mph)

AAAV Speed
72km/h
(45mph)

BMP-3 Speed
70km/h
(43mph)

M2 Bradley Speed
64km/h
(40mph)

BMP-3 Range
600km
(373 miles)

Bulldog Range
580km
(360 miles)

Warrior Range
660km
(410 miles)

Strategic Mobility: Operational Radius

Strategic mobility is the capability to cover long distances quickly. This allows a rapid advance to be maintained or the force to switch to another combat area and keep the enemy off balance. Good strategic mobility is also essential during the advance to contact with the enemy. Modern operations may be conducted over very long distances, and having to halt to refuel on a frequent basis is not acceptable. Thus it is not enough to merely move fast; an effective light armoured vehicle must be able to maintain a high average speed over a long distance.

Maximum Speed

Top speed is usually only attainable on a road or fairly flat ground. Racing cross-country or over obstacles is a thoroughly unpleasant experience for anyone aboard an armoured vehicle, no matter how good its suspension may be. It is, however, better than being hit by enemy fire.

Twenty-first Century Light Vehicles 1

Maximum Speed and Range

▶ **FV430 Bulldog**
▶ **M2 Bradley**
▶ **BMP-3**
▶ **Warrior**
▶ **AAAV**

Bulldog Speed
52km/h
(32mph)

AAAV Range
480km
(298 miles)

M2 Bradley Range
483km
(300 miles)

Light armoured vehicles are an essential part of modern warfare. Their primary function is to provide mobility to the personnel or systems they carry. Protection is a secondary, but important, consideration, and most are armed either for self-defence or to provide fire support to their troops.

Tactical mobility is the ability to operate in very rough terrain, crossing obstacles without becoming stuck. For this reason, many light armoured vehicles use tracks rather than wheels. This allows close co-operation with tanks. Infantry carried aboard light armoured transport are able to keep pace with the tank force and to smash through relatively light defences without dismounting. Cross-country speed is also a form of protection. A fast-moving target is hard to hit, and since these vehicles are less well protected than tanks, they may have to rely on mobility for defence.

LEFT: As with this British Warrior, the crew of an infantry fighting vehicle (IFV) remain aboard to operate its weapons and systems while infantry (referred to as 'dismounts') leave the vehicle to carry out their mission. The IFV may remain close by to provide fire support or may be given a new mission once its dismounts are delivered.

Twenty-first Century Light Vehicles 2

Personnel Capacity and Weapons Calibre

▶ **FV430 Bulldog**
▶ **M2 Bradley**
▶ **BMP-3**
▶ **Warrior**
▶ **AAAV**

By the time of the 1991 Gulf War, the armoured personnel carrier (APC) had largely given way to the infantry fighting vehicle, moving from a 'battle taxi' to a weapons platform that could support its infantry force in combat. Some older APCs mounting only a machine gun for self-defence were in use, but many of these vehicles had already been converted to other roles – for example, logistics vehicles, artillery observation vehicles, command posts, armoured ambulances and platforms for a range of specialist systems such as anti-aircraft defences.

This new generation of combat vehicle still had the same primary purpose: to provide protected transportation for an infantry force. Anti-personnel weapons that could hold up or even stop an infantry unit pose little threat to an armoured vehicle. However, many lighter anti-tank weapons, which would pose no real threat to a heavily armoured MBT, will easily penetrate the armour of an infantry fighting vehicle or armoured personnel carrier.

To many people, anything with tracks and some sort of gun is a tank, and an infantry fighting vehicle can indeed fulfil some of a tank's functions. Its primary role is infantry support, which frees real tanks to take on major threats the IFV cannot deal with. Similarly, the weapons mounted on an infantry fighting vehicle cannot be as heavy as those in a tank's turret; there is simply no room. Indeed, any IFV design must trade off its potency as a weapons platform against its carrying capacity. If too much room is given over to weapons, the vehicle becomes essentially an ineffective and excessively vulnerable light tank with an inadequate infantry force aboard. Striking the right balance, on the other hand, creates a highly potent combined infantry/light armour force capable of dealing efficiently with a wide range of situations.

AAAV

Bulldog
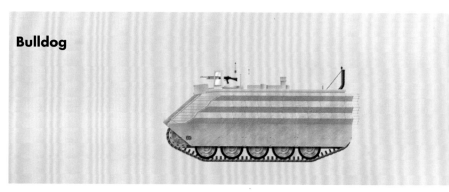

BMP-3

Warrior

M2 Bradley

Personnel Capacity

The crew required to operate the vehicle remains fixed at two or three personnel, depending on what weapons are mounted. These personnel are necessary, so any system that takes up internal space has to be fitted at the expense of troop-carrying capacity.

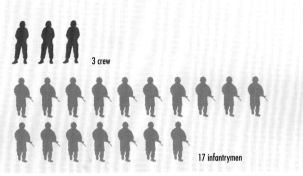

3 crew

17 infantrymen

2 crew

10 infantrymen

3 crew

7 infantrymen

3 crew

7 infantrymen

3 crew

6 infantrymen

Weapons Calibre

Most IFVs carry a machine gun for anti-personnel defence and usually a heavier weapon, such as an automatic cannon in the 20–30mm (0.79–1.2in) range, for harder targets. Some vehicles also mount anti-tank missiles.

Calibre
30mm
(1.2in)

Calibre
7.62mm
(0.3in)

Calibre
7.62mm
(0.3in)

Calibre
100mm
(3.9in)

Calibre
30mm
(1.2in)

Calibre
7.62mm
(0.3in)

Calibre
30mm
(1.2in)

Calibre
7.62mm
(0.3in)

Calibre
25mm
(1in)

Calibre
7.62mm
(0.3in)

Armoured Fighting Vehicles 59

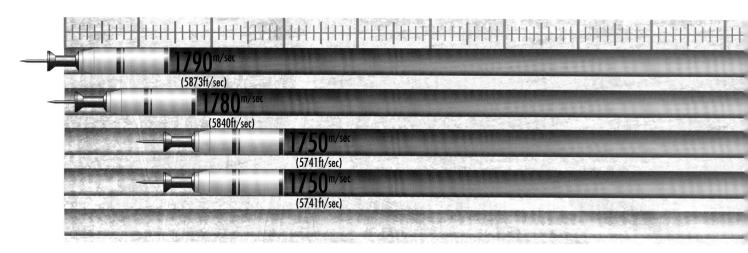

1790 m/sec
(5873ft/sec)

1780 m/sec
(5840ft/sec)

1750 m/sec
(5741ft/sec)

1750 m/sec
(5741ft/sec)

Muzzle Velocity

Modern tanks often engage at ranges of 2000–3000m (2187–3281yd). Even a projectile moving at the better part of 2000m/sec (6562ft/sec) may take a second and a half to travel from gun to target. A fast-moving tank can travel a long way in that time, reducing the chances of a hit.

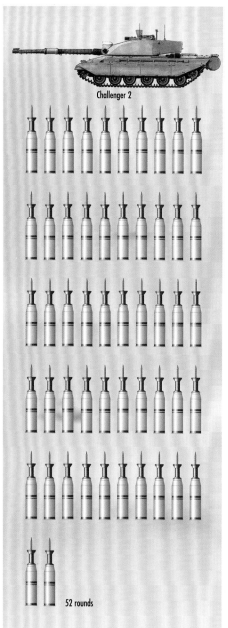

Challenger 2

52 rounds

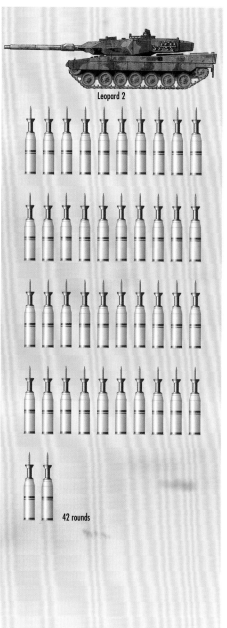

Leopard 2

42 rounds

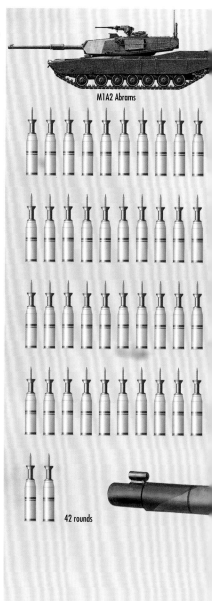

M1A2 Abrams

42 rounds

Number of Rounds

Modern armoured warfare takes place at a very high tempo, with no time for ammunition resupply in the middle of a battle. Thus a tank needs to carry enough ammunition for a protracted engagement, or several short fights during a forward deployment in which it is not practicable to take on more shells.

Main Battle Tanks Today 1

Muzzle Velocity and Number of Rounds

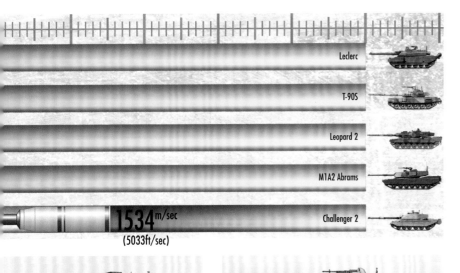

Leclerc

T-90S

Leopard 2

M1A2 Abrams

1534 m/sec
(5033ft/sec)

Challenger 2

▶ **M1A2 Abrams**
▶ **Leopard 2**
▶ **T-90S**
▶ **Challenger 2**
▶ **Leclerc**

Leclerc

T-90S

40 rounds

22 rounds

Modern MBTs mount a long gun capable of delivering a variety of ammunition types, each optimized to the characteristics of a different target. For anti-tank work it is most common to use an armour-piercing fin-stabilized discarding sabot (APFSDS) round, which relies for its destructive power upon impacting at high velocity. The muzzle velocity of the tank's gun is thus important in determining the penetrating power of the projectile. Shaped-charge ammunition relies less on impact velocity since its penetrative power comes from the detonation of the warhead. However, the warhead must still hit the target, and high muzzle velocity is useful here too. It equates to a flatter shell trajectory and less time between firing and hitting the target, thus reducing the chances that the target will move out of the way. Fast-moving shells are also less affected by wind, humidity and air temperature.

RIGHT: The French Leclerc main battle tank is fitted with a 120mm (4.7in) smoothbore gun. It has a theoretical rate of fire of 12 rounds per minute. If enough targets were available, a Leclerc could burn through its ready ammunition in just a few minutes of combat.

68940067

Main Battle Tanks Today 2

Main Gun Range and Rate of Fire

- ▶ **M1A2 Abrams**
- ▶ **Leopard 2**
- ▶ **T-90S**
- ▶ **Challenger 2**
- ▶ **Leclerc**

Tank guns are precision weapons with a limited ammunition supply, which makes the choice of which targets to engage a critical one. Every shot must be deliberate and precise, not least because a threat that appears while the gun is being loaded cannot be engaged. Under most circumstances a tank will not shoot as fast as it can, but reloading time can nonetheless be critical. A high theoretical rate of fire means that the tank will have a shot ready soon after firing, even if that shot is not immediately taken, and contributes to the overall effectiveness of the force.

Some tanks use autoloaders to speed up the loading process, though these devices tend to be mechanically complex and have at times been plagued with malfunctions. Otherwise, the gun is loaded in the traditional manner, by the gunner and possibly another crew member manhandling a heavy shell into the breech. Even with some mechanical assistance, this requires considerable strength, especially when working in the small and awkwardly shaped space of a tank's turret.

Ammunition is usually stored at the rear of the turret, in a compartment designed to protect the crew if the ammunition is detonated by a direct hit. Rapid fire is a test of the crew's endurance; hauling shells from storage to breech will tire the crew quickly and cause the tank's rate of fire to drop off. Good design makes the reloading process as easy as possible and reduces crew fatigue, as does firing at a measured and deliberate rate.

Rate of Fire

Rate of fire is usually more important in terms of reducing the time spent without a ready shot, rather than the ability to get rid of large amounts of ammunition. Of course, in a target-rich or desperate situation, the tank will be firing as fast as it can reload and a high rate of fire may be a big advantage.

Main Gun Range

Most tank guns can throw a shell further than their listed effective range, but the chances of a hit are minimal. There is no point in wasting ammunition in this manner; harassing fire is best left to the artillery.

M1A2 Abrams Gun Range
8000ᵐ
(8749yd)

Leclerc Gun Range
4000ᵐ
(4374yd)

Leclerc Rate of Fire
12
shots per minute

M1A2 Abrams Rate of Fire
10
shots per minute

Leopard 2 Gun Range
8000ᵐ
(8749yd)

T-90S Gun Range
4000ᵐ
(4374yd)

Challenger 2 Gun Range
3000ᵐ
(3281yd)

ABOVE: Like many earlier Russian tanks, the T-90 uses an autoloader. This allows the crew size to be reduced and makes space for other systems. Autoloader systems have traditionally been plagued by technical issues, and are not favoured by most Western tank designers.

Leopard 2 Rate of Fire
10
shots per minute

T-90S Rate of Fire
8
shots per minute

Challenger 2 Rate of Fire
10
shots per minute

Middle Eastern Main Battle Tanks 1

Operational Range

▶ **Ramses II**
▶ **Merkava**
▶ **Zulfiqar**
▶ **Al-Khalid**

Many Middle Eastern tank designs are derived from Russian or Chinese vehicles, often with overseas assistance. Egypt's Ramses II is an updated version of the Russian T-55; the Zulfiqar was developed from the Russian T-72. The Al-Khalid, fielded by Pakistan, was developed in conjunction with China using elements of several earlier Chinese and Russian designs. Developed versions such as these often improve on the originals but also carry forward compromises made in the original design.

The Israeli Merkava series of tanks was developed specifically to meet Israeli needs and to incorporate lessons learned in earlier conflicts. Unusually, it has a front-mounted engine, allowing the hull to incorporate a space at the rear that can be used to carry additional ammunition or even infantry.

The Merkava series has undergone a steady evolution since the Mk 1 was introduced, gaining additional armour, a new engine and weapons, and a lengthened hull. It has come as far from the original design as have many of its Middle Eastern rivals, even if, unlike them, it has retained the original design's name.

Operational range is an important factor in developing or updating a tank design. It does not merely dictate the distance the tank can advance during an offensive, but also indicates how long the tank can go on making small local movements when on the defensive or in close contact with the enemy. Everything a tank does eats up fuel, and a vehicle that runs out is essentially helpless.

OPPOSITE: The Merkava follows an unusual design philosophy. Doors at the rear of the hull allow easy resupply of stores or ammunition, and the tank can carry a squad of infantry in rather cramped safety. In an emergency, the tank can be used to rescue casualties, although this is wasteful of its capabilities.

1 The Israeli Merkava tank was a revolutionary design when it first appeared. Its sloping armour gives excellent protection, and it outguns most other MBTs in the Middle East. It is, however, heavier and slower than most of its adversaries.

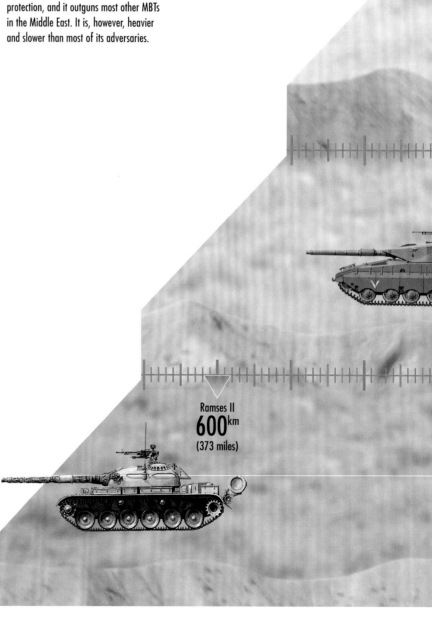

Ramses II
600km
(373 miles)

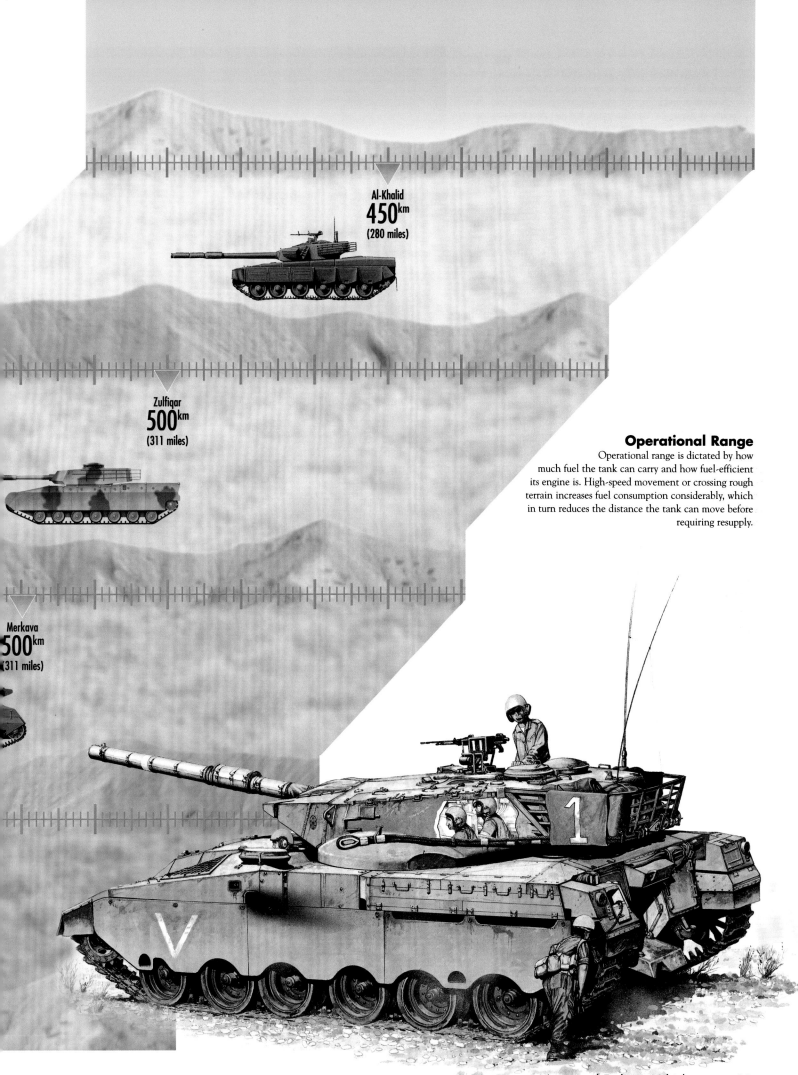

Al-Khalid
450^{km}
(280 miles)

Zulfiqar
500^{km}
(311 miles)

Merkava
500^{km}
(311 miles)

Operational Range
Operational range is dictated by how much fuel the tank can carry and how fuel-efficient its engine is. High-speed movement or crossing rough terrain increases fuel consumption considerably, which in turn reduces the distance the tank can move before requiring resupply.

Weight

A tank that is too lightly armoured will not survive on the battlefield. One whose weapons are inadequate will be ineffectual. Armament and protection are must-haves; designers have more leeway in terms of acceptable speed, and may decide to emphasize combat capability at the expense of pace.

1 Based on the Chinese Type 90-II, the Al-Khalid main battle tank has been developed for use by both the Pakistan and Chinese armed forces.

2 An Israeli Defence Force (IDF) Merkava tank stands watch somewhere in the Golan Heights region.

Zulfiqar Weight
40tonnes
(39.4 tons)

Ramses II Weight
45.8tonnes
(45.1 tons)

tonnes
40

tonnes
45.8

Zulfiqar Weight: 40 tonnes (39.4 tons)

Ramses II Weight: 45.8 tonnes (45.1 tons)

Ramses II Speed
72km/h
(45mph)

Al-Khalid Speed
72km/h
(45mph)

Zulfiqar Speed
70km/h
(43mph)

Middle Eastern Main Battle Tanks 2

Weight, Speed and Engine Power

▶ **Ramses II**
▶ **Merkava**
▶ **Zulfiqar**
▶ **Al-Khalid**

Al-Khalid Weight
47tonnes
(46.3 tons)

Merkava Weight
55.9tonnes
(55 tons)

	tonnes
	47

	tonnes
	55.9

Al-Khalid Weight: 47 tonnes (46.3 tons)

Merkava Weight: 55.9 tonnes (55 tons)

Merkava Speed
46km/h
(28.5mph)

To be effective, a tank needs to carry a number of very heavy systems. Its gun and ammunition weigh a lot, and these need a turret with a traversing mechanism capable of supporting them. This, along with the hull, is encased in armour. Making all of this metal move requires a powerful engine that propels the tank via a heavy transmission system and finally the tracks. In order to provide sufficient power, the engine must be large and, inevitably, heavy in weight.

The tank's top speed and its ability to cross rough terrain are both dictated by its weight and the power of its engine. A large engine takes up considerable space inside the tank, and fuel must also be carried; more powerful engines need more fuel to travel the same distance.

If it proves impossible to squeeze a suitable engine into a given hull design, then one solution is to enlarge the hull, but this increases the area that must be armoured and thus adds to weight, reducing speed or requiring a larger engine still.
A larger engine also adds its own weight to that of the tank – and the cycle continues.

Tank design is always a balancing act between power, weight and space required. Advanced engines with a high power-to-weight ratio offer many advantages, but ultimately any successful main battle tank design will fall within a typical range of power and weight values. There are good reasons why superlight and ultraheavy tanks are not fielded.

Maximum Speed

The Merkava trades mobility for protection, which is acceptable in a design intended mainly for defensive warfare. A relatively heavy (and slow) tank of this type is not well suited to sweeping breakthrough attacks and cannot readily redeploy to meet a new threat or take advantage of an opportunity.

Maximum Speed

Top speed is highly important, but it can only be maintained over good ground. Average speed of advance is dictated largely by the ability to cope with obstacles ranging from steep slopes and soft ground to water. All of these are likely to be encountered in a river crossing.

Fording Depth

Tank designers usually build some measure of wading capability into a modern MBT. Without it, operations can be severely restricted by water obstacles. However, deep wading requires specialist equipment such as raised engine intakes, which take up space and add weight to the tank.

K2 Speed
70km/h
(43mph)

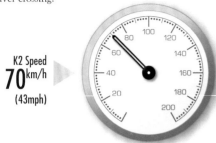

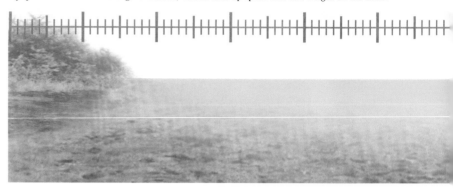

Type 90 Speed
70km/h
(43mph)

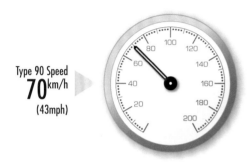

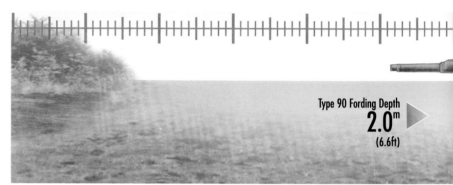

Type 90 Fording Depth
2.0m
(6.6ft)

T-80 Speed
60km/h
(37mph)

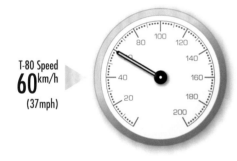

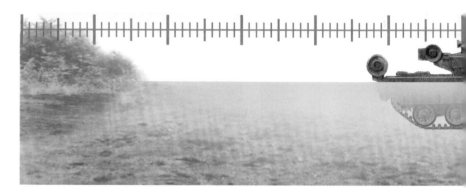

PT-91 Speed
60km/h
(37mph)

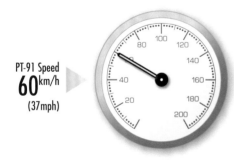

PT-91 Fording Depth
1.4m
(4.6ft)

Type 85-IIM Speed
57km/h
(35mph)

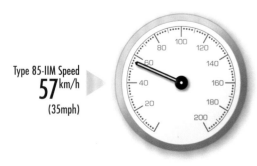

Type 85-IIM Fording Depth
1.4m
(4.6ft)

Eastern Main Battle Tanks

Maximum Speed and Fording Depth

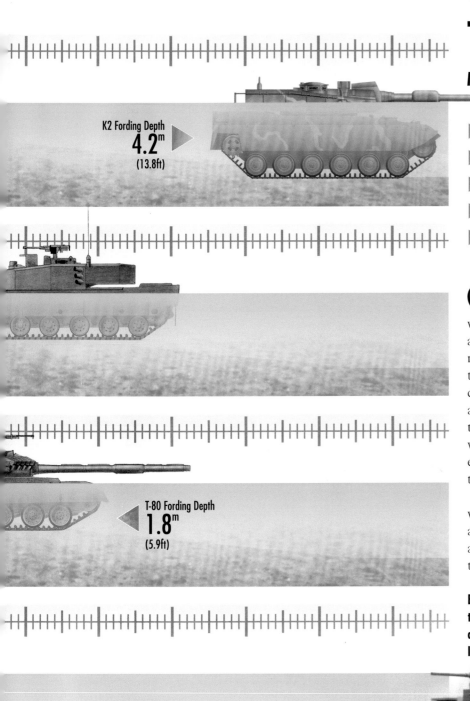

K2 Fording Depth
4.2m
(13.8ft)

T-80 Fording Depth
1.8m
(5.9ft)

▶ **Type 85-IIM**
▶ **K2 Black Panther**
▶ **PT-91**
▶ **T-80**
▶ **Type 90 Kyu-maru**

One of the most serious obstacles that can face an armoured force is a river or other body of water. For an MBT the only solution is to drive along the bottom. The ability to cross and keep moving is thus defined by the depth of water the tank can successfully negotiate and its ability to cope with underwater obstacles, loose ground and steep banks. In order to ford a river deeper than the bottom of its hull, a tank must be watertight. It must also be able to get air into the engine and exhaust gases out without flooding the engine compartment.

Some tanks must be prepared before entering water, but others, such as the K2 Black Panther, are equipped with a deep-wading kit as standard and can drive straight though any river within their depth capabilities.

BELOW: Developed in China from the unsuccessful Type 85, the Type 85-IIM was given a more powerful gun and an autoloader, plus improved electronics and fire-control systems. It has achieved some export success, with sales to Pakistan.

Infantry Fighting Vehicles of the 90s

Personnel Capacity and Weapons Calibre

▶ **M-60P**
▶ **BTR-80**
▶ **VCC-80 Dardo**
▶ **BTR-90**
▶ **KIVF K-200**

The infantry fighting vehicle (IFV) concept grew out of the armoured personnel carrier, but the transition was neither instant nor total. The line between the two remains blurry in places – a lightly armed IFV could arguably be called an APC, whatever classification its designers may give it. In order to provide adequate support for its troop contingent, an IFV needs at least a heavy machine gun and realistically should be armed with an automatic cannon of 20mm (0.79in) or greater calibre.

Some IFVs clearly show their lineage, being little more than upgunned APCs. The M-60P and BTR-80 are examples of this transition. Both are basically armoured personnel carriers rather than custom-designed IFVs.

The Korean K-200, on the other hand, was indirectly developed from the immensely successful US M113 APC, but was envisaged from the outset as an IFV. It can ford a shallow river and can also be used as a weapons carrier by adding heavier arms.

Many IFVs incorporate firing ports or even permanently mounted port weapons for troops, which theoretically allows them to fight from inside the vehicle. In practice, it is extremely hard to hit anything from a firing port, and using an IFV as a mobile firing position in this manner is somewhat inefficient. It might be better to replace the troop capacity with a heavier weapon and create a light combat vehicle. After all, an IFV's primary role is still to get infantry where they are going, and infantry, by definition, fight best when dismounted.

Personnel Capacity

The purpose of an IFV remains the same as that of its predecessor, the APC. It is intended to transport infantry quickly to the combat area whilst protecting them from anti-personnel threats such as snipers, machine guns and artillery-shell fragments.

M-60P

BTR-90

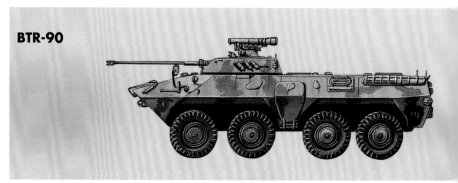

K-200

BTR-80

VCC-80

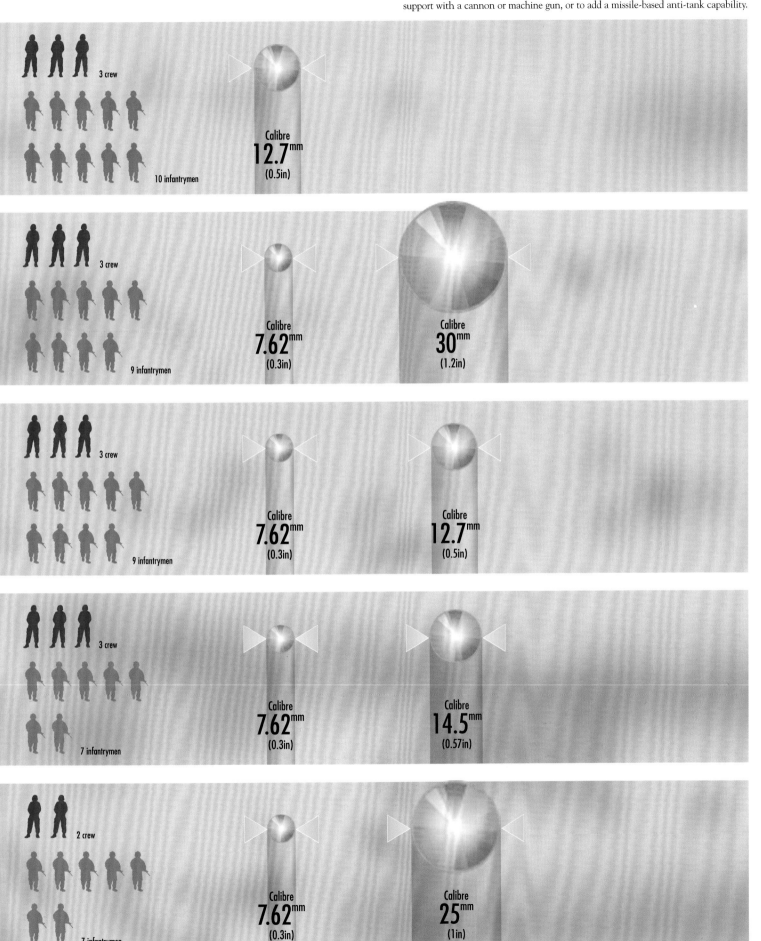

3 crew

10 infantrymen

Calibre
12.7mm
(0.5in)

3 crew

9 infantrymen

Calibre
7.62mm
(0.3in)

Calibre
30mm
(1.2in)

3 crew

9 infantrymen

Calibre
7.62mm
(0.3in)

Calibre
12.7mm
(0.5in)

3 crew

7 infantrymen

Calibre
7.62mm
(0.3in)

Calibre
14.5mm
(0.57in)

2 crew

7 infantrymen

Calibre
7.62mm
(0.3in)

Calibre
25mm
(1in)

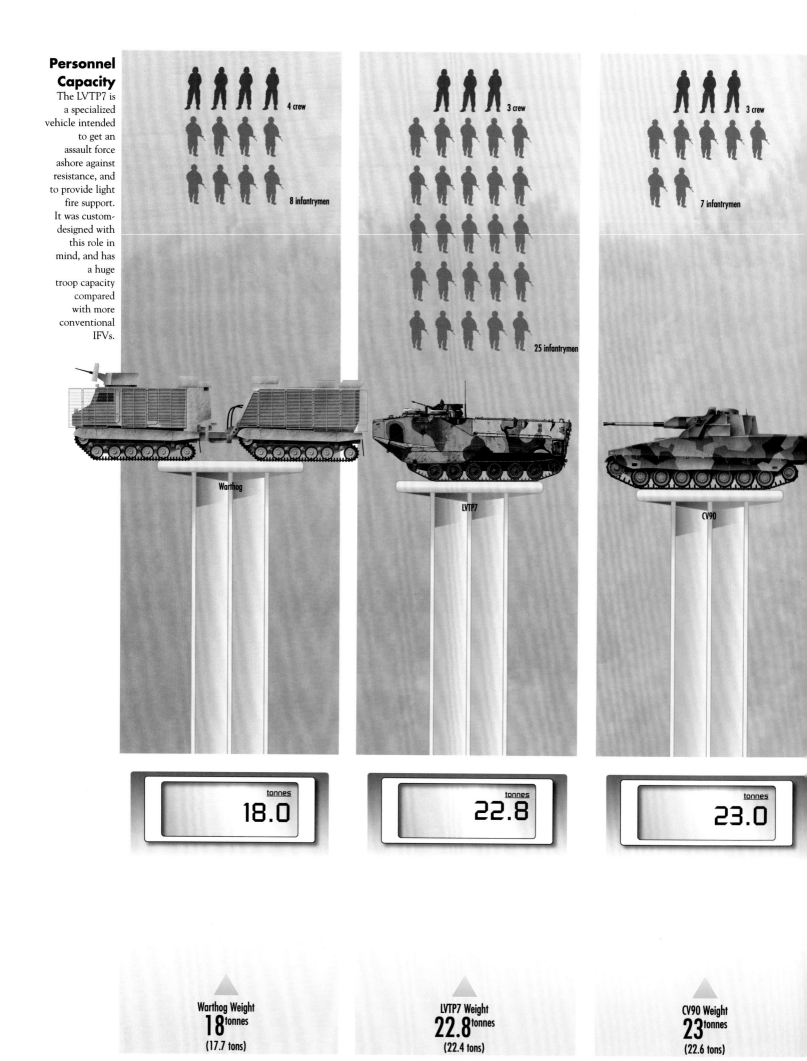

Personnel Capacity

The LVTP7 is a specialized vehicle intended to get an assault force ashore against resistance, and to provide light fire support. It was custom-designed with this role in mind, and has a huge troop capacity compared with more conventional IFVs.

4 crew

8 infantrymen

3 crew

25 infantrymen

3 crew

7 infantrymen

Warthog

LVTP7

CV90

tonnes	tonnes	tonnes
18.0	22.8	23.0

Warthog Weight
18 tonnes
(17.7 tons)

LVTP7 Weight
22.8 tonnes
(22.4 tons)

CV90 Weight
23 tonnes
(22.6 tons)

3 crew

7 infantrymen

Bionix 25

3 crew

9 infantrymen

Namer

tonnes

23.0

tonnes

60.0

Bionix 25 Weight
23tonnes
(22.6tons)

Namer Weight
60tonnes
(59.1 tons)

Tracked Infantry Fighting Vehicles

Weight and Personnel Capacity

▶ **LVTP7**
▶ **CV90**
▶ **Namer**
▶ **Warthog**
▶ **Bionix 25**

A number of innovative IFV designs have emerged in recent years, many of them from the industries of nations such as Singapore. Modern IFVs are designed with more than their immediate capabilities in mind, and often have 'growth potential' built into the design. The capacity to be adapted to the needs of an export customer or to accommodate lessons learned during a deployment allows a vehicle to be updated and modified rather than requiring replacement when operational needs change.

Many IFVs are part of a family of variants, which increases their attractiveness to buyers. A single vehicle that can be configured as a weapons carrier, field ambulance, command vehicle or mobile artillery observation post is far more efficient from a maintenance and spares-procurement point of view than several different designs. Thus vehicles such as the Warthog are attractive as they reduce the overall lifetime cost of operating a fleet of light armoured vehicles.

Today's IFV designs often use a modular system, allowing armament to be reconfigured as necessary. It is not uncommon for a relatively cheap base model to be offered, along with a number of upgrades and specialist configurations. This brings IFVs within the budget of forces that might otherwise simply not be able to afford them, and in turn increases the potential for export sales. However, custom-designed vehicles such as the US Advanced Amphibious Assault Vehicle (AAAV) are often more effective in their specialist role, making them a good choice for those forces that can afford them.

Weight
The Israeli Namer IFV was created by converting early-model Merkava tanks into personnel carriers. It is very heavy by IFV standards but is also extremely well protected. The weight saved by removing the turret and replacing it with a remotely operated light-weapons mount was used to add greater protection to the hull.

Wheeled Personnel Carriers 1

Maximum Speed

▶ **GTK Boxer**
▶ **LAV III**
▶ **LGS Fennek**
▶ **Stryker**

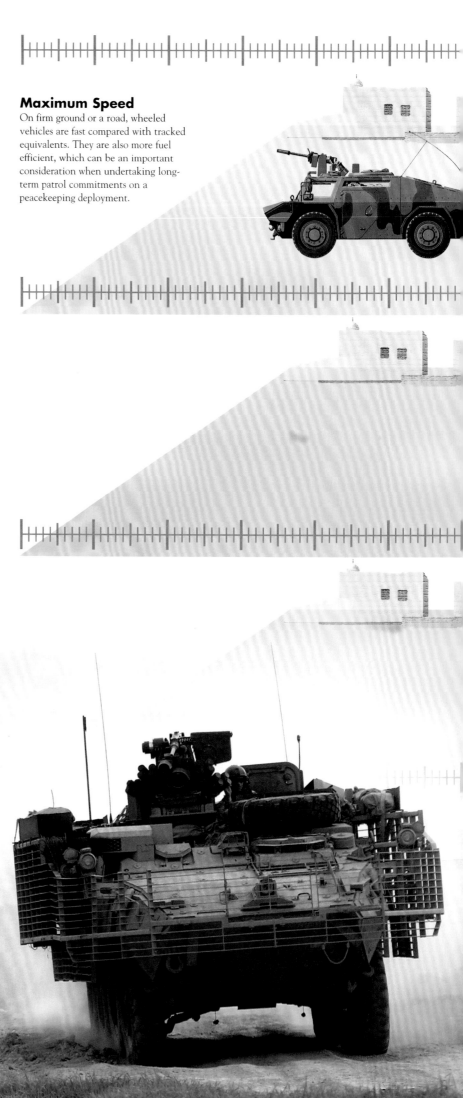

Maximum Speed

On firm ground or a road, wheeled vehicles are fast compared with tracked equivalents. They are also more fuel efficient, which can be an important consideration when undertaking long-term patrol commitments on a peacekeeping deployment.

Tracked vehicles require a great deal of support and maintenance, and are often difficult to deploy quickly or support in difficult conditions. Although their rough-terrain capability is lower, wheeled vehicles are often better suited to rapid-deployment operations. They are also cheaper and arguably better tailored to a peacekeeping or security deployment than a tracked vehicle. Many wheeled personnel carriers are part of a family of vehicles, and in another configuration might be considered a conventional armoured car suitable for use in providing fire-support or reconnaissance.

A wheeled APC cannot be as heavily protected as a tracked vehicle due to weight constraints, so will often rely upon speed for protection. The vehicle will be lightly armoured and should be able to protect its occupants from machine-gun fire and shell fragments. Many APCs have a secondary layer of protection around the crew area, which prevents small fragments from entering. While this will not help against a direct hit with an anti-tank weapon, it does greatly increase crew survivability against the commonest threats on the modern battlefield, and will usually allow the crew to escape with minor injuries even if the vehicle is disabled.

Successful designs are often used as the basis for further development. Thus the Piranha III, bought by several nations and designated LAV III in Canadian service, was used as the basis for the US Army's Interim Armoured Vehicle programme and entered service as the Stryker. A fire-support variant with a 105mm (4.1in) gun is built on the same chassis.

RIGHT: A US Army Styker vehicle carries out patrol duties. Wheeled vehicles generally impose less of a logistics burden than tracked equivalents, though they are also usually less capable in combat. The trade-off between more combat vehicles and individual combat capability makes selecting the right armoured vehicle a difficult choice.

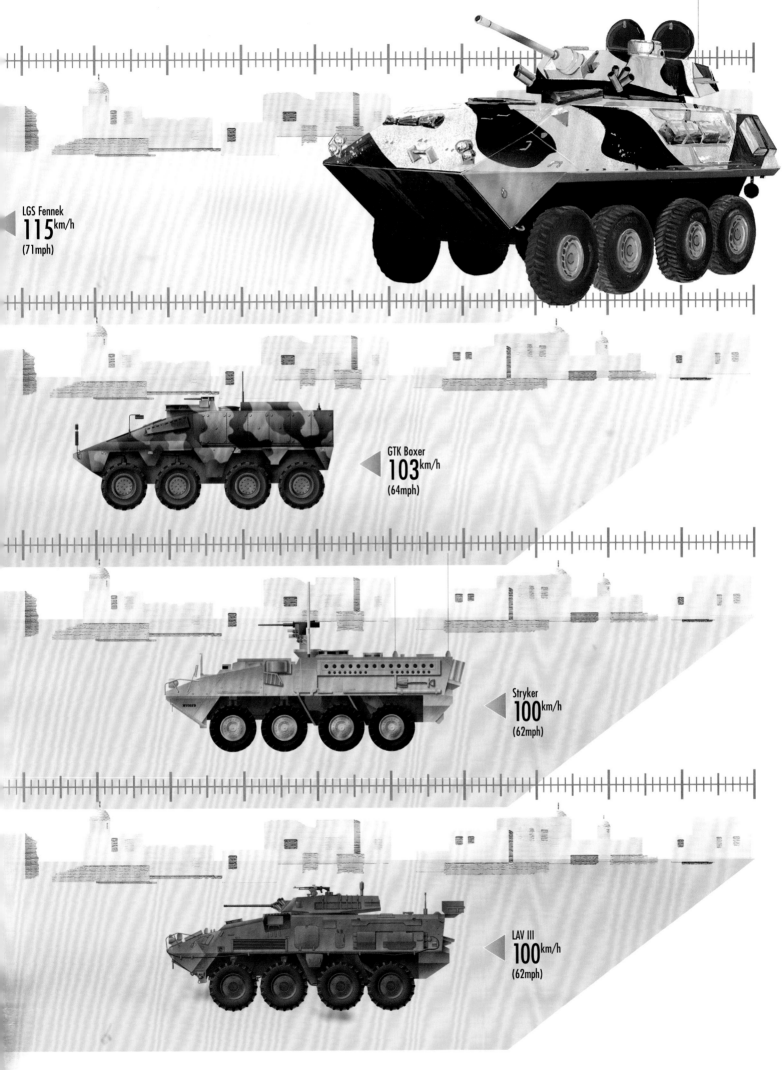

LGS Fennek
115km/h
(71mph)

GTK Boxer
103km/h
(64mph)

Stryker
100km/h
(62mph)

LAV III
100km/h
(62mph)

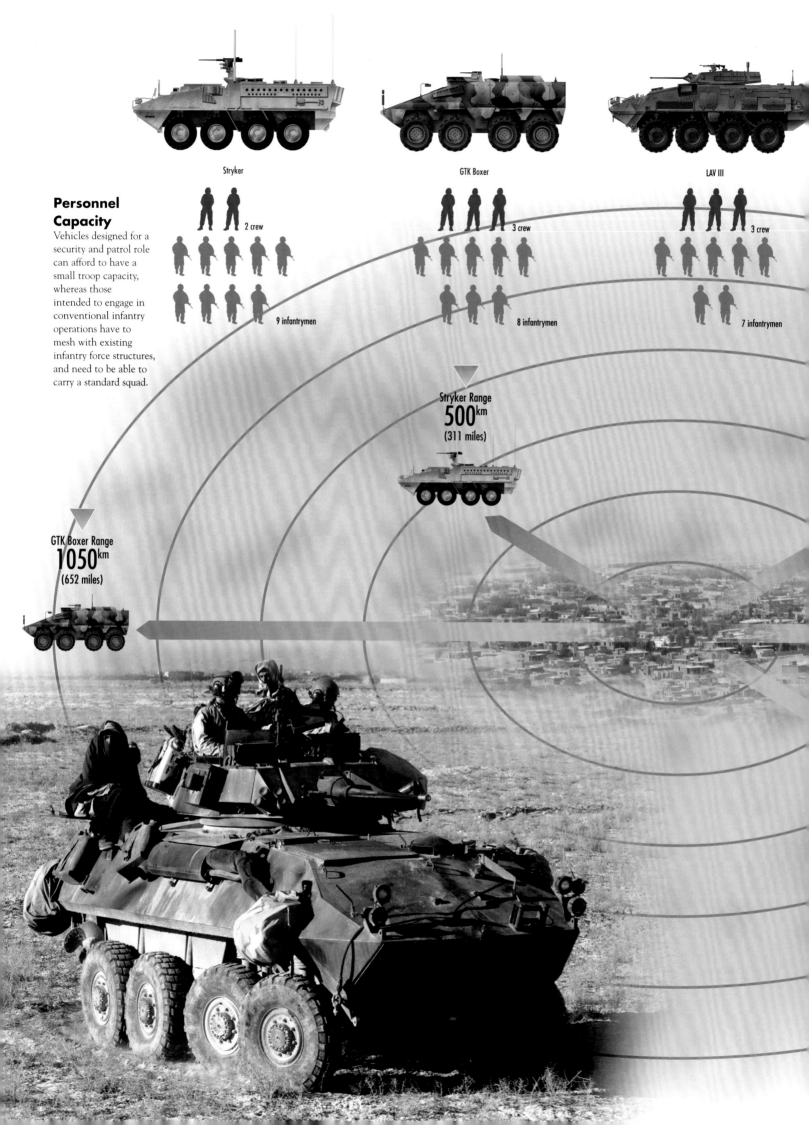

Stryker

GTK Boxer

LAV III

Personnel Capacity

Vehicles designed for a security and patrol role can afford to have a small troop capacity, whereas those intended to engage in conventional infantry operations have to mesh with existing infantry force structures, and need to be able to carry a standard squad.

2 crew

9 infantrymen

3 crew

8 infantrymen

3 crew

7 infantrymen

Stryker Range
500km
(311 miles)

GTK Boxer Range
1050km
(652 miles)

Mastiff PPV

LGS Fennek

2 crew

3 crew

4 infantrymen

Wheeled Personnel Carriers 2

Operational Range and Personnel Capacity

▶ **GTK Boxer**
▶ **Mastiff PPV**
▶ **LAV III**
▶ **LGS Fennek**
▶ **Stryker**

LAV III Range
450km
(280 miles)

Mastiff PPV Range
966km
(600 miles)

LGS Fennek Range
860km
(534 miles)

The majority of personnel carriers are designed around the ability to carry an infantry squad or section, of whatever size the owning nation normally deploys. Sometimes design trade-offs force changes of doctrine – for example, smaller squads or a different breakdown of sub-units within a force. In an emergency, such as when only a single vehicle is available to evacuate an infantry force from a dire situation, a surprisingly large number of fully equipped soldiers can be crammed into a small space. This is not conducive to operational efficiency, but it has saved lives.

Some vehicles, such as the Fennek, were designed as reconnaissance assets rather than troop carriers but are sometimes pressed into service to carry a small force when necessary. Others – the Mastiff, for instance – bridge the gap between recce/patrol assets and personnel carriers. The Mastiff was designed as a patrol vehicle which could carry troops, rather than a vehicle to transport troops into combat. It is primarily suited to peacekeeping and security operations, though it can be used as a combat asset at need.

Mines are a major threat to vehicles carrying out relatively predictable patrol operations, such as when on a peacekeeping deployment, and so many modern personnel carriers have excellent mine protection even if their overall armour is not all that heavy. Many wheeled combat vehicles are designed to remain drivable even with a wheel blown off, enabling them to drive out of trouble or to limp home even after serious damage.

Operational Range
A large radius of operation is vital to an effective combat vehicle, and even more so if it is to be used for patrol operations. Wheeled APCs are highly useful for security duties, patrolling supply routes and maintaining an 'armed presence' across a wide area.

OPPOSITE: The LAV III offers a good balance of firepower, transport capacity and mobility. It can serve as a utility supply vehicle at need, or provide security in areas where it is not considered appropriate to deploy tanks. Tracked vehicles are generally seen as more threatening than wheeled ones. Sometimes this is a good thing; when it is not, wheeled vehicles are a better option.

Missile-armed Combat Vehicles

Missile Range

▶ **BTR-90**
▶ **M901**
▶ **VBL**
▶ **M980**

Not all combat vehicles can carry a gun powerful enough to endanger another AFV, but missile systems can be fitted to most vehicles. They are, in general, light and recoilless, so that in theory it is possible to field a vast force of light, highly mobile tank slayers. However, missiles do have drawbacks. They are bulkier than gun rounds, reducing the number of shots available, and are usually expensive. They also produce a lot of backblast, which can reveal a launcher's position.

Despite these drawbacks, many nations field missile-equipped vehicles. They fill a niche once occupied by the gun-armed tank destroyer or the infantry anti-tank gun. Many of the weapons systems in use aboard these vehicles have other applications. The VBL uses MILAN, which is also deployed with infantry formations. This simplifies logistics and training, but infantry missile systems tend to be short-ranged and may lack the capability to destroy a heavily protected MBT.

Heavier missiles such as TOW and Konkurs, as used by the M901 and BTR-90 respectively, use wire-guidance, which allows an accurate attack at a great distance. Their warheads are powerful enough to be effective against most vehicles, but the missile's long flight time makes the launching vehicle vulnerable to return fire. The missile is guided from the vehicle, which must remain halted and exposed while the missile is in flight.

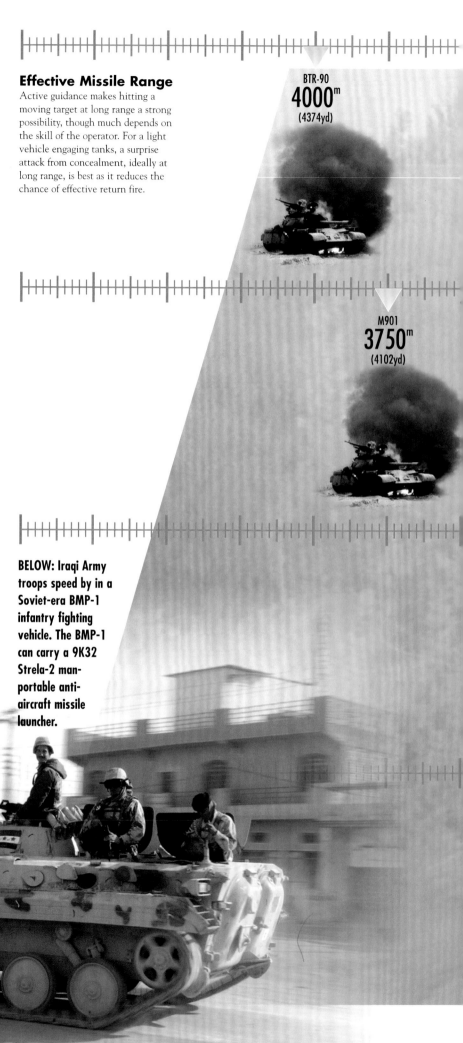

Effective Missile Range

Active guidance makes hitting a moving target at long range a strong possibility, though much depends on the skill of the operator. For a light vehicle engaging tanks, a surprise attack from concealment, ideally at long range, is best as it reduces the chance of effective return fire.

BTR-90
4000ᵐ
(4374yd)

M901
3750ᵐ
(4102yd)

BELOW: Iraqi Army troops speed by in a Soviet-era BMP-1 infantry fighting vehicle. The BMP-1 can carry a 9K32 Strela-2 man-portable anti-aircraft missile launcher.

BTR-90

M901

M980

3000^m
(3281yd)

M980

VBL

2000^m
(2187yd)

VBL

Big-gun Armoured Cars

Maximum Fording Depth, Gradient and Vertical Obstacles

- ▶ **Rooikat**
- ▶ **Piranha**
- ▶ **Renault VBC 90**
- ▶ **RPX-90**
- ▶ **Centauro**

The first armoured cars were exactly that – ordinary touring cars fitted with some armour and a weapon. Even as the concept matured into a capable combat vehicle, the armoured car was still associated with light weapons such as machine guns and automatic cannon. However, advances in technology, especially in recoil control, have made it possible for large armoured cars to carry a gun capable of threatening many tanks.

The main problem facing such heavy designs is cross-country mobility. The armoured car's main assets are cheapness, compared with tracked AFVs, and high speed. An armoured car that is unduly loaded down may lose much of its mobility, and attempts to remedy the problem can drive the cost up to the point where it is just as efficient to deploy tracked vehicles. There is an upper limit to how heavy an armoured car can be before it becomes an inferior light tank.

BELOW: The Centauro heavy armoured car has proven its worth on peacekeeping operations, where its combination of mobility and heavy firepower makes it ideal for controlling wide areas and protecting supply convoys.

Fording Depth

While some lighter armoured car designs are amphibious, most larger models are not. A relatively light weight and buoyant tyre can be a disadvantage when trying to gain purchase on a soft riverbed, meaning that armoured cars are often less able to ford fast-flowing water than a tracked vehicle of similar size.

Rooikat Fording Depth
1.5^m
(4.9ft)

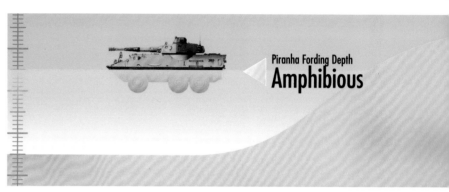

Piranha Fording Depth
Amphibious

Centauro Fording Depth
1.5^m
(4.9ft)

VBC 90 Fording Depth
1.2^m
(3.9ft)

RPX-90 Fording Depth
1.4^m
(4.6ft)

Gradients

Many armoured cars have impressive hill-climbing performance. However, traversing a slope is more of a problem. The Rooikat, for example, is challenged by traversing a 30-degree gradient. Anything steeper runs the risk of tipping the vehicle over.

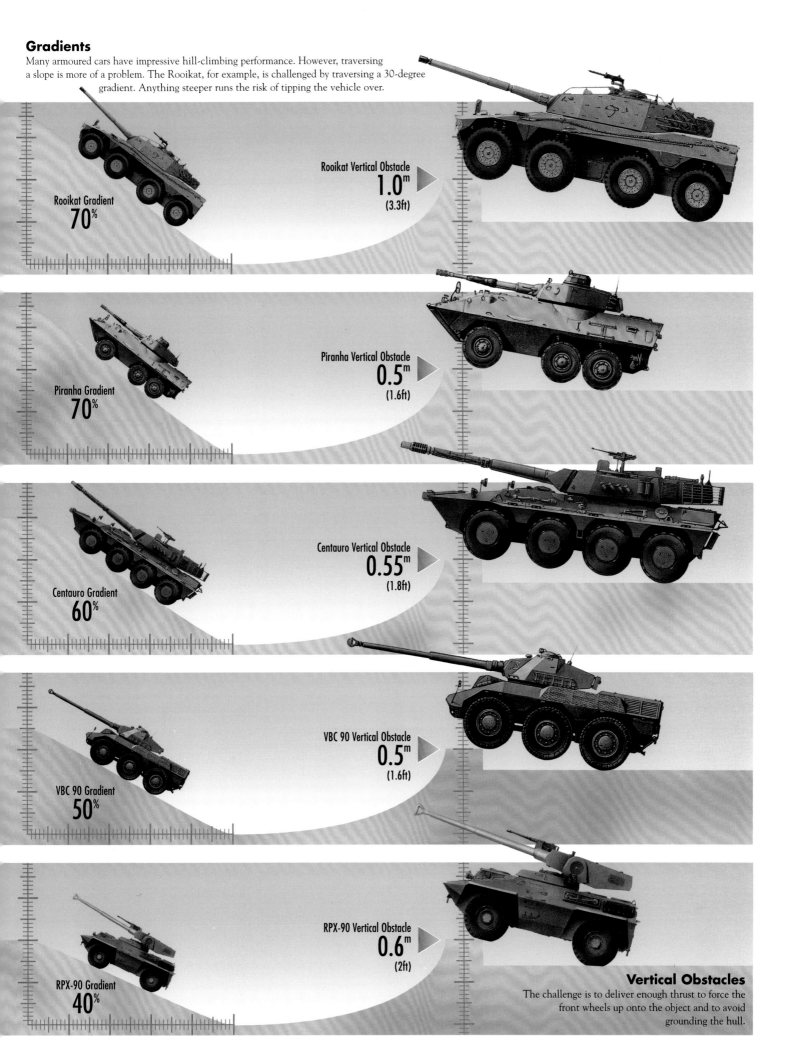

Rooikat Vertical Obstacle
1.0m
(3.3ft)

Rooikat Gradient
70%

Piranha Vertical Obstacle
0.5m
(1.6ft)

Piranha Gradient
70%

Centauro Vertical Obstacle
0.55m
(1.8ft)

Centauro Gradient
60%

VBC 90 Vertical Obstacle
0.5m
(1.6ft)

VBC 90 Gradient
50%

RPX-90 Vertical Obstacle
0.6m
(2ft)

RPX-90 Gradient
40%

Vertical Obstacles
The challenge is to deliver enough thrust to force the front wheels up onto the object and to avoid grounding the hull.

Maximum Speed

More wheels means lower ground pressure and better off-road performance once the vehicle exceeds a certain weight, but the wheels and their associated transmission systems also add to the weight of the vehicle, which reduces speed unless a larger engine is fitted.

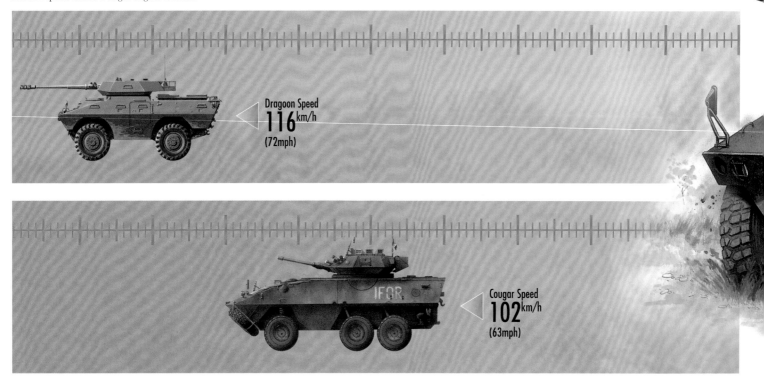

Dragoon Speed
116 km/h
(72mph)

Cougar Speed
102 km/h
(63mph)

Cascavel Speed
100 km/h
(62mph)

ERC 90 Speed
100 km/h
(62mph)

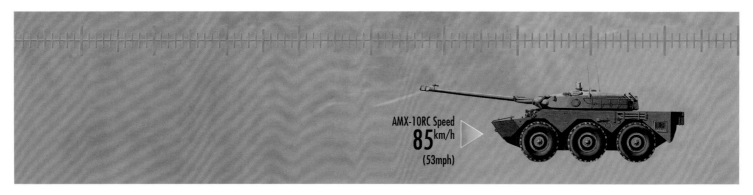

AMX-10RC Speed
85 km/h
(53mph)

Fire-support Armoured Cars

Maximum Speed and Engine Power

▶ **AMX-10RC**
▶ **Cougar**
▶ **Dragoon**
▶ **ERC 90**
▶ **Engesa EE-9 Cascavel**

Dragoon

Cougar

Cascavel

ERC 90

Dragoon Engine Power
223kW
(303.2hp)

Cougar Engine Power
160kW
(217.5hp)

Cascavel Engine Power
158kW
(214.8hp)

ERC 90 Engine Power
116kW
(157.7hp)

Cylinders
6

Cylinders
6

Cylinders
6

Cylinders
V6

A ny armoured-vehicle design is a trade-off between armour, firepower and speed, and where a main battle tank emphasizes the first two, armoured cars are characterized by speed. If they are also to carry heavy firepower then this must be at the expense of armour protection. As a result, most are protected only against shell splinters and light automatic weapons. Against heavier weapons their best defence is not to be hit, working on the principle that 'speed is armour'.

Many fire-support armoured cars mount a gun in the 90mm (3.5in) category, with some examples using heavier weapons. The Canadian-designed Cougar armoured car made use of an existing system by incorporating the entire turret of the Scorpion armoured reconnaissance vehicle, including its 76mm (3in) gun. This is quite adequate for fire-support work but insufficient for attacking tanks – the Cougar can fight its own kind but will come off worse in an engagement with anything better protected.

On the other hand, the 105mm (4.1in) gun carried by the French AMX-10RC is capable of penetrating many tanks and offers significantly greater firepower than the more common 90mm (3.5in) gun. However, this comes at a price. Although amphibious and possessing good mobility, the AMX-10RC is significantly slower than many competing designs. Under most circumstances this is not a major drawback, but there are times when high speed can make up for a lack of armour. It is perhaps significant that some of the AMX-10RCs deployed for the Gulf War were up-armoured.

Engine Power

A larger and more powerful engine will increase the vehicle's power-to-weight ratio, but it will also increase overall weight and bulk. If the cycle of increased size, power and weight gets out of hand, then an overly large vehicle will be the result; sometimes it is better to accept the lesser capabilities of a small, fast vehicle.

Light Tanks and Recce Vehicles 1

Weight vs Maximum Speed

▶ **VEC Cavalry Scout Vehicle**
▶ **OTO Melara R3 Capraia**
▶ **FV107 Scimitar**
▶ **Scorpion 90**
▶ **Stingray 2**

Speed and mobility are the primary assets of reconnaissance vehicles, enabling them to avoid contact with the enemy wherever possible. However, light vehicles of this sort are also highly useful as a source of rapidly deployable firepower. They are thus often used as the 'teeth' of fast-moving cavalry formations and to add firepower to an infantry force. Their small size and relatively low weight enables light vehicles to be transported by air and, in some cases, even dropped by parachute.

There are times when light armoured vehicles are the only ones available, and as a rule any armoured support is better than no armoured support. Thus for rapid-deployment forces or those operating in very distant areas, light vehicles are a good option. Weight and overall size become very important considerations when loading an amphibious warfare ship or a transport aircraft.

A variety of approaches are taken by light-armoured-vehicle designers, and there is no clear point where wheels or tracks are 'better'. The choice depends on a range of factors, including the sort of terrain the vehicle may have to operate in, the availability of good maintenance and support, and whether strategic or tactical mobility is more important. Experience has shown that there are places that a light tank such as a Scorpion or Scimitar can go that even infantry will struggle to get across. A wheeled vehicle would not be able to cope with such terrain, but on firmer ground a wheeled vehicle can travel faster for longer.

Weight

The acceptable weight of a vehicle depends upon what it is designed to do. The Scorpion and Scimitar were both intended primarily for the armoured reconnaissance role, whereas the Stingray is more of a combat or fire-support platform, and requires heavier armament and protection.

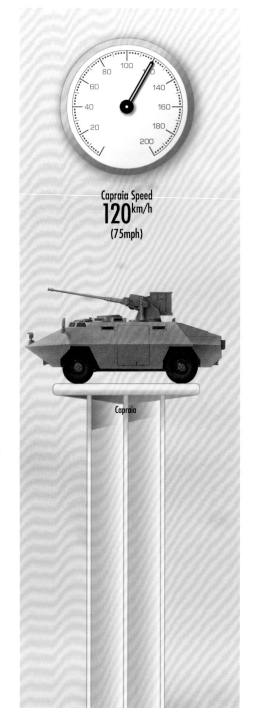

Capraia Speed
120km/h
(75mph)

Capraia

Scimitar Speed
80km/h
(50mph)

Scimitar

tonnes
3.2

tonnes
7.8

Capraia Weight
3.2tonnes
(3.1 tons)

Scimitar Weight
7.8tonnes
(7.7 tons)

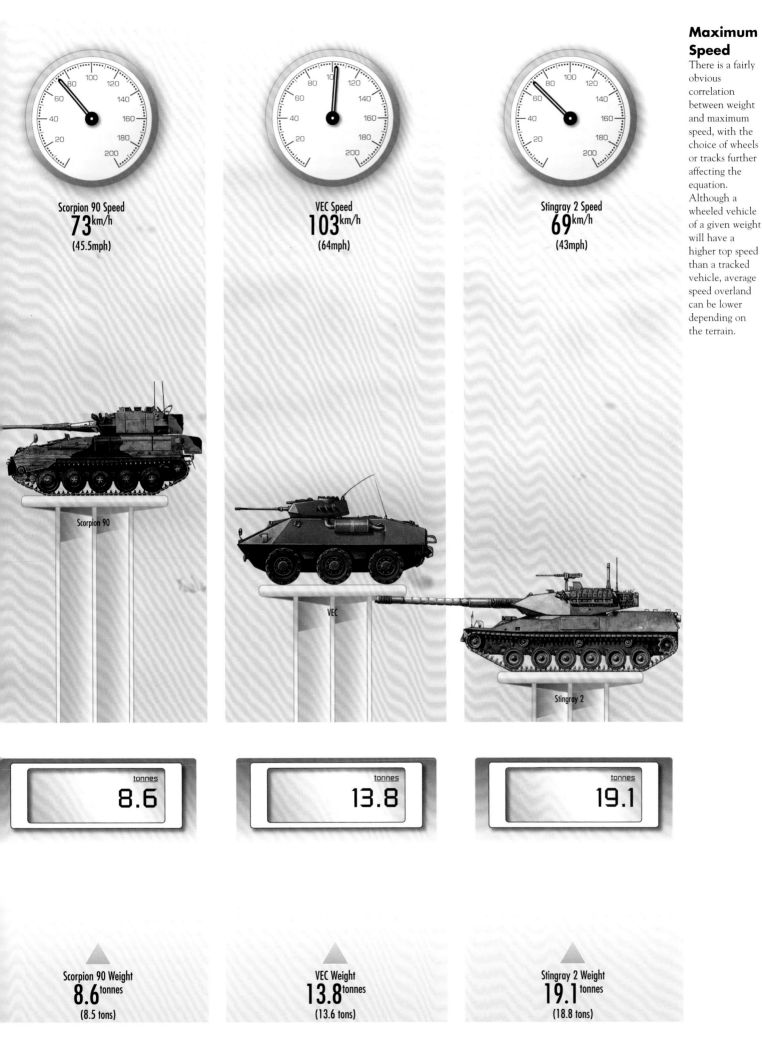

Scorpion 90 Speed
73km/h
(45.5mph)

VEC Speed
103km/h
(64mph)

Stingray 2 Speed
69km/h
(43mph)

Maximum Speed

There is a fairly obvious correlation between weight and maximum speed, with the choice of wheels or tracks further affecting the equation. Although a wheeled vehicle of a given weight will have a higher top speed than a tracked vehicle, average speed overland can be lower depending on the terrain.

Scorpion 90

VEC

Stingray 2

tonnes
8.6

tonnes
13.8

tonnes
19.1

Scorpion 90 Weight
8.6tonnes
(8.5 tons)

VEC Weight
13.8tonnes
(13.6 tons)

Stingray 2 Weight
19.1tonnes
(18.8 tons)

Light Tanks and Recce Vehicles 2

Operational Range and Weapons Calibre

▶ **VEC Cavalry Scout Vehicle**
▶ **OTO Melara R3 Capraia**
▶ **FV107 Scimitar**
▶ **Scorpion 90**
▶ **Stingray 2**

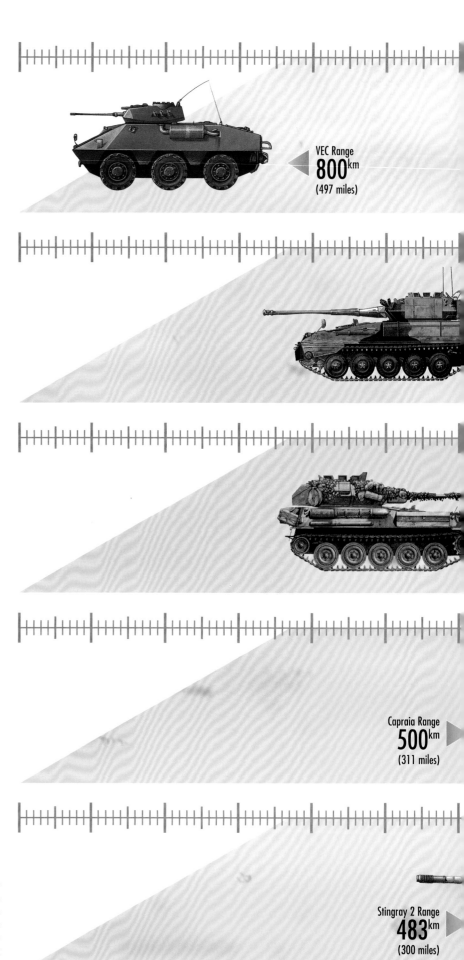

VEC Range
800km
(497 miles)

Capraia Range
500km
(311 miles)

Stingray 2 Range
483km
(300 miles)

The uses that light armoured vehicles are put to depends greatly upon what other weapons systems are available. Often there is no choice but to fight with whatever is at hand, but if 'real' tanks can reach the combat area quickly enough then light assets are better used for flank protection and reconnaissance. In the former role, the high speed of light tanks is a great advantage as they can move to counter any attempt to get around the flank of the main force, if necessary fighting a highly fluid delaying action while heavier assets redeploy to deal with the threat.

In order to keep their weight down and make them small targets, some light armoured vehicles use a relatively light weapon or a gun-over-hull configuration. The latter is an unarmoured weapon mounting controlled from within the vehicle, dispensing with the weight of a turret and its associated armour. A hit on the weapon will probably disable it, but the chances of being hit or even spotted are minimized by reducing the overall size of the vehicle.

Many light tanks are designed for the export market, and as such may be fitted into a variety of roles by the end user. The Stingray, for example, mounts a 105mm (4.1in) gun that enables its use as a light battle tank if necessary. It is really too lightly armoured for this role, but in some parts of the world it will not encounter first-line anti-tank weapons. In such an environment a relatively cheap vehicle may be able to fill in for heavier tanks without being excessively vulnerable.

Operational Range

Armoured reconnaissance often requires quite long forays into potentially hostile territory, and sometimes a rapid retreat becomes necessary. Operational range is calculated on the basis of a modest speed, but long range can translate into the ability to flee at top speed for a lengthy period. Whilst undignified, this is a survival trait in a reconnaissance vehicle.

Weapons Calibre

The most important 'weapon' aboard a reconnaissance vehicle is probably its radio; information gathered allows more powerful assets to be brought to bear. However, an effective weapons system is important to any vehicle likely to be in proximity to the enemy.

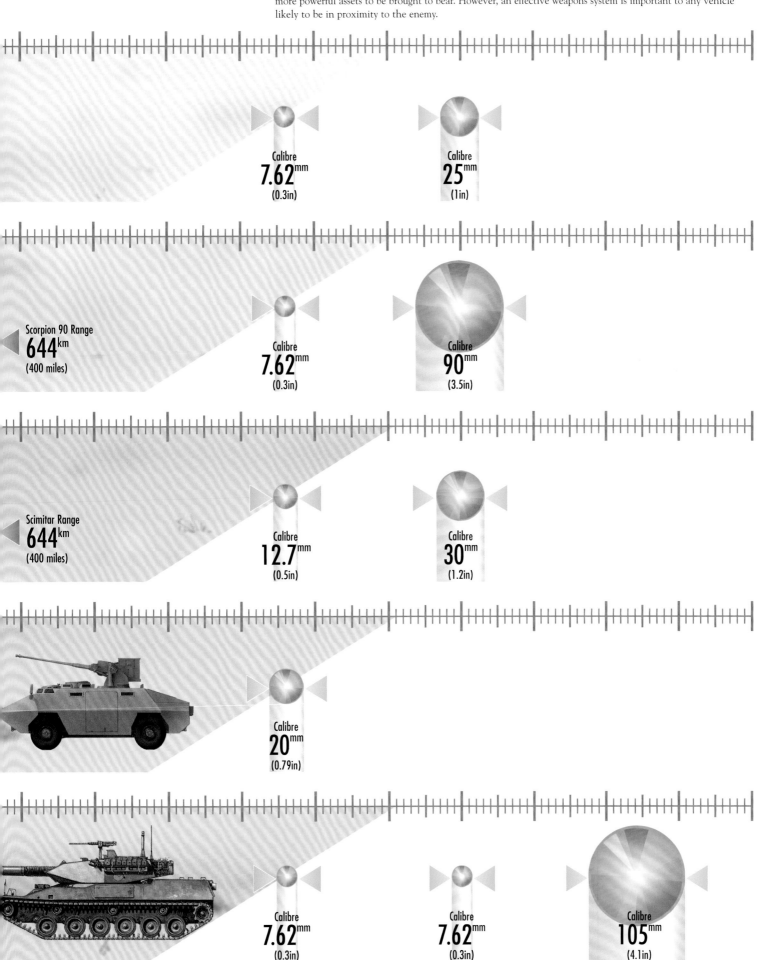

Calibre
7.62mm
(0.3in)

Calibre
25mm
(1in)

Scorpion 90 Range
644km
(400 miles)

Calibre
7.62mm
(0.3in)

Calibre
90mm
(3.5in)

Scimitar Range
644km
(400 miles)

Calibre
12.7mm
(0.5in)

Calibre
30mm
(1.2in)

Calibre
20mm
(0.79in)

Calibre
7.62mm
(0.3in)

Calibre
7.62mm
(0.3in)

Calibre
105mm
(4.1in)

Maximum Speed

A high road speed is important for patrol vehicles. Lacking significant armour, mobility is their best defence, and the ability to react rapidly to a situation developing some distance away is essential to maintaining control over an area.

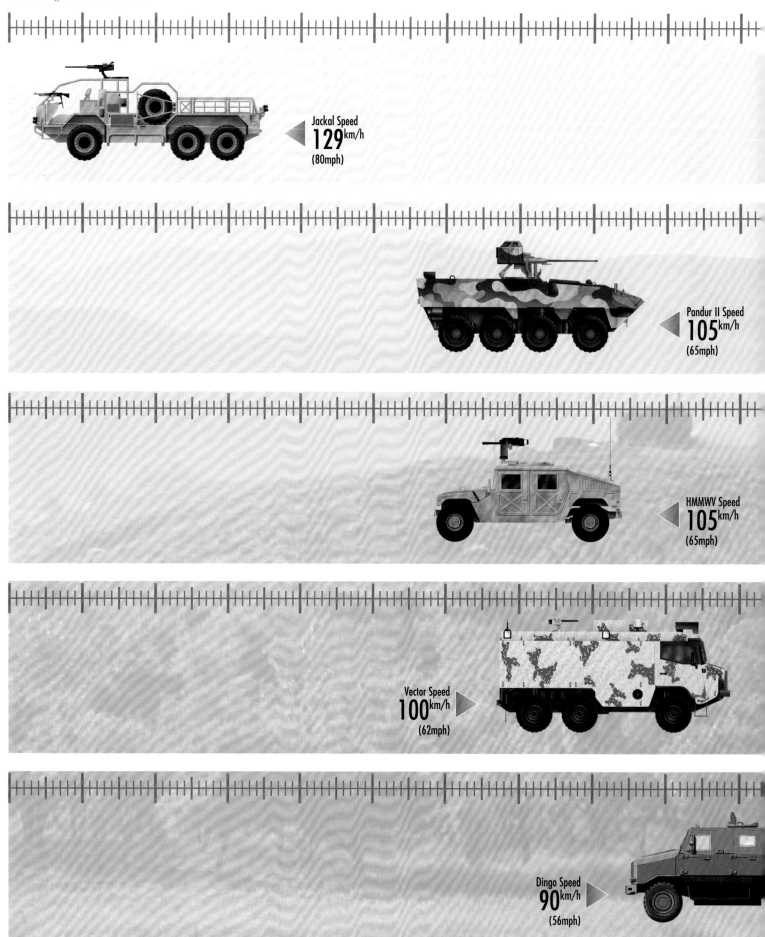

Jackal Speed
129km/h
(80mph)

Pandur II Speed
105km/h
(65mph)

HMMWV Speed
105km/h
(65mph)

Vector Speed
100km/h
(62mph)

Dingo Speed
90km/h
(56mph)

Multi-purpose Patrol Vehicles 1

Maximum Speed and Weight

▶ **M998 HMMWV**
▶ **AFT Dingo**
▶ **Jackal MWMIK**
▶ **Pandur II**
▶ **Pinzgauer Vector PPV**

In the post-Cold War world, there is still a need for heavy armoured forces and their supporting arms – self-propelled artillery and infantry fighting vehicles. However, these systems are extremely expensive and are not well suited to routine patrol and security operations. Heavy forces are best kept concentrated to deal with major threats or to crush opposition, leaving security work to lighter vehicles.

A large part of any modern military operation is security work. This includes protection of rear areas and lines of supply, but also the seemingly endless patrolling required to establish and maintain control over the countryside. Often, opposition forces are dispersed, and will try to influence an area or cause the security forces to lose control rather than engage in a direct large-scale confrontation that they will probably lose. A series of fleeting contacts is more likely than a set-piece battle, and the equipment required is rather different.

Light patrol vehicles are inexpensive enough that they can be deployed in fairly large numbers. Many use components from commercial vehicles, which reduces overall costs significantly. Carrying a support weapon such as a machine gun and a small group of infantry personnel, these light vehicles allow the security forces to maintain a presence over a wide area and to rush additional troops into the vicinity of any contact that occurs. Since they commonly operate in areas with poor infrastructure, patrol vehicles need to be relatively light in order to use local bridges and poor roads.

Weight

Many patrol vehicles are based on or developed from light civilian off-road trucks. Although they carry little protection compared with combat vehicles, adding armour increases the vehicle's weight significantly and often requires a redesigned chassis and/or suspension system.

Jackal Weight
6.7 tonnes
(6.6 tons)

tonnes
6.7

Pandur II Weight
15 tonnes
(14.8 tons)

tonnes
15.0

HMMWV Weight
3.9 tonnes
(3.8 tons)

tonnes
3.9

Vector Weight
6.6 tonnes
(6.5 tons)

tonnes
6.6

Dingo Weight
11.9 tonnes
(11.7 tons)

tonnes
11.9

Multi-purpose Patrol Vehicles 2

Operational Range and Personnel Capacity

▶ **M998 HMMWV**
▶ **AFT Dingo**
▶ **Jackal MWMIK**
▶ **Pandur II**
▶ **Pinzgauer Vector PPV**

Most patrol vehicles are resistant to small-arms fire and fragmentation but not to heavier weapons. While it is always desirable to provide the best possible protection, this must be balanced against vehicle weight and troop capacity. Design philosophies regarding the latter vary considerably, depending largely on the role envisaged for the vehicle and its troop complement.

In some cases the vehicle itself is the main asset, acting as an armed presence and mobile eyes. Vehicles such as the HMMWV and Jackal, with a very small troop capacity, fall into this category. As a weapons carrier with a couple of infantrymen in the back, a vehicle of this sort is a potent force in the local area but is limited in some ways. If it is desirable to send a ground force into an area inaccessible to the vehicle then additional personnel must be brought in by other means or several vehicles tasked as transport. Of course, in the latter case this does mean that the infantry force will be very well supported if combat begins.

With larger-capacity vehicles such as the Pandur or Dingo, the infantry force is the main asset and the vehicle acts as transport. Vehicles of this sort are better suited to deploying small foot patrols, which can enter a village or an area normally inaccessible to vehicles. The vehicle's support weapons will not be far away, but locals who are inclined to be friendly are more likely to interact with infantry personnel than with the crew of a heavily armed vehicle.

Personnel Capacity

Even a relatively small vehicle represents a significant investment for the owning force, and needs to be well suited to its task. A design such as the Pandur is essentially a light armoured personnel carrier; the HMMWV, however, represents a rather different approach to the problem.

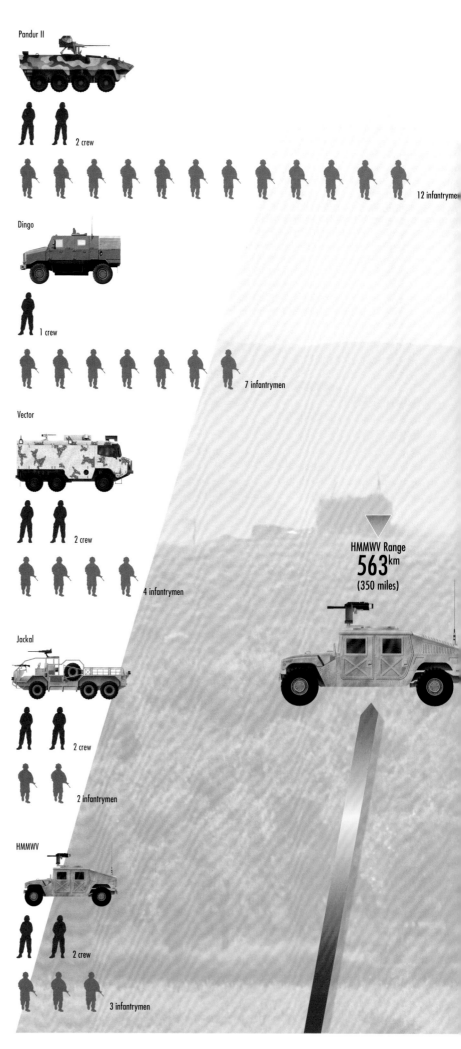

Pandur II
2 crew
12 infantrymen

Dingo
1 crew
7 infantrymen

Vector
2 crew
4 infantrymen

Jackal
2 crew
2 infantrymen

HMMWV
2 crew
3 infantrymen

HMMWV Range
563km
(350 miles)

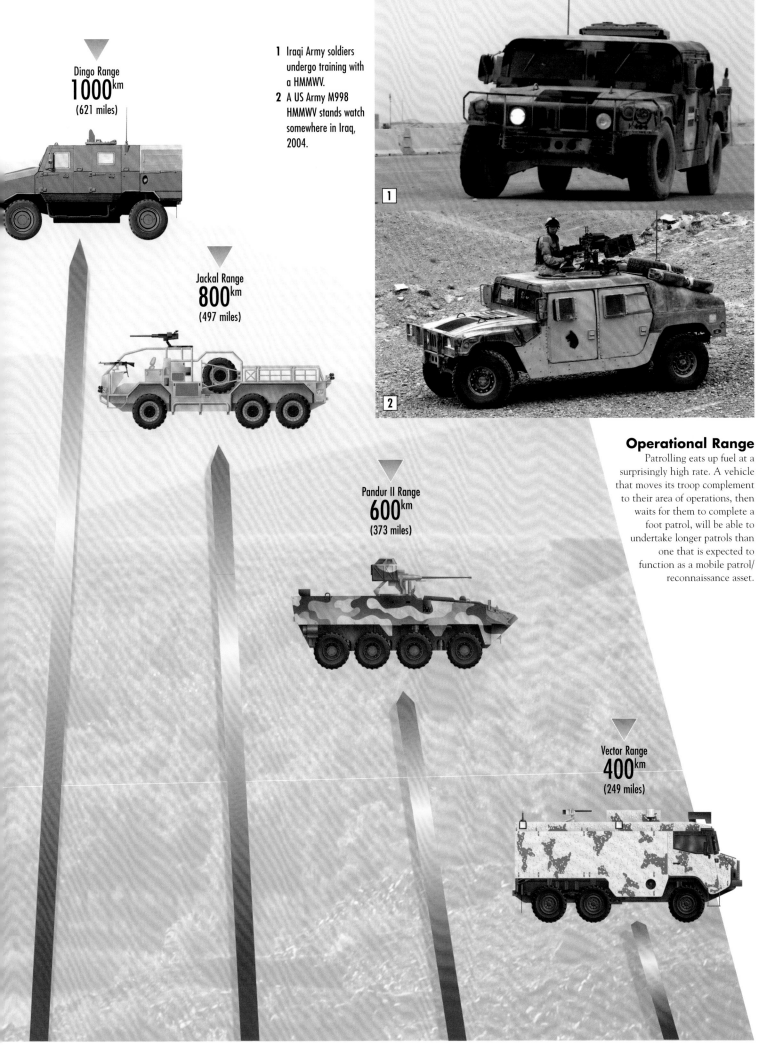

Dingo Range
1000km
(621 miles)

1 Iraqi Army soldiers undergo training with a HMMWV.
2 A US Army M998 HMMWV stands watch somewhere in Iraq, 2004.

Jackal Range
800km
(497 miles)

Operational Range

Patrolling eats up fuel at a surprisingly high rate. A vehicle that moves its troop complement to their area of operations, then waits for them to complete a foot patrol, will be able to undertake longer patrols than one that is expected to function as a mobile patrol/ reconnaissance asset.

Pandur II Range
600km
(373 miles)

Vector Range
400km
(249 miles)

Artillery, Bombs and Missiles

The function of artillery is to attack distant targets, usually by indirect fire with large quantities of explosives. Within this general concept there are several distinct roles, ranging from strategic nuclear strikes against targets on another continent to relatively short-range bombardment of enemy forces. Guided missiles may travel in a ballistic arc or fly like small aircraft, gaining the latter the name 'cruise missiles'. The addition of GPS guidance systems to many previously unguided rocket weapons has blurred the line between guided missiles and battlefield rocket systems.

Artillery weapons can be subdivided into two general types – rocket systems and 'tube' artillery, i.e. weapons that launch an unpowered projectile from a barrel. Traditionally, tube artillery includes mortars (very short-barrelled weapons firing in a very high arc), howitzers (short-barrelled low-velocity weapons firing in a high arc) and guns (long-barrelled, high-velocity weapons firing in a shallower arc). However, these distinctions have become less sharp due to the introduction of weapons that do not fit into any clear category.

LEFT: A battery of British AS-90 self-propelled guns from the Royal Horse Artillery fire rounds in Basra, Iraq, 2008.

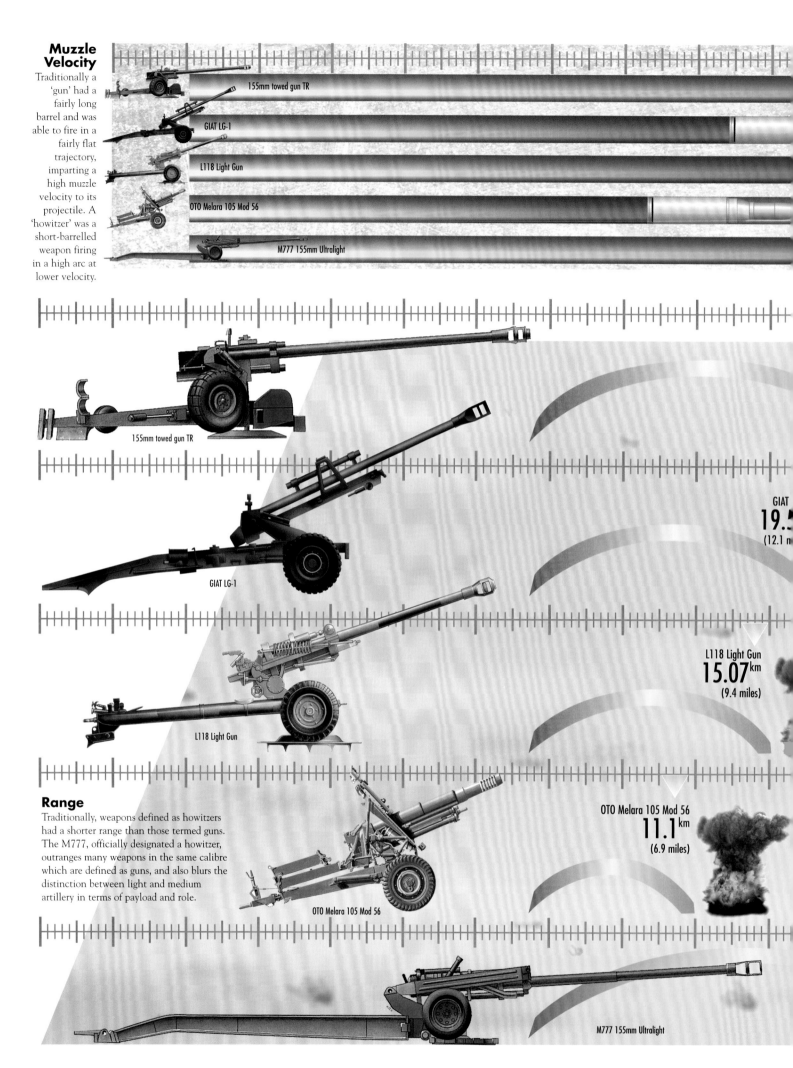

Muzzle Velocity

Traditionally a 'gun' had a fairly long barrel and was able to fire in a fairly flat trajectory, imparting a high muzzle velocity to its projectile. A 'howitzer' was a short-barrelled weapon firing in a high arc at lower velocity.

155mm towed gun TR

GIAT LG-1

L118 Light Gun

OTO Melara 105 Mod 56

M777 155mm Ultralight

155mm towed gun TR

GIAT LG-1

L118 Light Gun

OTO Melara 105 Mod 56

M777 155mm Ultralight

GIAT
19.5
(12.1 m

L118 Light Gun
15.07 km
(9.4 miles)

OTO Melara 105 Mod 56
11.1 km
(6.9 miles)

Range

Traditionally, weapons defined as howitzers had a shorter range than those termed guns. The M777, officially designated a howitzer, outranges many weapons in the same calibre which are defined as guns, and also blurs the distinction between light and medium artillery in terms of payload and role.

Light and Medium Artillery

Range vs Muzzle Velocity

▶ **155mm towed gun TR**
▶ **GIAT LG-1**
▶ **L118 Light Gun**
▶ **OTO Melara 105 Mod 56**
▶ **M777 155mm Ultralight**

155mm towed gun TR
24^{km}
(14.9 miles)

BELOW: The US M119 was developed from the L118 Light Gun for use by infantry formations. It is easily air transportable and can be towed behind a HMMWV or similar light vehicle.

M777 155mm Ultralight
40^{km}
(24.9 miles)

Light artillery has the advantage of being relatively easy to move around. Guns can be transported by air or towed by light vehicles. However, this has traditionally limited the calibre and thus the hitting power of light-artillery weapons. A calibre of 105mm (4.1in) is standard, although recent developments in technology have allowed more powerful weapons to be fielded. These include the 155mm (6.1in) M777, which was designed from the outset to create a heavier-calibre weapon that could still operate within light-artillery parameters. Such weapons blur the line between light and medium artillery; by calibre they might be considered medium guns, but they can fulfil both the light and the medium roles.

The invention of weapons capable of performing both functions caused the term gun-howitzer to come into being, but it is more common to define a weapon as a gun or howitzer based on the preference of the designers. Thus the short-barrelled Oto Melara 105 is termed a howitzer, as is the long-barrelled M777. The L118 Light Gun, with the same muzzle velocity as the OTO Melara, is a gun, but the higher-velocity LG-1 is a howitzer. There seem no longer to be any hard-and-fast rules about designation.

Heavy Artillery

Effective Range, Calibre and Elevation

▶ **Palmaria**
▶ **2S4 Tyulpan**
▶ **M110**
▶ **Primus 155mm**
▶ **2S7 Pion**

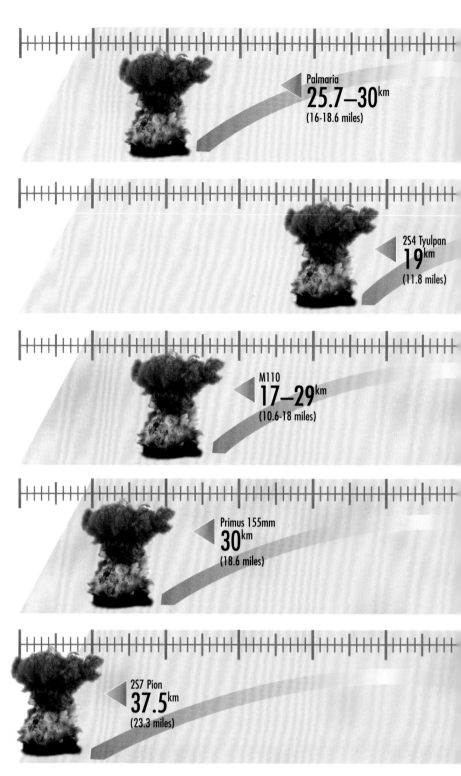

Palmaria
25.7–30km
(16-18.6 miles)

2S4 Tyulpan
19km
(11.8 miles)

M110
17–29km
(10.6-18 miles)

Primus 155mm
30km
(18.6 miles)

2S7 Pion
37.5km
(23.3 miles)

Many heavy artillery systems use very powerful weapons, with guns of 203mm (8in) or even greater calibre being common. However, 'heavy artillery' is arguably a role rather than a class of weapons. Its function is to deliver as much indirect firepower as possible on the enemy at long range, usually against large or static targets such as troop concentrations or fortifications. If very heavy guns are not available, then the heavy artillery role falls on whatever weapons are there to be called on.

The US M110 and Russian 2S7 Pion are true self-propelled heavy artillery weapons, mounting 203mm (8in) guns. The lighter 155mm (6.1in) guns of the Primus and Palmaria weapons systems can serve a similar function at comparable ranges, but they deliver a smaller payload per shell and may not be effective against some targets. On the other hand, lighter weapons systems are more flexible; when not attempting to fill the heavy-artillery niche they can be quickly redeployed for other artillery tasks. The 2S4 Tyulpan mounts an extremely heavy (240mm/9.45in) weapon, which is defined as a breech-loading mortar rather than a gun. The barrel is short relative to the weapon's calibre, which greatly reduces the weapon's weight but also its effective range.

With advanced extended-range ammunition, the Tyulpan can rival some gun systems for range, but its normal projectiles have a range of only about 10km (6.2 miles). Extremely heavy, short-ranged weapons of this sort are primarily useful when attacking fortifications. In a fluid battle environment they will frequently be unable to get into range of the enemy.

RIGHT: A Cold War-era M110 SP gun takes part in exercises. Artillery gives a force the capability to strike at a distant enemy and to pound defensive positions into wreckage. It cannot capture an objective nor win battles alone, but artillery support can make the task facing other arms much easier.

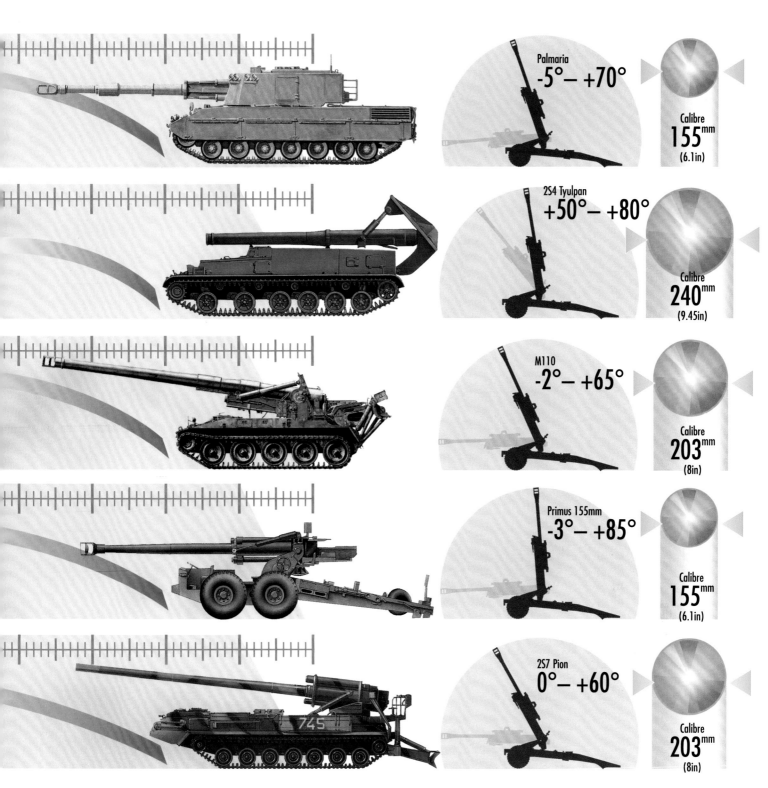

Palmaria
-5° — +70°
Calibre
155mm
(6.1in)

2S4 Tyulpan
+50° — +80°
Calibre
240mm
(9.45in)

M110
-2° — +65°
Calibre
203mm
(8in)

Primus 155mm
-3° — +85°
Calibre
155mm
(6.1in)

2S7 Pion
0° — +60°
Calibre
203mm
(8in)

Elevation and Calibre

An artillery shell (or any other projectile) will travel furthest when fired upwards at a 45-degree angle. However, this may not be sufficient to clear obstructions. A greater elevation allows the shell to be lobbed over intervening objects and dropped almost vertically down into the target area, which negates much of the protection available to a dug-in enemy force.

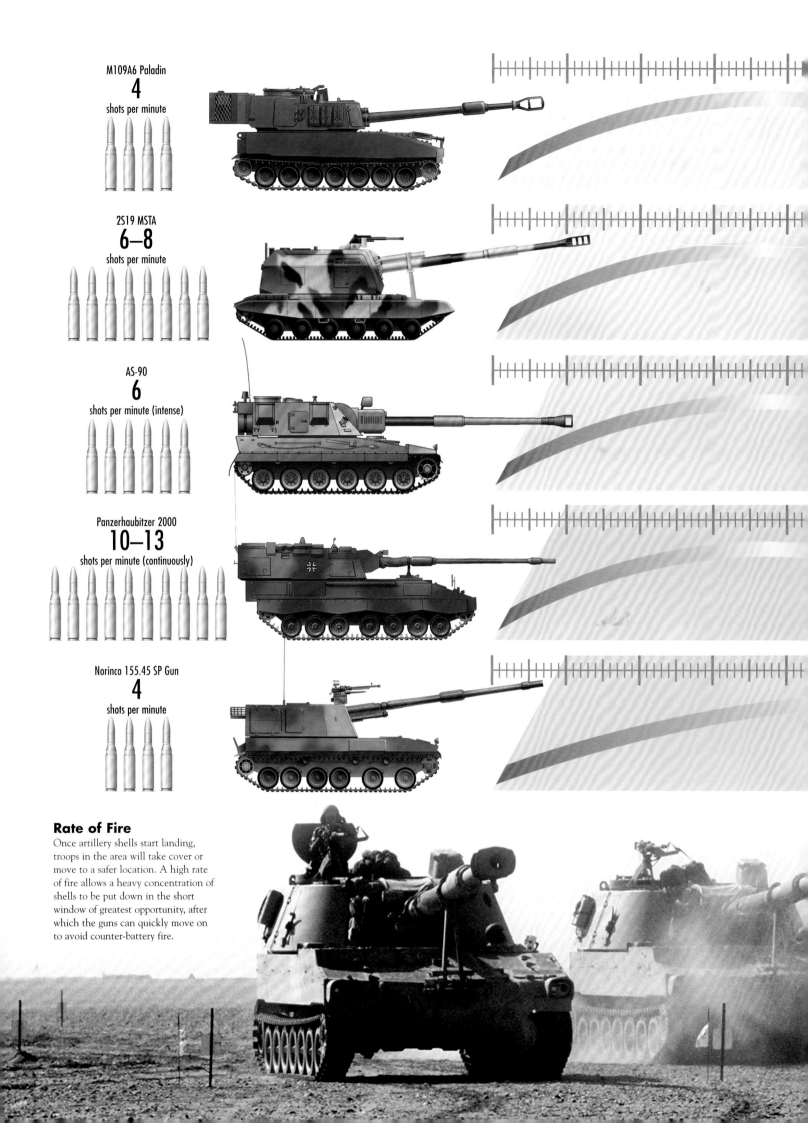

M109A6 Paladin
4
shots per minute

2S19 MSTA
6–8
shots per minute

AS-90
6
shots per minute (intense)

Panzerhaubitzer 2000
10–13
shots per minute (continuously)

Norinco 155.45 SP Gun
4
shots per minute

Rate of Fire

Once artillery shells start landing, troops in the area will take cover or move to a safer location. A high rate of fire allows a heavy concentration of shells to be put down in the short window of greatest opportunity, after which the guns can quickly move on to avoid counter-battery fire.

M109A6 Paladin Range
24–30km
(14.9-18.6 miles)

2S19 MSTA Range
29km
(18 miles)

AS-90 Range
30km
(18.6 miles)

Panzerhaubitzer 2000 Range
30km
(18.6 miles)

Norinco 155.45 SP Gun Range
39km
(24.2 miles)

Effective Range

Long-range fire capability allows the guns to remain safely behind friendly forces, and gives greater flexibility in terms of firing position. Shorter-range guns may have to shoot from predictable locations in order to hit a given target, and can offer support only to friendly formations in the nearby area. Long range increases the number of friendly units that the battery can support.

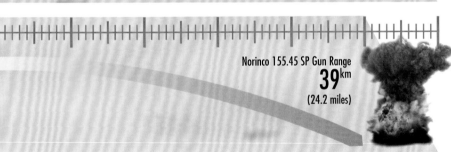

Self-propelled Guns 1
Effective Range and Rate of Fire

▶ **M109A6 Paladin**
▶ **2S19 MSTA**
▶ **AS-90**
▶ **Panzerhaubitzer 2000**
▶ **Norinco 155.45 SP Gun**

The 'industry standard' for medium artillery is 155mm (6.1in) calibre, with a 39-calibre barrel being common. This means that the gun's length is 39 times its calibre, a size that experience has shown gives a good combination of range and mobility. The 39-calibre, 155mm (6.1in) gun was standardized by several NATO members in 1963, with the result that many artillery systems based on this agreement have very similar performance characteristics.

A longer gun would increase range, and some militaries have chosen to experiment with such weapons, typically using 52-calibre guns. Very long guns are prone to damage when moving rapidly cross-country. Self-propelled (SP) artillery is often called upon to do so, and even with a barrel support, the weight of the gun can be a problem. However, there are other ways to improve the range of artillery weapons, such as advanced munitions. Some of these use a rocket to boost the shell after launch, though this extra range comes at the price of a reduced warhead. Alternatively, the shell can be shaped to improve its aerodynamic performance, increasing range without altering the payload.

Most self-propelled artillery systems are capable of a high rate of fire for a short time. Even with autoloaders and power-assisted shell handling, there is a limit to how fast the gun can load and shoot at maximum intensity, and after a period of rapid fire the rate must be reduced. Thus artillery systems have a maximum rate of fire and a much slower sustained rate, which avoids excessive barrel over-heating.

OPPOSITE: As with many SP guns, the barrel of the US M109A6 Paladin is clamped into a rest when travelling. This provides support and stability for the long gun, which might otherwise be damaged or distorted by the stresses of rapid cross-country movement.

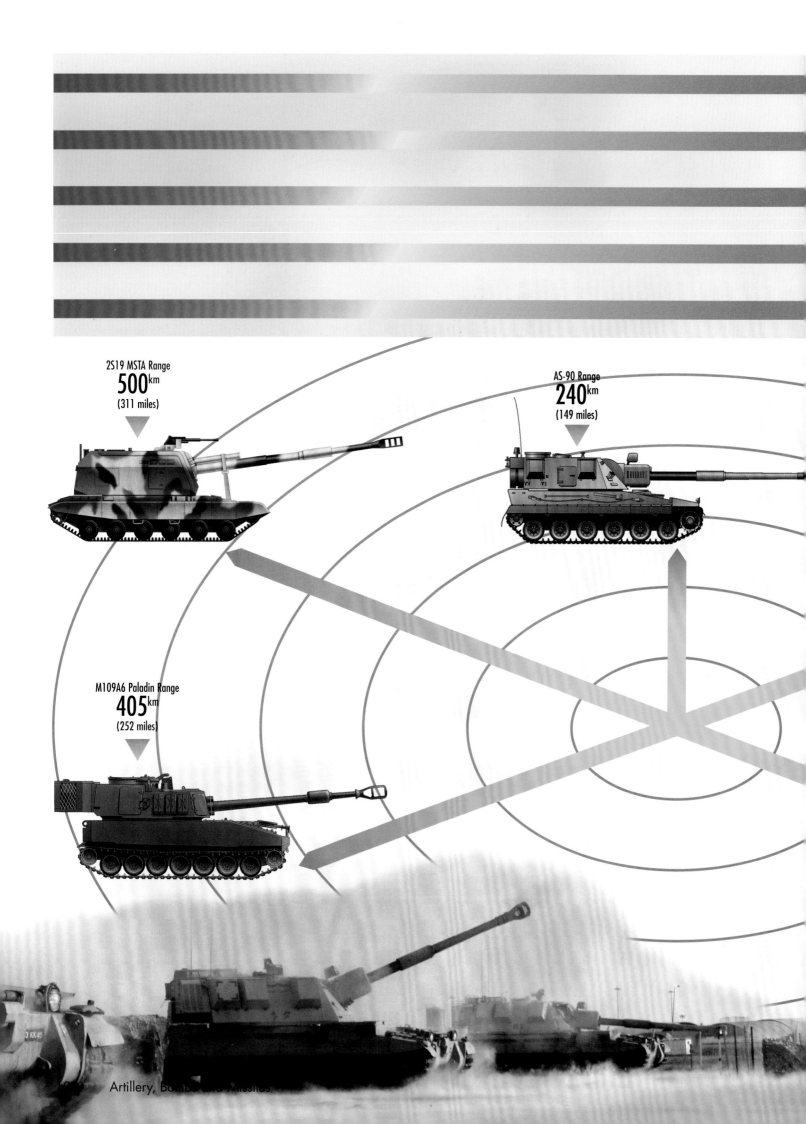

2S19 MSTA Range
500km
(311 miles)

AS-90 Range
240km
(149 miles)

M109A6 Paladin Range
405km
(252 miles)

Self-propelled Guns 2

Tactical Mobility: Speed and Road Range

▶ **M109A6 Paladin**
▶ **2S19 MSTA**
▶ **AS-90**
▶ **Panzerhaubitze 2000**
▶ **Norinco 155.45 SP Gun**

Norinco 155.45 SP Gun
56 km/h
(34.8mph)

Panzerhaubitze
Speed
60 km/h
(37.3mph)

AS-90
55 km/h
(34.2mph)

2S19 MSTA
60 km/h
(37.3mph)

M109A6 Paladin
56 km/h
(34.8mph)

Speed

The speed of a self-propelled gun system is to some extent dictated by the forces it must support. The guns must be able to keep pace with armoured or mechanized-infantry formations, whilst the ability to move faster than the tanks or infantry fighting vehicles is an advantage that will rarely be useful.

Panzerhaubitzer 2000 Range
420 km
(261 miles)

Road Range

The operational radius of SP guns varies considerably. It is acceptable for a gun system to require frequent refuelling, as it will rarely be in close proximity to the enemy and thus does not expose its support elements to enemy fire.

Norinco 155.45 SP Gun Range
450 km
(280 miles)

Self-propelled artillery first emerged during World War II, when the need was perceived for artillery that could keep pace with rapidly advancing tank formations. Early designs were crude, being little more than a field-artillery piece mounted on an obsolete tank chassis. Within a few years, the modern self-propelled gun began to emerge. Self-propelled artillery can go anywhere that a tank can. However, this does mean that self-propelled guns suffer from some of the same limitations. Tracked vehicles tend to be fuel-hungry and require a great deal of maintenance. This is less of a problem when they are integrated into an armoured formation, as much of the necessary maintenance and repair capability is already in place.

Self-propelled guns are far more lightly armoured than tanks, as in theory they are unlikely to encounter serious anti-tank weaponry. Their armour will usually protect their crew and systems from shell fragments, but more commonly the vehicles will avoid counter-battery fire by 'shoot and scoot' tactics, firing several shots in rapid succession and then moving to a new position before the enemy can respond.

SP guns can be pushed into a close-support role, sometimes with great success. Any armoured vehicle is a serious threat to an infantry force, and one armed with a very large gun can blast defenders out of their positions with ease. During operations in Beirut in the 1980s, Israeli forces found it effective to create small battle groups of infantry supported by one tank and one self-propelled gun.

OPPOSITE: The British AS-90 was introduced in 1993 as a replacement for the 105mm Abbot self-propelled howitzer. Mounting the NATO compatible 155mm L31 gun, it is capable of firing three rounds in a 10-second burst, six rounds per minute for up to three minutes, or two rounds per minute for a duration of one hour.

Wheeled SP Guns

Travel Range and Speed

▶ **G6**
▶ **Archer**
▶ **Caesar**
▶ **DANA**

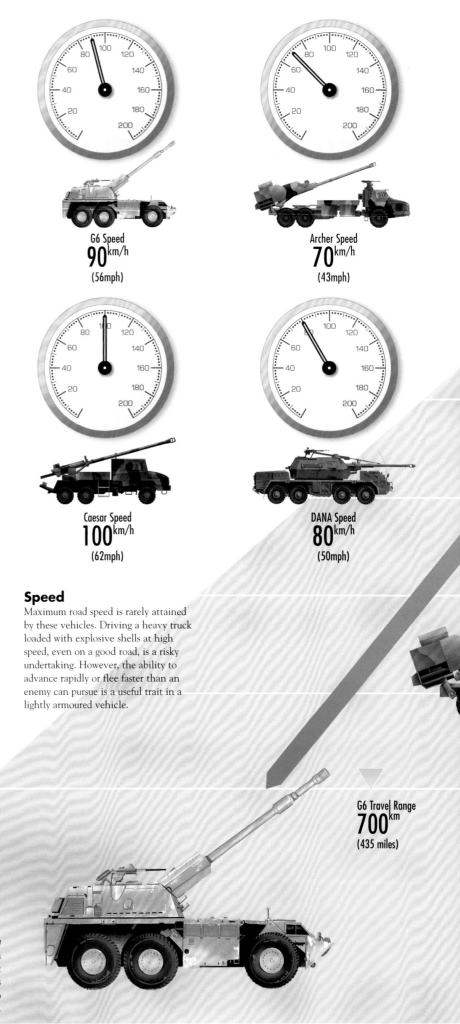

G6 Speed
90 km/h
(56mph)

Archer Speed
70 km/h
(43mph)

Caesar Speed
100 km/h
(62mph)

DANA Speed
80 km/h
(50mph)

Traditionally, self-propelled artillery systems were mounted on tracked chassis, often those of obsolete battle tanks. This not only gave the vehicle good cross-country mobility but also enabled it to absorb the recoil of a powerful gun. Recent developments in recoil-management technology have enabled a 155mm (6.1in) gun to be mounted on a wheeled chassis, whose off-road performance may be inferior to that of a track-laying vehicle but which can attain a higher speed over a longer distance on roads or reasonably level countryside.

Most wheeled self-propelled guns are built on a six-wheeled chassis, often one developed from off-road truck designs. Weight can be saved by dispensing with an armoured turret, and instead mounting the gun over the vehicle hull. The crew areas and engine are still armoured, and turretless vehicles are overall not significantly less well protected than more conventional equivalents. Most self-propelled artillery is lightly armoured in any case, and defends itself best by avoiding contact with enemy forces.

While the Caesar and Archer systems use an open configuration, vehicles such as the DANA and G6 use a more conventional turret, housing the gun crew, loading mechanism and ammunition supply. The DANA was a ground-breaking design when it appeared in the 1970s; not only did it use a wheeled chassis but the weapon's autoloader was capable of operating even with the gun fully elevated. This feature was successful enough to become standard on later designs, and the DANA gun system has since evolved through several upgraded and export versions.

Speed

Maximum road speed is rarely attained by these vehicles. Driving a heavy truck loaded with explosive shells at high speed, even on a good road, is a risky undertaking. However, the ability to advance rapidly or flee faster than an enemy can pursue is a useful trait in a lightly armoured vehicle.

G6 Travel Range
700 km
(435 miles)

Travel Range

Wheeled gun systems offer up to twice the strategic mobility of an equivalent track-laying vehicle such as the M109A6 Paladin, but that is only part of the picture. Wheeled vehicles require less support in the field and are a good choice for forces needing to obtain more 'teeth' than 'tail' for their procurement dollars.

1 A Swedish-made Archer takes part in exercises during winter. The system is fully automated, with a remote-controlled weapon station mounted on a modified 6x6 chassis of the Volvo A30D all-terrain articulated hauler.

Archer Travel Range
500km
(311 miles)

Caesar Travel Range
600km
(373 miles)

DANA Travel Range
600km
(373 miles)

Short- to Medium-range Rocket Artillery Systems

Effective Range and Rate of Fire

▶ **BM-21 Grad**
▶ **TOS-1 MRL**
▶ **M77 Oganj MLRS**
▶ **ASTROS II**

The original artillery rockets were destructive but rather random, sometimes even turning back on their launchers. The invention of propellants that burn more evenly, along with a better understanding of aerodynamics, has enabled the artillery rocket to become a reliable support system in the modern era. Rocket systems are still less accurate than 'tube' artillery – i.e. guns and howitzers – but they can achieve a good effective range and carry a powerful payload.

Rockets are launched in quick succession, so the vehicle can move soon after opening fire and thus avoid counter-battery fire. A gun could only deliver a couple of shells in the time that a rocket system can launch up to 40 rockets.

The inaccuracy of the rockets can sometimes be an advantage; a salvo launched at the same spot will spread out in flight and create a larger beaten zone. At shorter ranges, the salvo will remain concentrated and many warheads will hit a small area in a short period.

Effective Range

Rocket systems lack the range of tube artillery, and are less precise. Their primary role is in saturating a target area with warheads in a very short space of time. The two primary advantages of rocket systems are cheapness and the ability to dump a large payload onto a target in a few seconds. A rocket system can be built onto a fairly standard truck, as it does not have to absorb the recoil of a heavy gun, and can fire from any fairly level and firm surface without much preparation. This creates an inexpensive and easy-to-maintain artillery capability.

BM-21 Grad
20km
(12.4 miles)

TOS-1 MRL
3.5km
(2.2 miles)

M77 Oganj MLRS
20km
(12.4 miles)

ASTROS II
9–30km
(5.6-18.6 miles)

LEFT: A Saudi Arabian Avibras ASTROS II SS-30 rocket leaves its launch system, mounted on the back of a Tectran 6x6 AV-LMU truck, during Operation Desert Shield.

BM-21 Grad

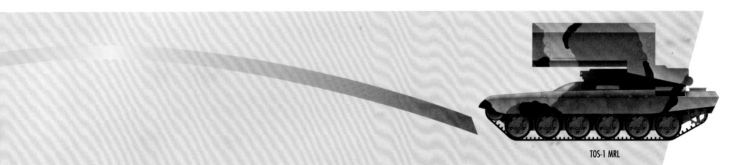

TOS-1 MRL

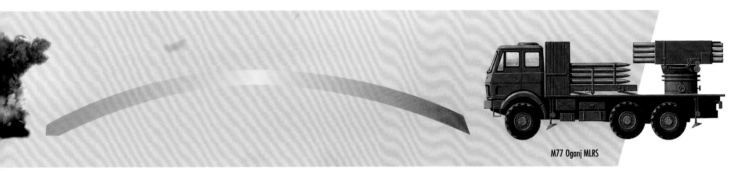

M77 Oganj MLRS

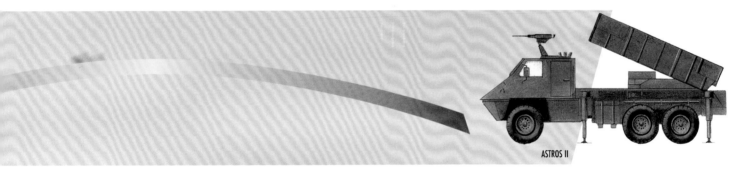

ASTROS II

Rate of Fire

Once loaded, a rocket system can fire off all its ammunition in a period of just a few seconds. Reloading can be a lengthy process, however, so sustained fire rates are not very high.

BM-21 Salvo
2
rockets per sec

BM-21 Grad

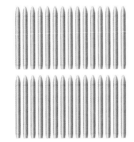

TOS-1 Salvo
30
rockets in 15 secs

TOS-1 MRL

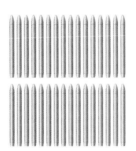

M77 Oganj Salvo
32
rockets in 20 secs

M77 Oganj MLRS

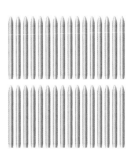

ASTROS II Salvo
32
rockets

ASTROS II

Long-range Rocket Artillery Systems

Effective Range and Rate of Fire

- ▶ **Type 89 MLRS**
- ▶ **BM-30 Smerch**
- ▶ **AR1A MLRS**
- ▶ **GMLRS**
- ▶ **HIMARS**

Rockets are not powered all the way to the target. They accelerate continuously until their fuel burns out, then follow a ballistic arc like any other projectile. A rocket is larger and has more wind resistance than a shell, and is far more prone to wind effects during its flight. Over short distances this may not be very significant, but traditionally long-range rocket systems have been notoriously inaccurate and primarily useful for harassing fire against 'area' targets.

Modern rocket systems are assisted by ballistic computers that can take input from satellites, existing maps, and data sent from other combat formations to calculate the optimum firing solution. However, even if the system tries to take into account known wind conditions, wind is inherently variable and can still cause significant inaccuracy. One solution is to fit rockets with a GPS (Global Positioning System) guidance system, turning them into something between a traditional unguided rocket and a guided missile.

Using GPS is cheap compared with conventional missile guidance, as it relies on a satellite system that is already in place, but it is not as precise as a true missile-guidance system. GPS enables a rocket to guide itself to a position with reasonable accuracy, but there is no guarantee that the target will be there when it arrives. A GPS-guided rocket attacks a point on the ground; it is up to the user to determine if a suitable target will be present when the rocket gets there.

LEFT: The US M270 Multiple Launch Rocket System (MLRS) has been in service since the mid-1980s. A salvo of 12 rockets can saturate a one kilometre square (0.4-square-mile) area with bomblets, delivering ferocious firepower in an instant.

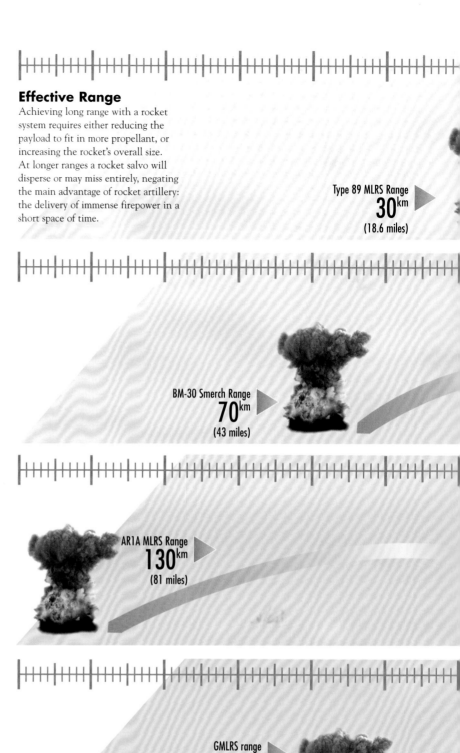

Effective Range

Achieving long range with a rocket system requires either reducing the payload to fit in more propellant, or increasing the rocket's overall size. At longer ranges a rocket salvo will disperse or may miss entirely, negating the main advantage of rocket artillery: the delivery of immense firepower in a short space of time.

Type 89 MLRS Range
30km
(18.6 miles)

BM-30 Smerch Range
70km
(43 miles)

AR1A MLRS Range
130km
(81 miles)

GMLRS range
60km
(37 miles)

HIMARS Range
32km
(19.9 miles)

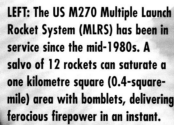
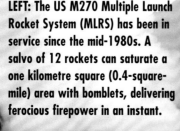

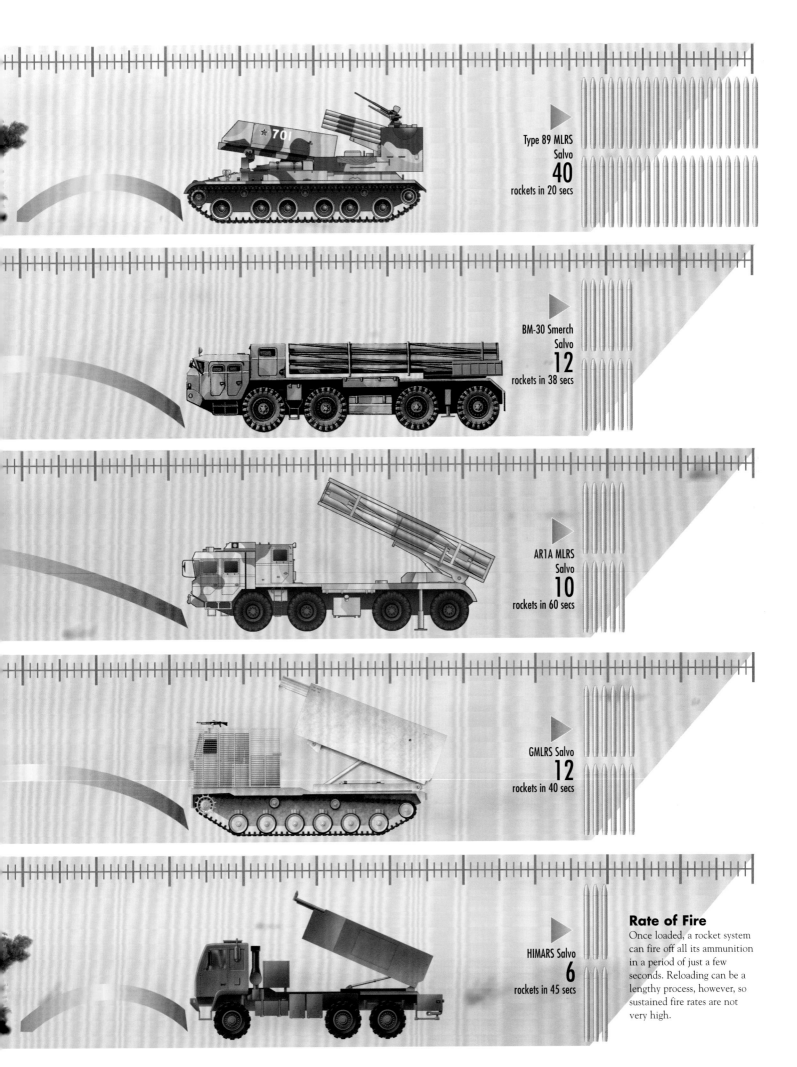

Type 89 MLRS
Salvo
40
rockets in 20 secs

BM-30 Smerch
Salvo
12
rockets in 38 secs

AR1A MLRS
Salvo
10
rockets in 60 secs

GMLRS Salvo
12
rockets in 40 secs

HIMARS Salvo
6
rockets in 45 secs

Rate of Fire
Once loaded, a rocket system can fire off all its ammunition in a period of just a few seconds. Reloading can be a lengthy process, however, so sustained fire rates are not very high.

Anti-aircraft Artillery

Effective Range and Rate of Fire

▶ **PGZ95 SPAAA**
▶ **Sidam 25**
▶ **9K22 Tunguska**
▶ **Type 87 SPAAG**

The need for mobile anti-aircraft weaponry that could move with an armoured formation was demonstrated during World War II. At the same time the practice of using obsolete armoured-vehicle chassis as platforms for anti-aircraft artillery (AAA) was established. Although AAA units are not intended to come into direct contact with the enemy's ground forces, nothing is guaranteed in warfare.

Although missiles have proved their worth in the anti-aircraft role, especially against distant or fast-moving threats, there is still a place for guns. For close-range air defence against fixed-wing aircraft, especially helicopters, rapid-fire gun systems can be highly effective.

Hybrid gun/missile systems offer a range of options, though these come at the price of increased cost and complexity. Missiles are used for area defence, engaging any aircraft that ventures within their reach, with the guns as a back-up for use against close-range targets. The primary advantage of pure gun systems is cheapness, allowing more potential targets to be protected for the same amount of budget dollars.

Effective Range

The effective range of a gun-based anti-aircraft system is fairly short compared with that of a missile. Unguided projectiles take time to reach their target at longer range and the point of aim cannot be corrected once they are fired, greatly increasing the chances of a miss.

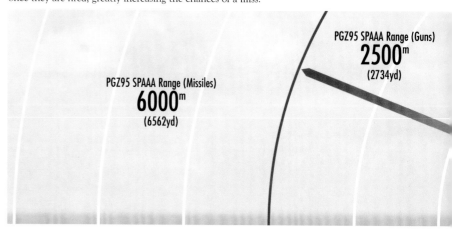

PGZ95 SPAAA Range (Guns)
2500ᵐ
(2734yd)

PGZ95 SPAAA Range (Missiles)
6000ᵐ
(6562yd)

Sidam 25 Range
5000ᵐ
(5468yd)

BELOW: A Russian 9K22 Tunguska parades through Moscow. Modern air-defence vehicles must be able to track and engage targets as diverse as fast-moving strike jets, low, slow helicopters and possibly small reconnaissance drones or even enemy missiles. A gun system may have a secondary use as a high-firepower ground-combat asset.

9K22 Tunguska Range (Missiles)
8000ᵐ
(8749yd)

9K22 Tunguska Range (Guns)
3500ᵐ
(3828yd)

Type 87 SPAAG Range
4000ᵐ
(4374yd)

Rate of Fire

In order to hit and damage a fast-moving target, AAA systems attempt to throw what amounts to a wall of projectiles in the path of the aircraft. The more rounds are passing through the same volume of air as the target, the greater the chances of a hit.

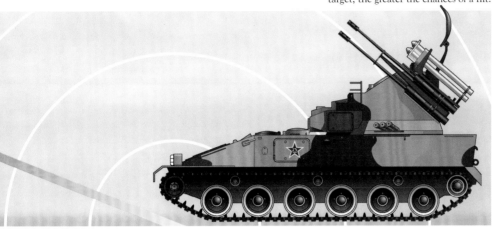

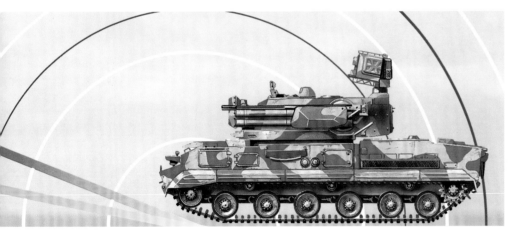

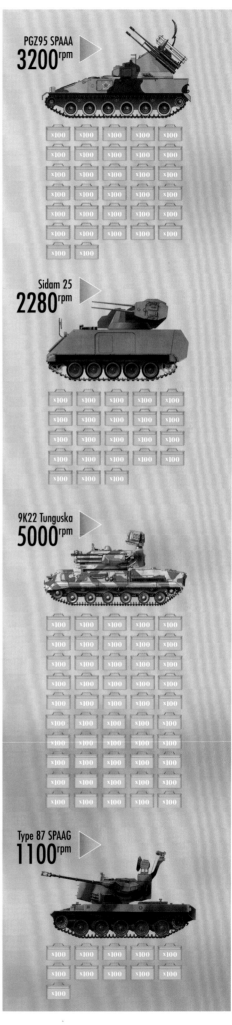

PGZ95 SPAAA
3200rpm

Sidam 25
2280rpm

9K22 Tunguska
5000rpm

Type 87 SPAAG
1100rpm

Air-defence Missile Launchers

Effective Range and Ceiling

▶ **ADATS**
▶ **2K12 KUB (SA-6 'Gainful')**
▶ **Crotale Mk 3**
▶ **S-300PMU (SA-10 'Grumble')**
▶ **MIM-104 Patriot**

Two of the critical factors for an air-defence missile are its range and ceiling. Ceiling is the maximum height at which an interception is possible. Light, man-portable air-defence missiles have a low ceiling and are primarily useful against helicopters or low-flying ground-attack aircraft. Weapons of this sort can be used to defend a point target but are ineffective against high-flying aircraft, whether they are attacking or simply flying over on their way to another target.

Longer-range missiles can be used for area defence, intercepting enemy aircraft at higher altitudes and greater distances. This can allow a launcher to cover a greater radius, or permit a missile to chase down an aircraft that attempts to flee out of range. A long-range missile system can dominate local airspace and make air operations in the area extremely hazardous. Ironically, perhaps, this makes it a high-priority target for enemy air forces, requiring that the heavy launchers be protected by shorter-range weapons.

In order to achieve long range and a high intercept ceiling, a large and expensive missile is needed, and this must be partnered with a suitable launcher. Thus most militaries field a mix of air-defence weapons, with a few powerful, long-range systems for area defence and a greater number of short-range missiles to protect specific targets. Close-in defence is often supplemented by rapid-fire guns. The US-designed ADATS (Air Defence Anti-Tank) missile system is unusual, in that it is designed to launch the same missiles against aircraft or ground targets. Its range is short, but a warhead capable of crippling a tank will leave little of an aircraft it hits.

Effective Range

Attack aircraft often carry stand-off missiles, and can defeat many short-range air-defence systems by launching their weapons from beyond the system's engagement range, then retiring. Longer-range systems can cover a larger area and intercept intruders earlier.

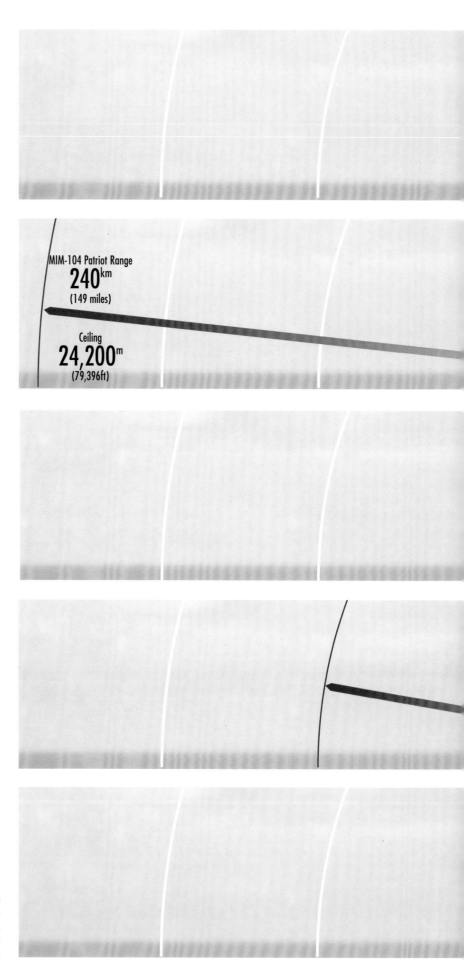

MIM-104 Patriot Range
240km
(149 miles)

Ceiling
24,200m
(79,396ft)

Ceiling

The largest air-defence missiles can intercept a high-flying bomber or even a short-range ballistic missile. Decades ago it was possible to defeat air defences by simply flying above their engagement envelope. Today, a low-level, high-speed penetration offers a better chance of success.

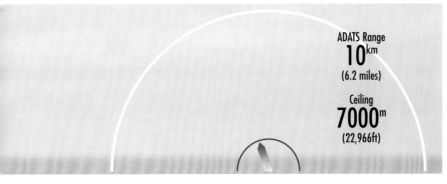

ADATS Range
10km
(6.2 miles)

Ceiling
7000m
(22,966ft)

ADATS

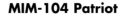

MIM-104 Patriot

Crotale Mk 3 Range
16km
(9.9 miles)

Ceiling
9000m
(29,528ft)

Crotale Mk 3

S-300PMU Range
150km
(93 miles)

Ceiling
25,000m
(82,021ft)

S-300PMU

2K12 KUB Range
20km
(12.4 miles)

Ceiling
7000m
(22,966ft)

2K12 KUB

Stand-off Missiles

Effective Range and Warhead Weight

▶ **AGM-86C CALCM**
▶ **AGM-154 JSOW**
▶ **Hsiung Feng II**
▶ **Storm Shadow**
▶ **AGM-129 ACM**

A cruise missile is, in many ways, a small automated aircraft which can travel autonomously to its target area before making an attack. During this 'cruise' part of the mission, guidance may be provided by an inertial or GPS system, or by terrain-matching. This compares radar data with known terrain features and allows the missile to find its way to a programmed destination. Some missiles use inertial and GPS guidance for the terminal attack phase; others have a thermal-imaging system.

Many cruise missiles are air launched, allowing a stand-off strike without exposing the launch platform to enemy air defences. The small, low-flying missile is better able to penetrate a defended area than an aircraft, and many cruise missiles are designed to be 'stealthy', making them difficult to detect or target. Other designs can be deployed on ground launchers or naval vessels; in many cases there are variants of the same missile that can be launched from different platforms.

The US AGM-86 CALCM (Conventional Air Launched Cruise Missile) was developed from a nuclear-armed weapon to meet changing operational requirements. It permitted the B-52 strategic bomber to become a launch platform for precise non-nuclear strikes.

Warhead Types

Most cruise missiles can carry various warheads, including cluster bombs or penetrator warheads intended to punch deep into a bunker before exploding. This mission requires great precision. Storm Shadow achieves it by using a thermal camera in its nose. At the start of the attack phase, the missile gains altitude then dives, enabling the camera to seek the target from above.

AGM-86C CALCM

AGM-154 JSOW

Hsiung Feng

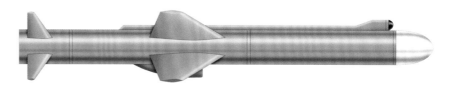

Storm Shadow

AGM-129 ACM

BELOW: Cruise missiles can be carried aboard mobile container-launchers, which can shift position to avoid attack.

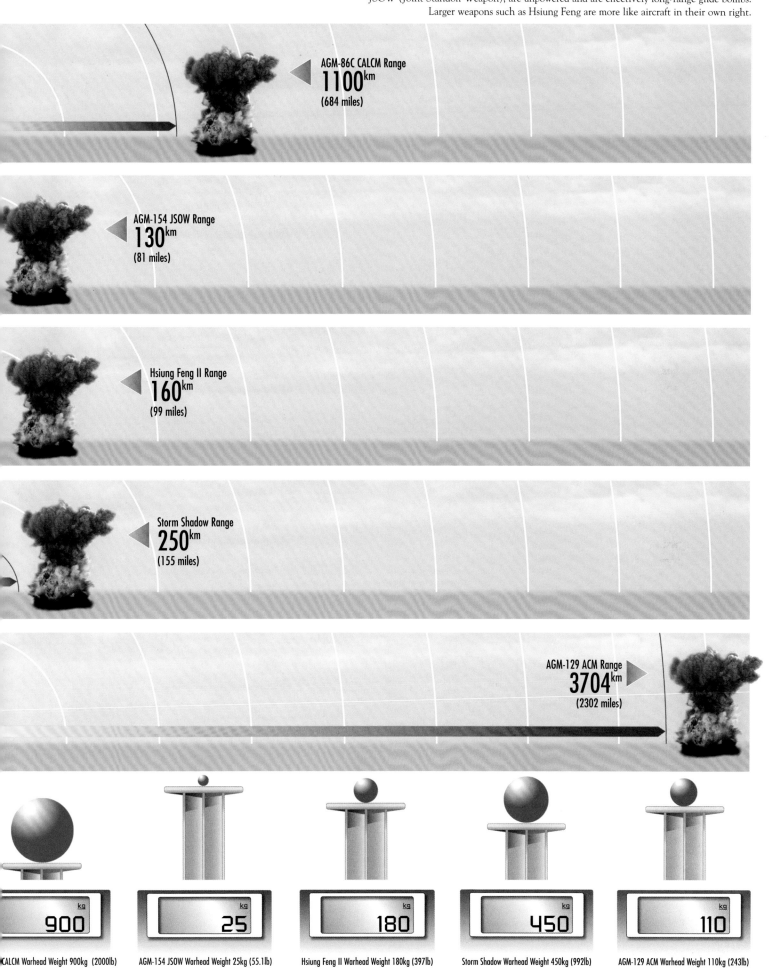

The range of a stand-off missile depends on its role. Smaller examples, such as the AGM-154 JSOW (Joint Standoff Weapon), are unpowered and are effectively long-range glide bombs. Larger weapons such as Hsiung Feng are more like aircraft in their own right.

AGM-86C CALCM Range
1100km
(684 miles)

AGM-154 JSOW Range
130km
(81 miles)

Hsiung Feng II Range
160km
(99 miles)

Storm Shadow Range
250km
(155 miles)

AGM-129 ACM Range
3704km
(2302 miles)

kg
900

kg
25

kg
180

kg
450

kg
110

CALCM Warhead Weight 900kg (2000lb)

AGM-154 JSOW Warhead Weight 25kg (55.1lb)

Hsiung Feng II Warhead Weight 180kg (397lb)

Storm Shadow Warhead Weight 450kg (992lb)

AGM-129 ACM Warhead Weight 110kg (243lb)

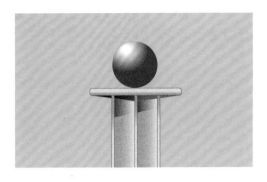

AGM-84H SLAM-ER Warhead Weight 221kg (487lb)

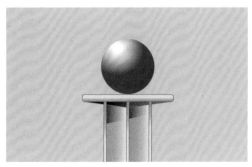

Kh-59MK (AS-18 'Kazoo') Warhead Weight 320kg (705lb)

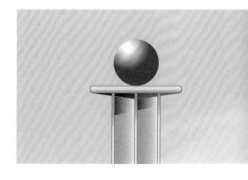

AGM-130 Warhead Weight 240kg (529lb)

Warhead Weight

The warhead is often a relatively small part of the weight of the missile, although its size determines the magnitude of impact the missile will have.

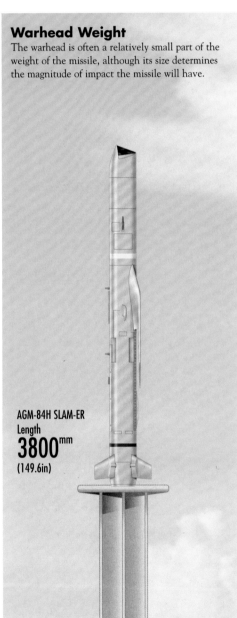

AGM-84H SLAM-ER
Length
3800^{mm}
(149.6in)

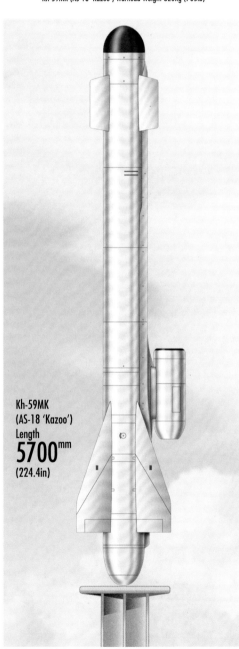

Kh-59MK
(AS-18 'Kazoo')
Length
5700^{mm}
(224.4in)

AGM-130
Length
3920^{mm}
(154.3in)

AGM-84H SLAM-ER Launch Weight 691kg (1523lb)

Kh-59MK (AS-18 'Kazoo') Launch Weight 930kg (2050lb)

AGM-130 Launch Weight 1323kg (2917lb)

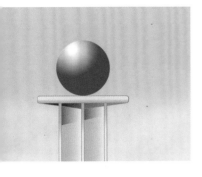

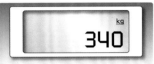

GBU-67 Zoobin Warhead Weight 340kg (750lb)

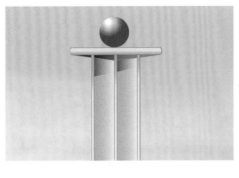

Brimstone Warhead weight not known

Modern Tactical Air-to-Surface Missiles 1

Warhead Weight, Launch Weight and Length

▶ **AGM-84H SLAM-ER**
▶ **Kh-59MK (AS-18 'Kazoo')**
▶ **AGM-130**
▶ **GBU-67 Zoobin**
▶ **Brimstone**

Hitting a ground target from a fast-moving platform such as an aircraft is a challenge at the best of times. Even with a good ballistic computer, 'dumb' bombs are extremely inaccurate. Bombs also require the attacking aircraft to fly over the target, which may be heavily defended. Guided missiles offer both greater precision and the ability to launch the weapon at a distance from the target. This 'stand-off' capability increases survivability for attack aircraft.

A bomb can be mostly payload, but a missile needs to give up space for propellant, guidance fins and its targeting system. This reduces the size of payload that a missile of a given size can carry. The proportions of payload to overall missile weight vary considerably, but as a rule, if long range is desired, then this can only come at the expense of payload, or else a bigger missile will have to be constructed. This remains an option, but there is a limit to how big a missile can get and still be carried by a typical strike aircraft.

By way of comparison, a Mk 83 bomb, often referred to as a 500kg or 1000lb bomb although its exact weight can vary, carries a 200kg (441lb) warhead in a package about 3000mm (118.1in) long. The 430kg (948lb) warhead of a Mk 84 bomb (925kg/2039lb total weight) is carried in a casing 3280mm (129.1in) long. Bombs do offer more 'bang per kilo' than missiles, which may be important when considering the load an aircraft can carry, but this must be balanced against stand-off-attack capability and precision.

Launch Weight

Air-launched weapons tend to be designed to fit existing aircraft capabilities. The weapon's performance must be balanced against the capability of strike aircraft to carry it, forcing weapon designs into several rough categories determined by previous generations of weaponry.

-67 Zoobin
gth
180mm
5.2in)

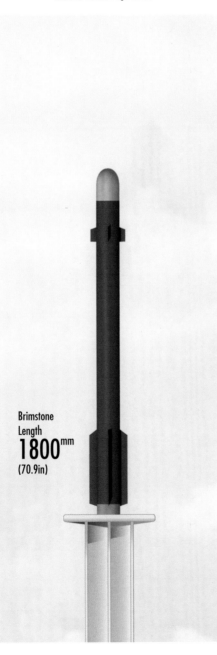

Brimstone
Length
1800mm
(70.9in)

GBU-67 Zoobin Launch Weight 560kg (1235lb)

Brimstone Launch Weight 48.5kg (107lb)

Modern Tactical Air-to-Surface Missiles 2

Effective Range

▶ **AGM-84H SLAM-ER**
▶ **Kh-59MK (AS-18 'Kazoo')**
▶ **AGM-130**
▶ **GBU-67 Zoobin**
▶ **Brimstone**

The addition of guidance systems to freefall ordnance (i.e. bombs) has created a new role for unpowered munitions, somewhere between a traditional bomb and a missile. A bomb normally falls away from under an aircraft, accelerating downwards whilst retaining much of the launching platform's airspeed. This seriously limits the range of a bomb, unless it is dropped from a great height. In the past, high-altitude bombing led to low accuracy, but the advent of guidance systems negated this problem.

A bomb can be given increased range by 'tossing' it. Instead of flying straight and level to drop its bombs, the aircraft pulls up sharply at high speed, launching the bomb in a high arc which extends its range significantly. The bomb's guidance system can, however, only alter its flight path from side to side, or shorten its flight. An unpowered bomb cannot glide or extend its range in the way that a missile can.

Thus, missiles offer greater flexibility than guided bombs. A missile can accelerate or gain height in order to reach a distant target, and in some cases can be given a re-attack capability. A missile with this function can turn around and have another try if it misses its target. Thrust can also be useful if the target is moving and in the case of missiles that can be retargeted in flight. A missile can change its aim point to anywhere within its maximum range and will often arrive at the target area at higher speed than a bomb, making defensive fire problematical.

RIGHT: Carrying one air-to-surface missile on each of its underwing pylons, a single aircraft can make stand-off strikes against several high-value targets in the course of a single mission. A similar number of attacks with short-range weapons might pose an unacceptable level of risk to the aircraft and its pilot.

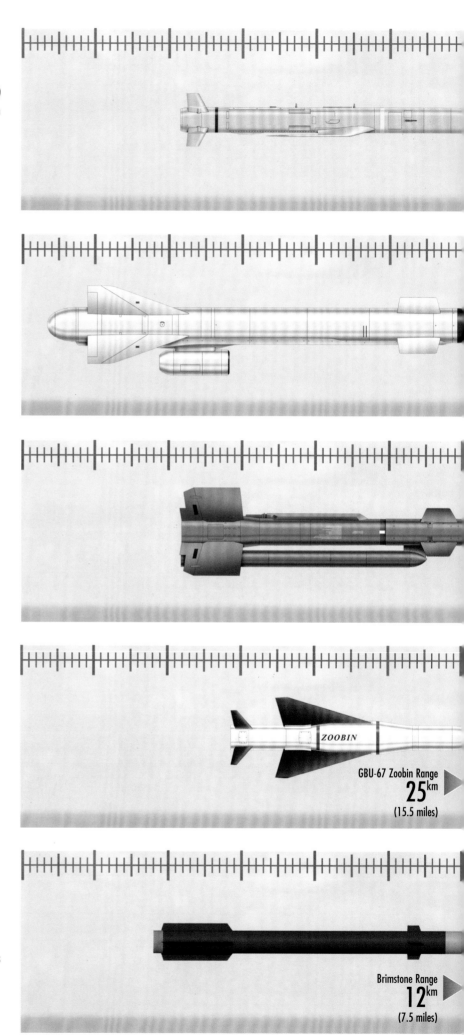

GBU-67 Zoobin Range
25km
(15.5 miles)

Brimstone Range
12km
(7.5 miles)

Range

Longer-range missiles are, in general, larger and more expensive than short-range weapons. They must carry guidance systems for the approach to the target area as well as for the final attack, and often require larger and more sophisticated launch platforms.

AGM-84H SLAM-ER Range
124km
(77 miles)

Kh-59MK (AS-18 'Kazoo') Range
200km
(124 miles)

AGM-130 Range
60km
(37 miles)

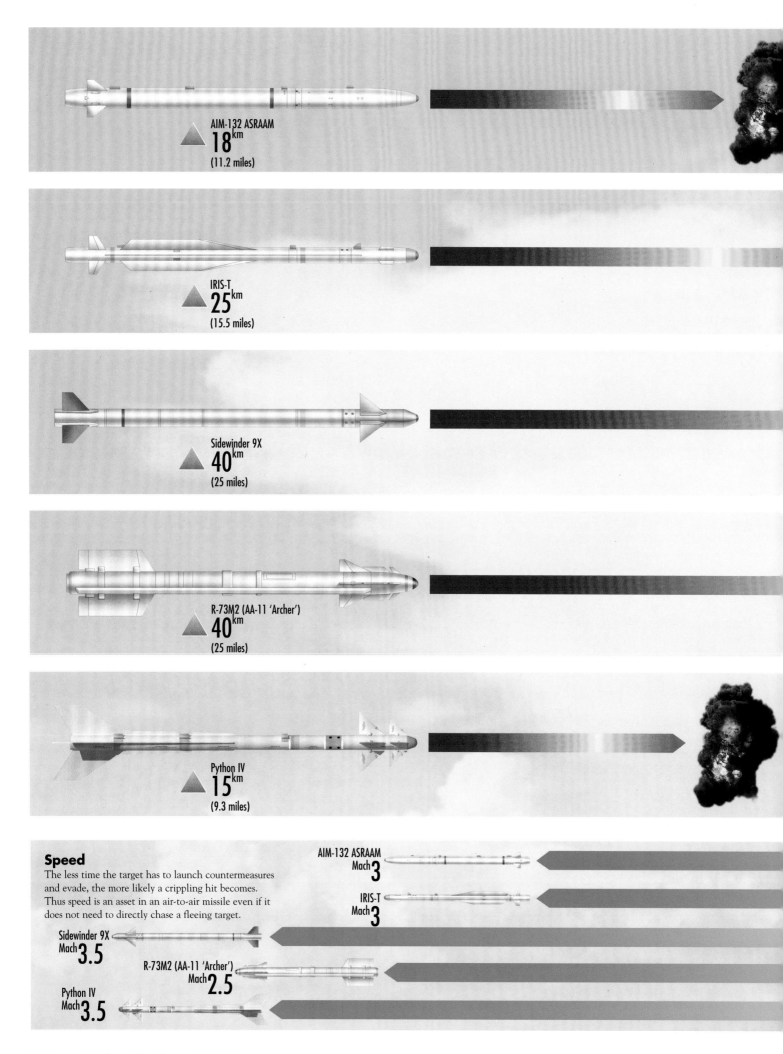

AIM-132 ASRAAM
▲ **18**km
(11.2 miles)

IRIS-T
▲ **25**km
(15.5 miles)

Sidewinder 9X
▲ **40**km
(25 miles)

R-73M2 (AA-11 'Archer')
▲ **40**km
(25 miles)

Python IV
▲ **15**km
(9.3 miles)

Speed
The less time the target has to launch countermeasures and evade, the more likely a crippling hit becomes. Thus speed is an asset in an air-to-air missile even if it does not need to directly chase a fleeing target.

AIM-132 ASRAAM
Mach **3**

IRIS-T
Mach **3**

Sidewinder 9X
Mach **3.5**

R-73M2 (AA-11 'Archer')
Mach **2.5**

Python IV
Mach **3.5**

Air-to-Air Missiles

Effective Range and Speed

▶ **AIM-132 ASRAAM**
▶ **IRIS-T**
▶ **Sidewinder 9X**
▶ **R-73M2 (AA-11 'Archer')**
▶ **Python IV**

Long-range air-to-air missiles are normally guided by radar, and may be fired at a target that is too distant to see. Shorter-range missiles, sometimes referred to as 'dogfight' missiles, generally use infrared homing. Early infrared seekers were rather primitive and would lock onto the largest heat source in their arc of vision. This was sometimes the sun, and even if the missile locked onto the hot engine exhaust of an enemy aircraft it could easily be distracted by flares dropped as a countermeasure.

Modern heat-seeking missiles are much less likely to be distracted by other heat sources, but can still be confused by flares dropped by the target aircraft. A combination of flares and well-timed evasive manoeuvres can cause a missile to overshoot its intended target. However, a missile does not necessarily need to make a direct hit. A contact explosion is highly destructive, but missiles are fused to explode in proximity to the target if a hit is not obtained. This creates a shower of missile fragments that can inflict crippling damage on an enemy aircraft.

A new generation of missiles is emerging, which can lock onto a target that is not in front of the launching aircraft. By means of a targeting system fitted to the pilot's helmet, a missile can be locked onto any target the pilot can see, swerving violently after launch to begin its pursuit. An attack on a target outside the normal arc is known as an 'over the shoulder launch'.

Effective Range

Long-range missiles give the user a massive advantage in air-to-air combat, as they can down some of the enemy force before they get close enough to launch their own weapons.

BELOW: A Eurofighter Typhoon fires an MBDA ASRAAM (Advanced Short-Range Air-to-Air Missile) during target practice.

Air-launched Anti-tank Missiles

Effective Range and Length

▶ **AGM-114K Hellfire II**
▶ **Brimstone**
▶ **Nimrod**
▶ **Mokopa**

During World War II, all manner of aircraft were converted to the 'tank-buster' role, including some that were highly inappropriate, such as large bombers. Tank busters of the era attacked at low altitude, flying relatively slowly compared with today's strike jets, and although some used cannon, most delivered their attack with rockets. From these inaccurate but nevertheless effective weapons were developed a new generation of guided anti-armour weapons, which permit a fast-moving aircraft to destroy a single enemy tank with great precision.

The Hellfire missile was designed from the outset to be usable by both fixed-wing aircraft and helicopters. Most early Hellfire models were laser-guided, with some using radar guidance. The ability to receive guidance from other sources than the launching platform allowed a missile strike to be delivered and the aircraft to leave the vicinity or seek cover behind terrain while a designator on the ground or aboard a helicopter took over control of the missiles.

Hellfire set the standard for many following missiles. The Nimrod was designed to be used by CH-53 assault helicopters. The South African Mokopa missile was developed largely due to an international arms embargo that prevented imports, while Brimstone started out as a developed version of Hellfire. Brimstone initially used radar guidance, but operational experience showed that a 'man in the loop' was often necessary, and a dual-mode variant was introduced, which can use autonomous radar guidance or semi-active laser homing. The latter requires manual targeting using a laser designator, allowing the missile to be precision guided.

Although developed as anti-tank weapons, many missiles have matured into multi-role precision systems, capable of carrying a range of payloads for use against bunkers, ships and personnel concentrations.

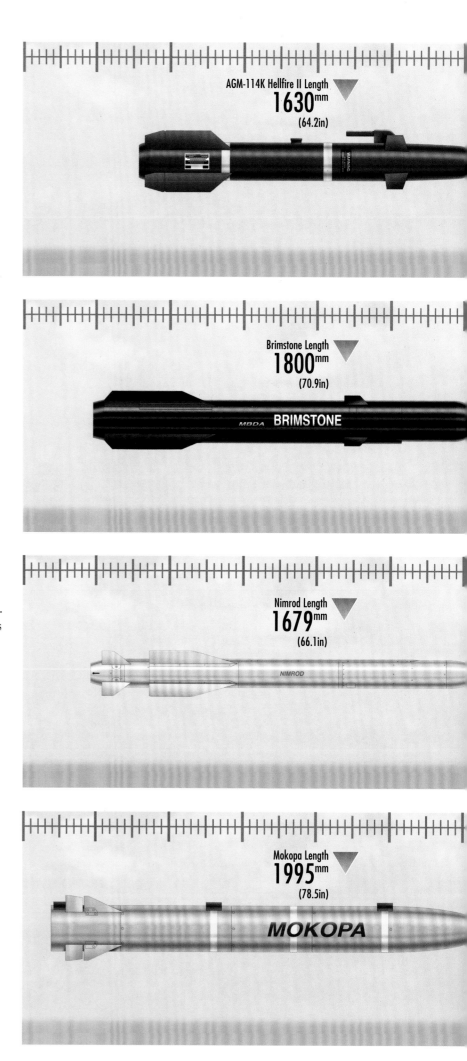

AGM-114K Hellfire II Length
1630mm
(64.2in)

Brimstone Length
1800mm
(70.9in)

Nimrod Length
1679mm
(66.1in)

Mokopa Length
1995mm
(78.5in)

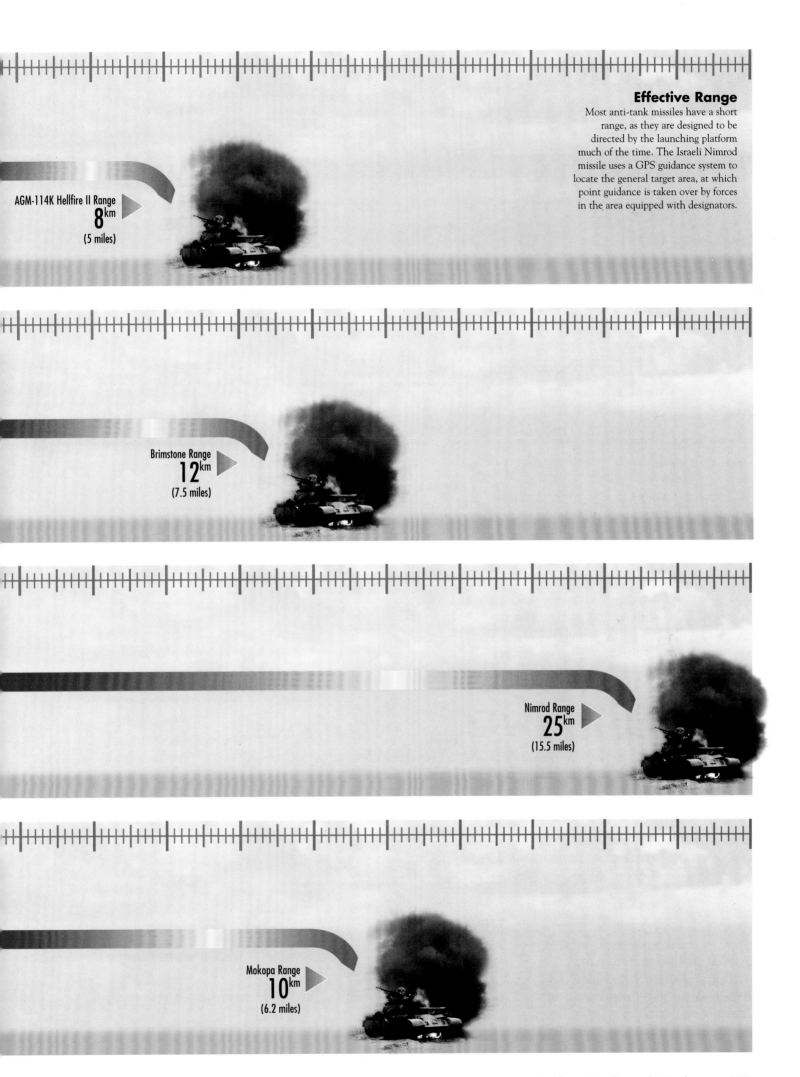

Most anti-tank missiles have a short range, as they are designed to be directed by the launching platform much of the time. The Israeli Nimrod missile uses a GPS guidance system to locate the general target area, at which point guidance is taken over by forces in the area equipped with designators.

AGM-114K Hellfire II Range
8km
(5 miles)

Brimstone Range
12km
(7.5 miles)

Nimrod Range
25km
(15.5 miles)

Mokopa Range
10km
(6.2 miles)

Anti-tank Guided Weapons Systems

Effective Range and Weight

▶ **FGM-148 Javelin**
▶ **Spike-MR**
▶ **Raytheon Griffin**

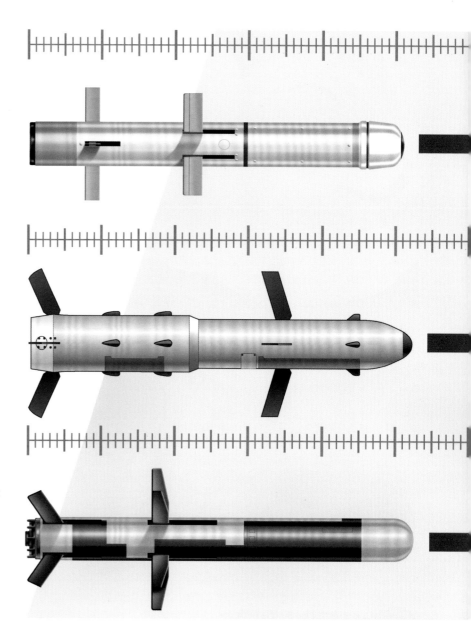

The ability to destroy tanks, or at least to pose a threat to them, is one of the most important capabilities a military force can possess. It has been suggested that 'if you can't fight tanks, you can't fight', which underlines the importance of having an anti-armour capability within infantry forces. In the past, it was sufficient to provide rocket-propelled grenades and disposable unguided weapons, but modern advanced main battle tanks (MBTs) are too well armoured to be seriously damaged by such weapons, though they remain useful against lighter vehicles, and targets such as bunkers.

The new generation of guided anti-tank weapons allows infantry to attack armoured vehicles from a greater distance with a good chance of a hit, and in many cases these weapons can be switched to a different target while the missile is in flight. The guidance systems of missiles such as Javelin and Spike permit top-attack mode to be selected. The armour of a tank or other combat vehicle tends to be weakest on top. Wherever possible, this is the preferred mode of attack.

The increasing levels of protection provided to armoured vehicles has necessitated a gradual expansion in warhead size since the introduction of the first light anti-armour weapons. There is a limit to how large and powerful a warhead can be and remain man-portable, so warhead technology has also had to advance. Some missiles use tandem warheads, which make two attacks on the same spot in rapid succession, as a countermeasure against reactive armour.

RIGHT: The Javelin missile system uses a 'soft launch' to avoid injuring the operator. A short-duration rocket motor drives the missile out of the tube, after which it coasts for a short distance before the main motor ignites. This greatly reduces backblast, though it is still unsafe to be directly behind the launcher.

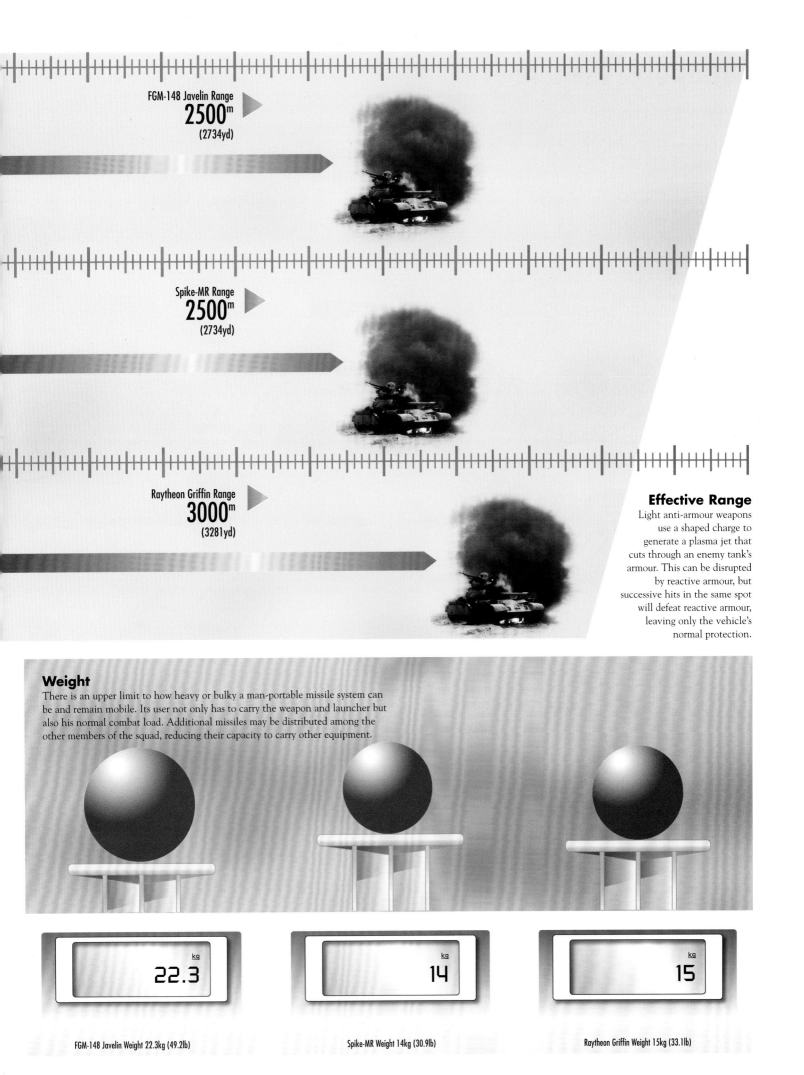

FGM-148 Javelin Range
2500^m
(2734yd)

Spike-MR Range
2500^m
(2734yd)

Raytheon Griffin Range
3000^m
(3281yd)

Effective Range
Light anti-armour weapons use a shaped charge to generate a plasma jet that cuts through an enemy tank's armour. This can be disrupted by reactive armour, but successive hits in the same spot will defeat reactive armour, leaving only the vehicle's normal protection.

Weight
There is an upper limit to how heavy or bulky a man-portable missile system can be and remain mobile. Its user not only has to carry the weapon and launcher but also his normal combat load. Additional missiles may be distributed among the other members of the squad, reducing their capacity to carry other equipment.

kg
22.3

kg
14

kg
15

FGM-148 Javelin Weight 22.3kg (49.2lb)

Spike-MR Weight 14kg (30.9lb)

Raytheon Griffin Weight 15kg (33.1lb)

Weapons Dispensers

Weight and Submunitions

▶ **RBK-250**
▶ **Kite**
▶ **JP233**
▶ **CBU-100 Rockeye**
▶ **Bombkapsel 90 (BK90)**

Submunition dispensers are simply vehicles which carry a large number of smaller weapons to the target area. Many are air-dropped, and are often constructed to the same dimensions as a conventional bomb. The payload is normally anti-personnel bomblets, or cluster bombs, but can also include anti-tank munitions, mines or more exotic payloads such as anti-electrical bomblets designed to damage power-transmission stations. Specialist submunitions also potentially include chemical weapons or propaganda leaflets, and runway-denial systems. The latter often incorporate both direct-attack munitions and delayed-detonation mines to make clearance and repair more difficult.

The purpose of using submunitions rather than a single warhead is to saturate the target area, which has caused some controversy, as cluster munitions are regarded as indiscriminate weapons in some quarters. While it is true that everyone and everything in the target area is attacked by exploding bomblets, the same is true for any weapon with a blast radius, such as conventional bombs, missiles and artillery shells. Cluster munitions simply do the same job more efficiently, over a wider area.

Cluster munitions can be delivered with great precision to a target area, but once there they are designed to saturate the area with great lethality. A near miss with a bomb or shell may be survivable, but the hail of fragments caused by anti-personnel bomblets has so much overlap that unprotected personnel are unlikely to escape.

The dispenser itself may be unguided or may incorporate various forms of guidance, including inertial, GPS or laser designation. This permits the payload to be delivered with great accuracy, though, as already noted, the submunitions will then be scattered so as to give maximum coverage of the target area. Weapons of this sort cannot be used for pinpoint attacks, but are extremely effective against area targets such as concentrations of vehicles or troops.

Submunitions

Submunitions vary in size. Anti-personnel bomblets can be very small, whilst anti-armour submunitions must pack a larger punch. The intensity of coverage depends on how many submunitions are carried and how widely they are scattered.

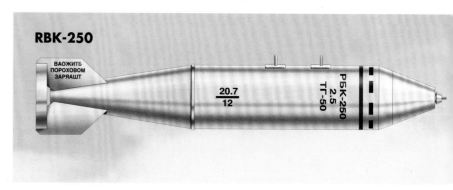

RBK-250

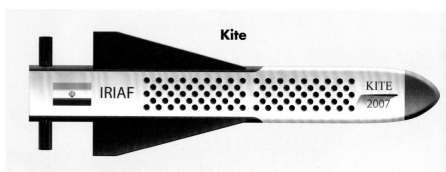

Kite

JP233

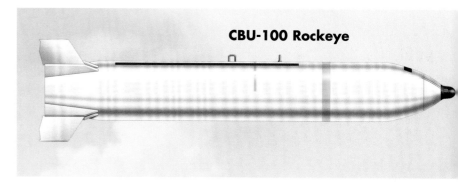

CBU-100 Rockeye

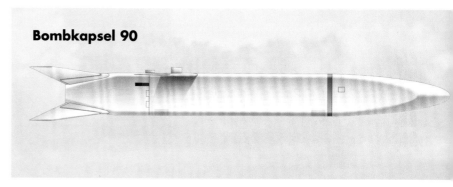

Bombkapsel 90

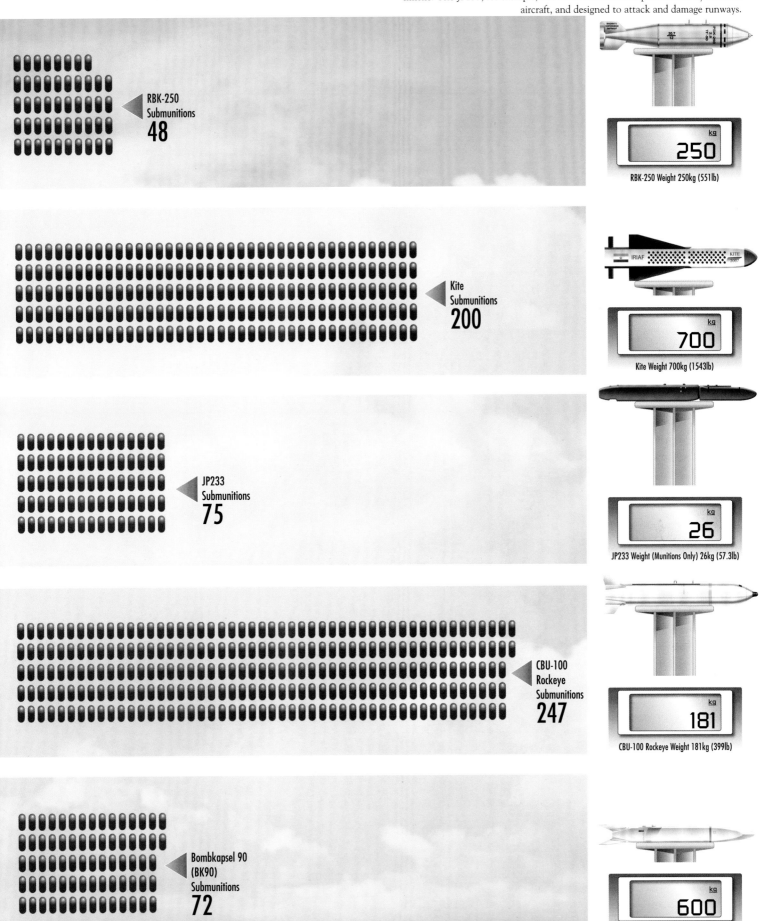

Submunition dispensers vary considerably in size and weight. Those intended to be deployed from aircraft normally correspond to the dimensions of an existing bomb or missile. The JP233, for example, was based on container pods carried by Tornado aircraft, and designed to attack and damage runways.

RBK-250
Submunitions
48

RBK-250 Weight 250kg (551lb)

kg
250

Kite
Submunitions
200

Kite Weight 700kg (1543lb)

kg
700

JP233
Submunitions
75

JP233 Weight (Munitions Only) 26kg (57.3lb)

kg
26

CBU-100
Rockeye
Submunitions
247

CBU-100 Rockeye Weight 181kg (399lb)

kg
181

Bombkapsel 90
(BK90)
Submunitions
72

Bombkapsel 90 (BK90) Weight 600kg (1323lb)

kg
600

Bombs

Payload

▶ **Mk 82**
▶ **Mk 83**
▶ **Mk 84**
▶ **FAB-1500**

Unguided bombs are, at best, highly inaccurate. Precision can be improved by delivering the bombs at a very low level, but this action can pose a hazard to the launching aircraft. For this reason, retarded bombs were developed, which deploy air brakes after being dropped. These slow the bomb and allow the aircraft to clear the blast area. 'Dumb' bombs can also be converted into guided weapons by fitting a GPS guidance kit, creating weapons that lack the precision of laser-guided bombs but which are still far more accurate than unguided equivalents.

The basic bomb in all these cases is much the same: an aerodynamic casing carrying as large a warhead as possible. The United States uses three standard sizes of bomb, designated Mk 82, Mk 83 and Mk 84, modelled on the traditional 500lb (227kg), 1000lb (454kg) and 2000lb (907kg) bombs. Decisions about what mix of bombs is most likely to be effective on a given mission must be based on the nature of the target and the delivery platform – some aircraft cannot carry the heavier bombs on their pylons.

Standard bomb payloads have remained more or less the same since World War II, when extensive experience was gained of the trade-off between bomb weight and effectiveness. A larger, single warhead is more effective against a point target like a bunker, but a pattern of smaller bombs will cause more destruction to a supply dump or troop concentration.

The Russian equivalent to the US Mk 80 series is designated FAB (from the Russian for 'General Purpose Bomb'). These weapons, too, come in standard sizes modelled on traditional bomb payloads. Equivalents to the Mk 82, Mk 83 and Mk 84 all exist and can be delivered by tactical aircraft; there are also much more powerful FAB-1500 (1500kg/3307lb) and FAB-3000 (3000kg/6614lb) bombs which can only be delivered by heavy bombers.

1 US Air Force ground crew load up M117 bombs under the wings of a B-52H longe-range bomber.

FAB-1500
1500kg
(3307lb)

Payload
Conventional general-purpose bombs offer a lot of 'bang for buck' as they give up little mass for guidance or propulsion systems, and thus can carry a proportionally larger warhead than a missile of the same nominal weight.

kg
1500

Weight 1500kg (3307lb)

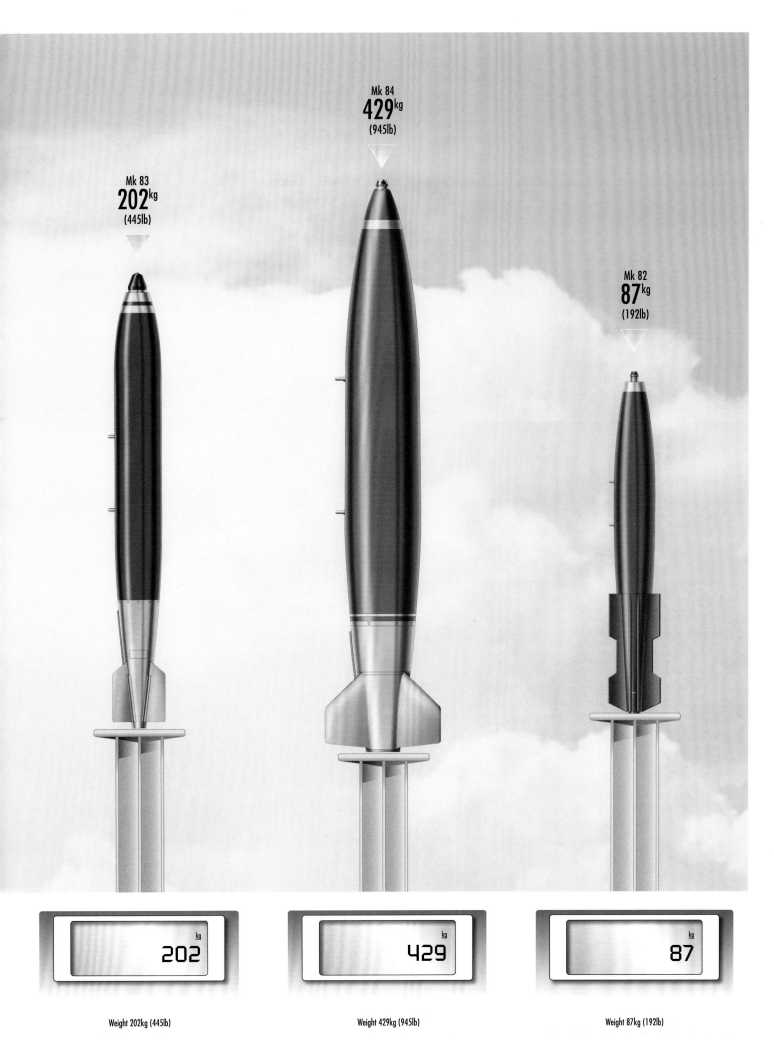

Mk 83
202kg
(445lb)

Mk 84
429kg
(945lb)

Mk 82
87kg
(192lb)

202 kg

429 kg

87 kg

Weight 202kg (445lb)

Weight 429kg (945lb)

Weight 87kg (192lb)

US Nuclear Bombs

Approximate Blast Radius of Effect

▶ **B57**
▶ **B61**
▶ **B83**

In addition to an electromagnetic pulse (EMP), which can disrupt communications and electronic equipment over a wide area, a nuclear explosion creates a massive amount of thermal (infrared) radiation, which will incinerate nearby personnel and objects, and start fires over a wider area. The flash may cause temporary blindness in anyone looking at it, and the detonation also emits a surge of ionizing radiation, which may irradiate the immediate surroundings.

The fireball will destroy anything within its radius and create a crater as well as sending a high-pressure wave of air (blast) outwards. This is powerful enough to flatten nearby structures and will cause damage over a wide area. Air rushing back into the low-pressure area created by the blast causes secondary damage and also brings in dust that is then thrown upwards to create the characteristic 'mushroom cloud'. This dust, which includes radioactive material and irradiated debris, then settles as 'fallout' wherever the wind carries it.

The area over which these effects take place depends upon the yield of the weapon, rated in kilotons. One kiloton equates to 1016 tonnes (1000 tons) of TNT. The US B61 nuclear bomb is a variable-yield weapon, which can be set to deliver a given intensity of blast depending on the chosen target. The B61 can be delivered by a variety of aircraft, including the Lockheed Martin F-35 Lightning II. Its maximum yield is 340 kilotons for the 'strategic' role, and can be set as low as 0.3 kiltotons for 'tactical' targets. By comparison, the B57 bomb was designed as a series of fixed-yield warheads ranging from 5 to 20 kilotons. The B83 is the largest US nuclear weapon and has a variable yield, with a maximum of 1.2 megatons.

RIGHT: The total destruction radius created by a nuclear weapon is perhaps smaller than many people might imagine, but this is only one of the weapon's effects. Near the impact or burst point, absolutely nothing will survive.

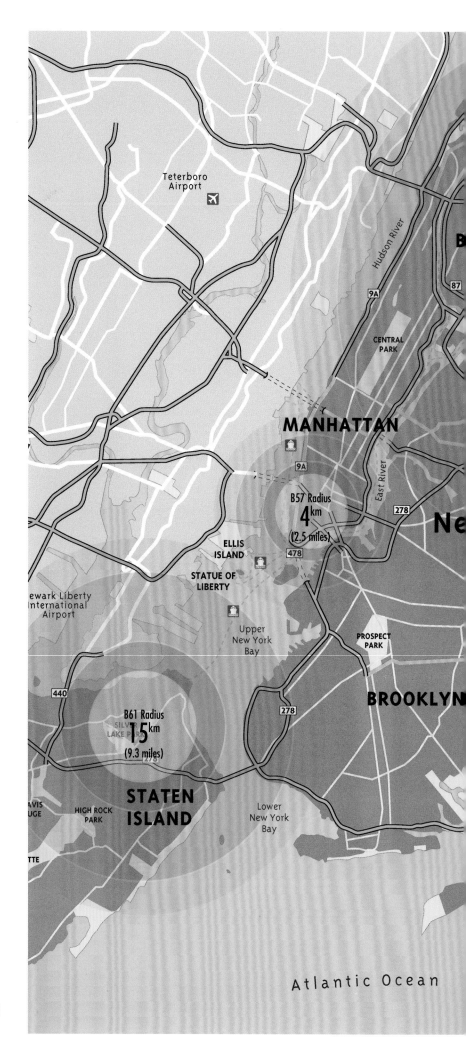

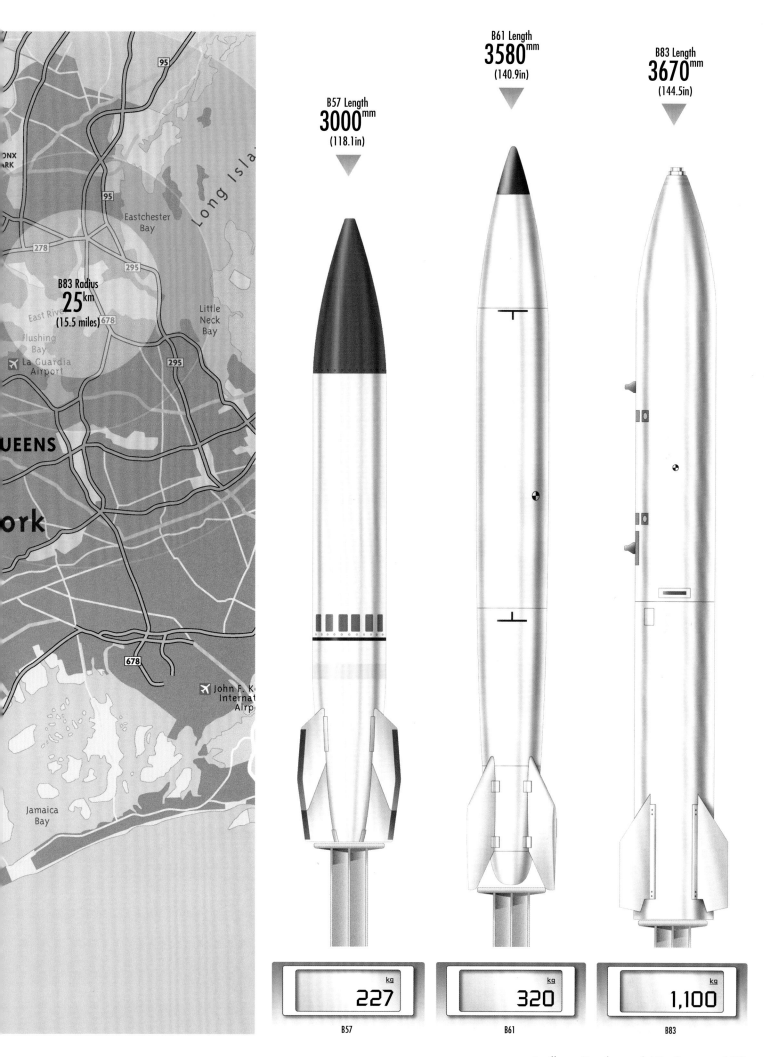

B57 Length
3000mm
(118.1in)

B61 Length
3580mm
(140.9in)

B83 Length
3670mm
(144.5in)

B83 Radius
25km
(15.5 miles)

	kg
	227

B57

	kg
	320

B61

	kg
	1,100

B83

Nuclear Explosion: Number of Kilotons

Fallout Range

▶ **0.1 Kiloton**
▶ **1 Kiloton**
▶ **10 Kiloton**

The precise effects of a nuclear detonation depend on its location. A high-altitude (above 30km/18.6 miles) detonation does not produce a mushroom cloud or radioactive fallout. The fireball will not touch the ground, but direct radiation effects may be considerable. High-altitude bursts would normally be used to produce an electromagnetic pulse (EMP) and thereby damage electronic equipment. A lower air burst will cause mainly blast and thermal effects, and is more hazardous to people than structures.

A subsurface burst, where the warhead penetrates the ground before exploding, will cause heavy radioactive contamination of the area and very severe local effects, but smaller secondary effects. When a weapon is detonated on or close to the ground, local blast and thermal effects will be severe, and fallout will be considerable due to contaminated debris drawn up into the mushroom cloud. The diagram shows the effects of various warhead detonations within a major urban area.

Within the severe damage zone (red), few structures will remain intact and personnel casualties will be almost total. The area will also be heavily contaminated. Within the moderate damage zone (orange), strongly built structures (e.g. concrete) may survive more or less intact, but lighter buildings will be destroyed or heavily damaged. Personnel casualties are likely to be high, due to both the weapon's effects and secondary causes such as fires and collapsing buildings. Within the light damage zone (yellow), windows will be broken and buildings will suffer light structural damage. Damage patterns will be varied, as blast can rebound and be funnelled by structures. Immediate casualties are unlikely to be severe and will mostly be from secondary causes.

RIGHT: Damage zones are not clear-cut and may be patchy due to terrain and weather effects. Nearer to the point of detonation (Ground Zero), damage becomes more uniform and more severe until, close to Ground Zero, destruction becomes total.

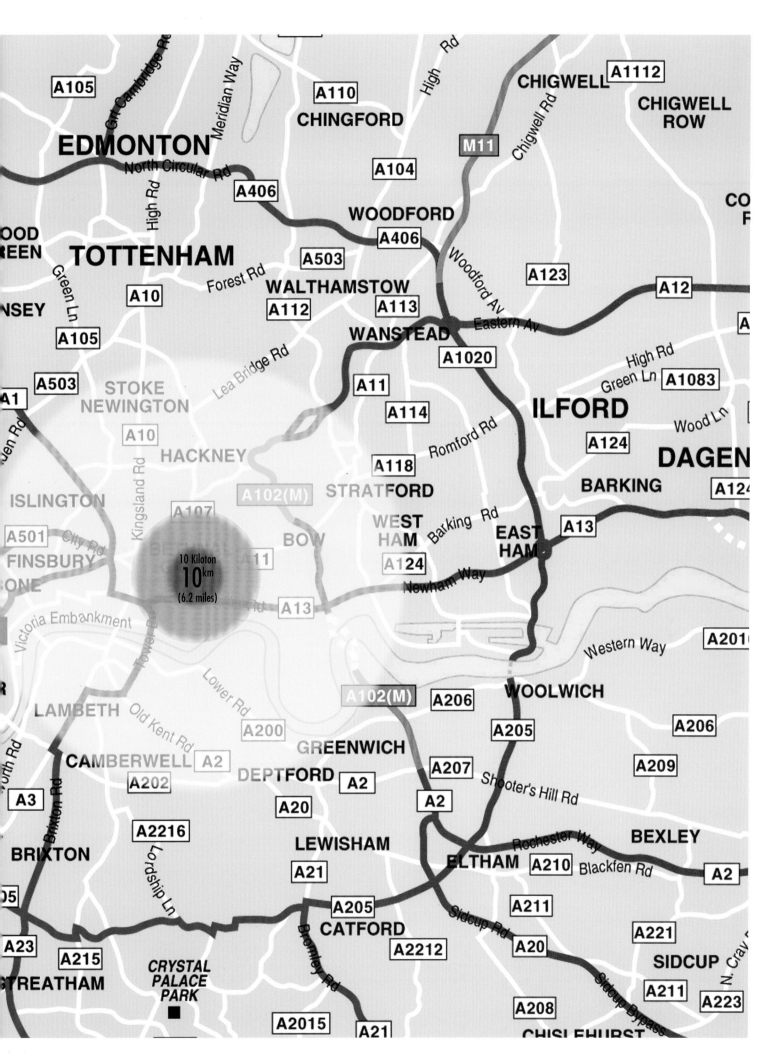

Moscow

New York

CSS-4
12,900km
(8016 miles)

LGM-30G
13,000km
(8077 miles)

SS-18
16,000km
(9942 miles)

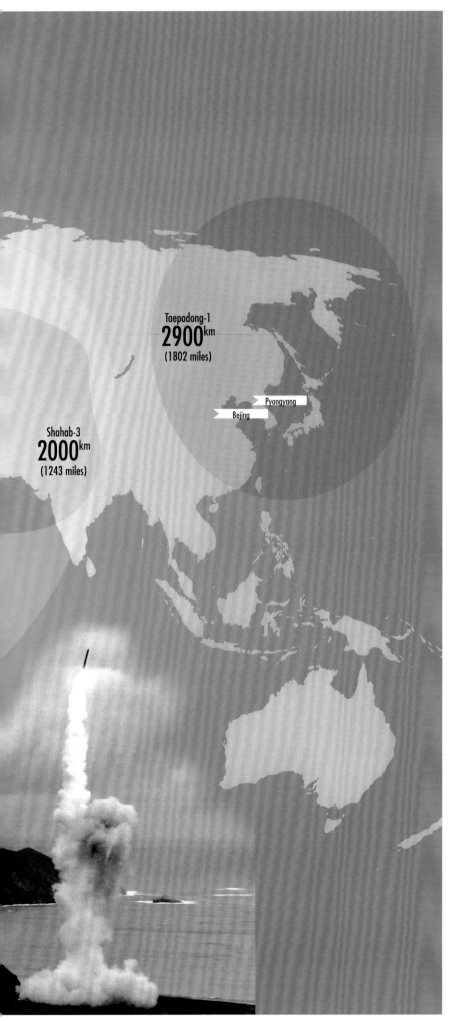

Taepodong-1
2900km
(1802 miles)

Shahab-3
2000km
(1243 miles)

Pyongyang

Bejing

Intercontinental Ballistic Missiles

Range

▶ **LGM-30G (United States)**
▶ **SS-18 (Russia)**
▶ **CSS-4 (China)**
▶ **Shahab-3 (Iran)**
▶ **Taepodong-1 (North Korea)**

Early nuclear bombs were sufficiently large and heavy that they could only be delivered by strategic bombers, and this required that the bombers penetrate deep into enemy airspace and then make a hazardous return flight after their attack. The invention of air-launched cruise missiles increased the survivability of the nuclear-bomber force, and therefore also the chance that weapons would actually reach their targets. However, it was the ballistic missile that made reliable delivery of nuclear weapons possible, and thus greatly increased the credibility of a deterrence policy. A ballistic missile is extremely hard to intercept, and can cover the distance between launcher and target in a fraction of the time required to fly there in a bomber. Missile accuracy has steadily increased over time, but this is only important when attacking very hard targets such as missile silos. Against population centres and industrial areas, a near miss with a nuclear warhead is every bit as effective as a direct hit.

Theatre ballistic missiles are intended to be able to attack any target within their 'theatre of war', defined as within 3500km (2175 miles) of the launch point. The term has replaced earlier ones such as medium-range ballistic missile or intermediate-range ballistic missile. The longest-ranged missiles, those capable of attacking targets on another continent, are extremely large, expensive and difficult to develop, and are termed intercontinental ballistic missiles (ICBMs). Some nations protect their missile launch capabilities with hardened bunkers, while others use submarines to hide their weapons in the world's oceans.

LEFT: A Minuteman III missile takes off from somewhere on US soil. The LGM-30G Minuteman III is the only land-based ICBM in service in the United States. It has a range of approximately 13,000km (8078 miles).

Naval Power

The seas are vitally important to international trade, and can be used to project power into distant areas. Controlling a sea area, or at least denying it to the enemy, is a vital part of maritime strategy. Naval forces must deal with threats from submarines, surface vessels and aircraft, necessitating a mixed armament and the sensor systems to make these weapons useful.

A cheap, lightly armed vessel can undertake patrol work and 'show the flag' but may be vulnerable to attack. Conversely, an excessively complex or expensive vessel may not justify its cost, especially if the owning nation has extensive commitments. Thus most navies operate a range of vessels, most of which can undertake a variety of duties. Few navies can afford enough specialist ships to ensure that one is available to meet any given situation; for this reason multi-role vessels are currently popular as they provide at least a modest capability in all areas.

LEFT: USS *Seawolf* (SSN-21), lead boat of the US Navy's Seawolf class of nuclear attack submarines, conducts sea trials off the coast of Connecticut, 1997. The aerial image shows the sail from a starboard angle, looking forward.

Corvettes and Patrol Craft

Speed and Displacement

▶ **Visby Class**
▶ **Houbei Class**
▶ **Eilat Class**

Large ocean-going warships are inefficient in some applications, such as the defence of a coastline or patrol operations close to the shore. A much smaller and less expensive vessel can provide a credible deterrent in the form of an 'armed presence' and can deal with most minor incidents. There is a limit to the amount of weaponry that can be crammed into a small hull of course, but these smaller vessels can still pose a threat to a major warship.

Today's small surface combatants are generally armed with highly effective anti-ship missiles, which can cripple or even sink a major warship. It does not matter how large or small, expensive or basic the launching platform is; what matters is its ability to get its missiles into a suitable firing position. Speed is important when attempting an interception or trying get into missile range, as pis an effective set of defences.

Anti-aircraft and anti-missile defences in the form of decoys, electronic countermeasures, missiles and guns can all increase the survivability of a surface vessel, but perhaps the best defence of all is not to be attacked. Modern corvettes such as the Visby class and missile boats such as the Chinese Houbei class are designed to have a minimal radar return. Their 'stealth' is in part due to small size, and partly due to the use of shaping and advanced materials to absorb or scatter radar energy rather than returning a clear signal.

ABOVE: The Swedish Visby-class corvette is clearly a 'stealth boat'. It has a minimum of angles and projections to reflect radar energy, and uses angled planes to prevent a clean return. It is not invisible to radar, but can only be detected at relatively short range, which may enable it to launch a surprise attack.

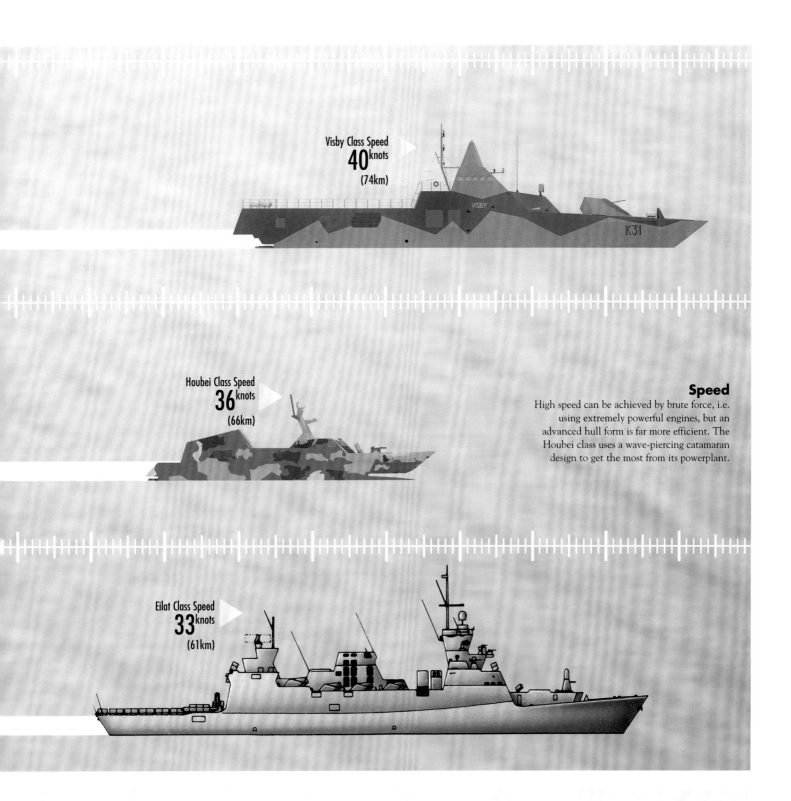

Visby Class Speed
40knots
(74km)

K31

Houbei Class Speed
36knots
(66km)

Speed

High speed can be achieved by brute force, i.e. using extremely powerful engines, but an advanced hull form is far more efficient. The Houbei class uses a wave-piercing catamaran design to get the most from its powerplant.

Eilat Class Speed
33knots
(61km)

Displacement

The size of a vessel is indicated by the amount of water it displaces. A larger ship generally needs deeper water to operate in so cannot come as far inshore, and also makes a bigger target.

Visby Class Displacement
640tonnes
(630 tons)

Houbei Class Displacement
224tonnes
(220 tons)

Eilat Class Displacement
1075tonnes
(1058 tons)

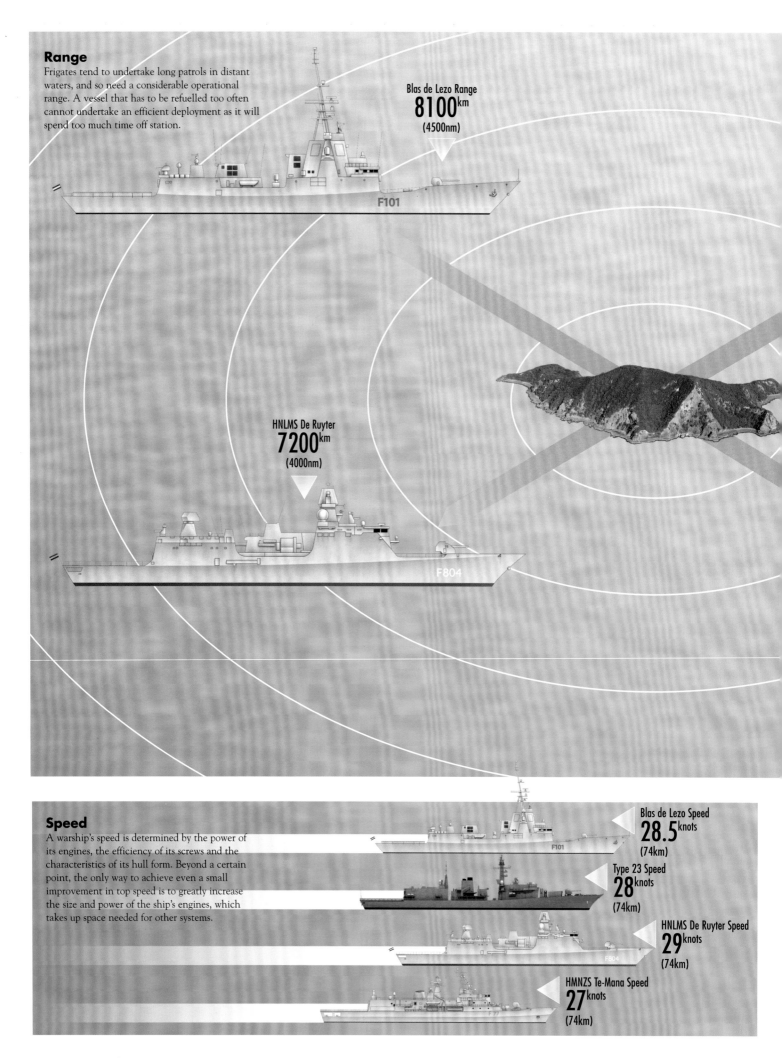

Range

Frigates tend to undertake long patrols in distant waters, and so need a considerable operational range. A vessel that has to be refuelled too often cannot undertake an efficient deployment as it will spend too much time off station.

Blas de Lezo Range
8100km
(4500nm)

F101

HNLMS De Ruyter
7200km
(4000nm)

F804

Speed

A warship's speed is determined by the power of its engines, the efficiency of its screws and the characteristics of its hull form. Beyond a certain point, the only way to achieve even a small improvement in top speed is to greatly increase the size and power of the ship's engines, which takes up space needed for other systems.

Blas de Lezo Speed
28.5knots
(74km)
F101

Type 23 Speed
28knots
(74km)

HNLMS De Ruyter Speed
29knots
(74km)
F804

HMNZS Te-Mana Speed
27knots
(74km)

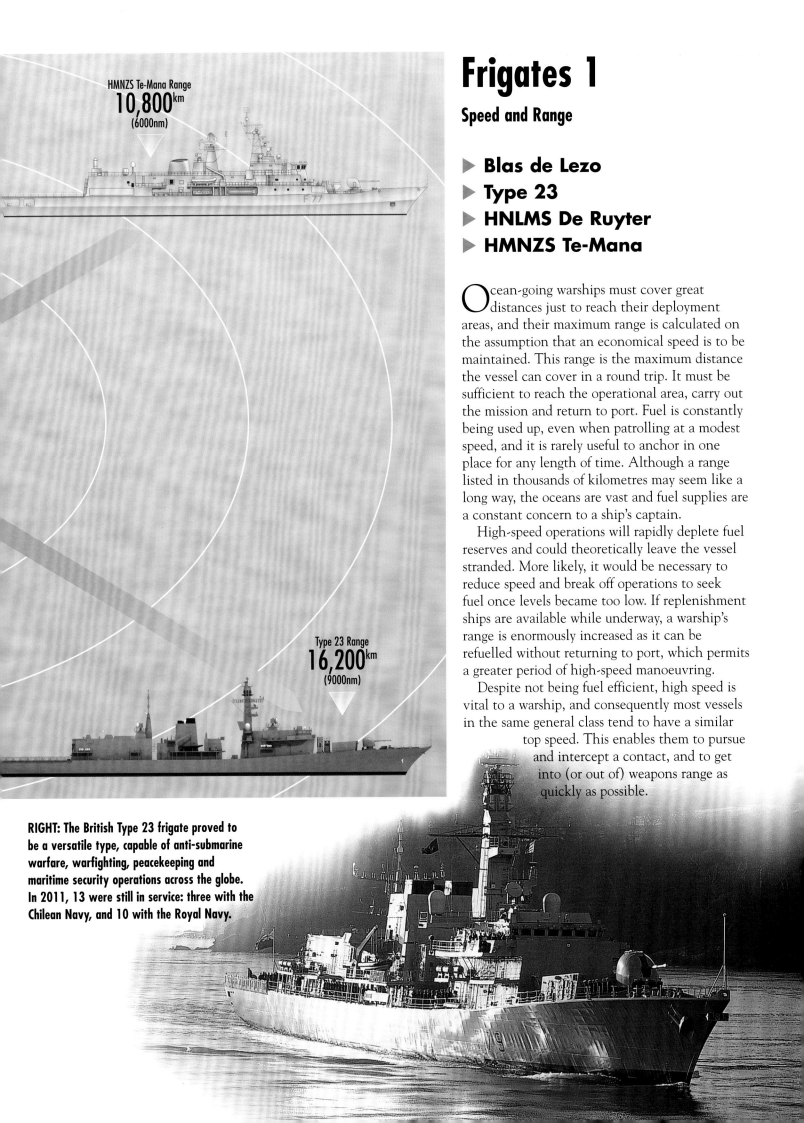

HMNZS Te-Mana Range
10,800km
(6000nm)

Type 23 Range
16,200km
(9000nm)

Frigates 1
Speed and Range

▶ **Blas de Lezo**
▶ **Type 23**
▶ **HNLMS De Ruyter**
▶ **HMNZS Te-Mana**

Ocean-going warships must cover great distances just to reach their deployment areas, and their maximum range is calculated on the assumption that an economical speed is to be maintained. This range is the maximum distance the vessel can cover in a round trip. It must be sufficient to reach the operational area, carry out the mission and return to port. Fuel is constantly being used up, even when patrolling at a modest speed, and it is rarely useful to anchor in one place for any length of time. Although a range listed in thousands of kilometres may seem like a long way, the oceans are vast and fuel supplies are a constant concern to a ship's captain.

High-speed operations will rapidly deplete fuel reserves and could theoretically leave the vessel stranded. More likely, it would be necessary to reduce speed and break off operations to seek fuel once levels became too low. If replenishment ships are available while underway, a warship's range is enormously increased as it can be refuelled without returning to port, which permits a greater period of high-speed manoeuvring.

Despite not being fuel efficient, high speed is vital to a warship, and consequently most vessels in the same general class tend to have a similar top speed. This enables them to pursue and intercept a contact, and to get into (or out of) weapons range as quickly as possible.

RIGHT: The British Type 23 frigate proved to be a versatile type, capable of anti-submarine warfare, warfighting, peacekeeping and maritime security operations across the globe. In 2011, 13 were still in service: three with the Chilean Navy, and 10 with the Royal Navy.

Frigates 2
Complement and Full-load Displacement

▶ **Blas de Lezo**
▶ **Type 23**
▶ **HNLMS De Ruyter**
▶ **HMNZS Te-Mana**

The term 'frigate' has meant different things at various times in history. Today, a frigate is a workhorse vessel capable of undertaking a variety of roles. Frigates may operate independently or escort high-value vessels. They must be capable of dealing with submarine, air and surface threats, though many designs are optimized for one of these roles and retain the others as a secondary capability. Thus a frigate must carry a mix of guns, missiles and torpedoes, plus helicopters and the specialist sensors required to track surface, air and underwater targets. All these systems require specialist crew members to operate and maintain them. Recent frigate designs include a number of innovative measures designed to improve efficiency. Thus the British Type 23, which was developed as an anti-submarine platform at the end of the 1970s, requires far more crew members to operate it than the multi-role FREMM frigate recently designed by France and Italy, despite the FREMM class ships being much larger. However, automation is not the only factor that determines a ship's displacement and the crew size needed. Greater capability always comes at the cost of increased displacement and crew requirements.

Complement

Adding a weapon or sensor system requires not only personnel to man it, but also increases the quantity of support personnel and supplies the vessel must carry. Machinery can only go so far towards replacing people, after which the vessel becomes critically vulnerable to casualties or fatigue due to overwork.

Blas de Lezo Complement
250 men

Type 23 Complement
181 men

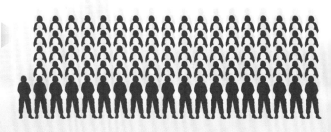

HNLMS De Ruyter Complement
202 men

LEFT: Modern frigates such as the Type 23 are light, fast and manoeuvrable.

HMNZS Te-Mana Complement
163 men

One way to keep displacement down is to create a vessel with deliberately limited capabilities, or one optimized for a single role with only a token capability in other areas. However, this can lead to a vessel simply being too small to accommodate necessary new equipment as operational requirements change.

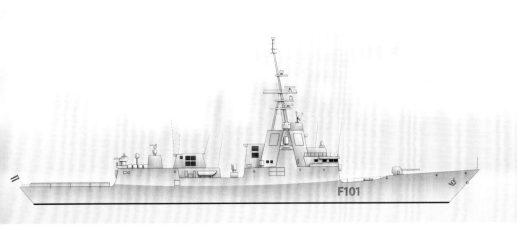

Blas de Lezo Displacement
5800 tonnes
(5710 tons)

Type 23 Displacement
4270 tonnes
(4200 tons)

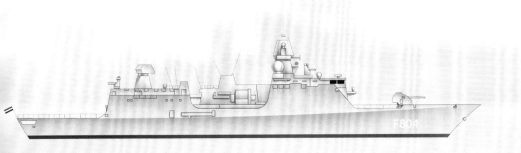

HNLMS De Ruyter Displacement
6050 tonnes
(5955 tons)

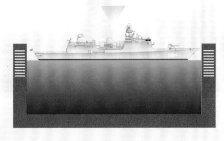

HMNZS Te-Mana Displacement
3600 tonnes
(3545 tons)

Anti-Submarine Torpedoes

Modern anti-submarine torpedoes have to be able to track and hit a deep-diving submarine in open water and also function in the cluttered and confusing shallow-water environment close to shore. Older weapons lacked one or both of these capabilities, limiting their usefulness.

Type 054A
7.3km
(4.5 miles)

Detonation

If a contact detonation is accomplished, the warhead does not need to be especially big to do crippling or fatal damage. Submarines are not armoured; their best defence lies in remaining undetected or denying the enemy a clear signature to home in on.

Frigates: Anti-Submarine Warfare

Torpedo Range

Type 23
11km
(6.8 miles)

Sachsen Class
10km
(6.2 miles)

▶ **Type 23**
▶ **Sachsen Class**
▶ **Type 054A**

In the past, a range of anti-submarine weapons have been used, including depth charges dropped over the stern of a surface vessel or fired from a launcher. Rockets and mortars have also been used to scatter contact-fused bombs over the suspected position of a submarine. These measures required the surface vessel to approach very closely, whereas torpedoes greatly increase the reach of the anti-submarine vessel.

Most frigates engage submarines using lightweight torpedoes from deck-mounted launchers. The weapons have a significant range, but this is exceeded by that of a heavyweight guided torpedo from a submarine. However, it is not just the range of the weapons that dictates the distance at which the vessel can engage; it is also the efficiency of its sensors. A stealthy submarine may not be detected until it is fairly close, reducing the effectiveness of long-range anti-submarine weapons.

An anti-submarine torpedo must be fast enough to reach the target before it moves out of range, and must be able to home in on a stealthy boat that is trying to creep away. Its targeting processor must be sophisticated enough to discern the real signature of the boat from background ocean noise, decoys and other distractions.

RIGHT: The *Sachsen* **receives supplies. The anti-submarine role has traditionally been a job for frigates. Most classes carry at least one helicopter to extend their sensor reach with 'dipping' sonar and to deliver an attack against a distant contact. Helicopter-delivered torpedoes are normally the same as those launched from warships.**

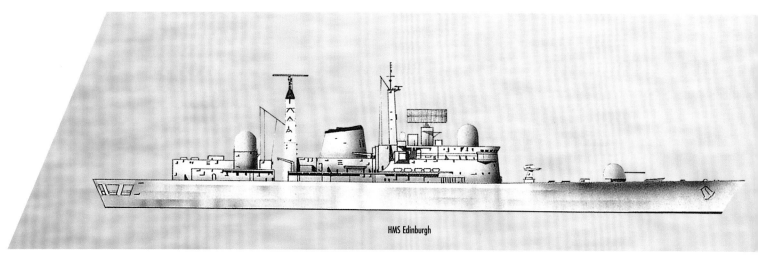

HMS Edinburgh

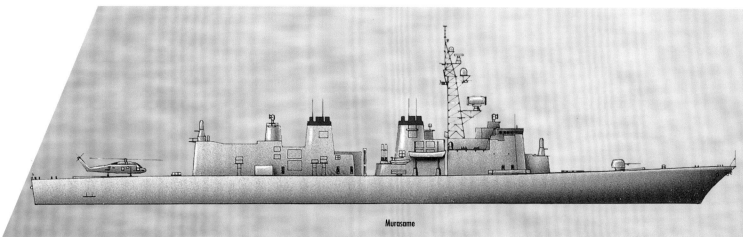

Murasame

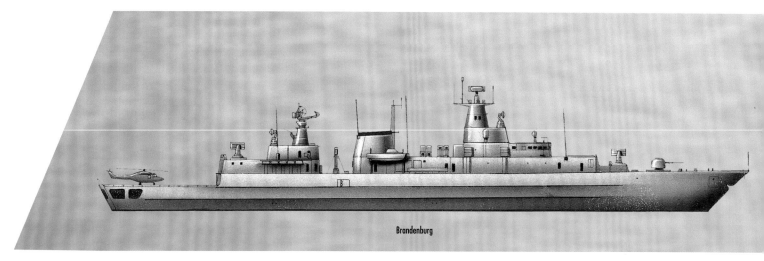

Brandenburg

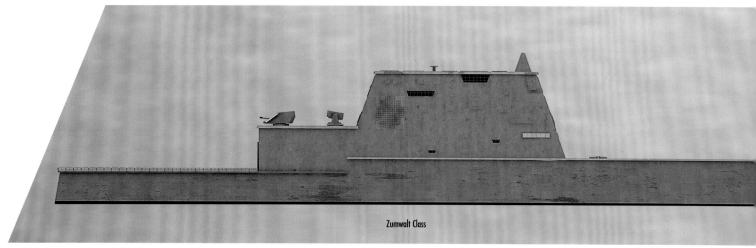

Zumwalt Class

Armament

Besides a recent tendency towards larger guns, there has been a move from fixed or trainable missile launchers to vertical-launch systems (VLS). A VLS system can launch several different types of missiles, and can deliver the salvo much faster than a trainable launcher that has to be reloaded. VLS systems have no blind arcs blocked by the ship's superstructure, as the missile climbs above the vessel before turning towards the target.

Sea Dart launcher
1

114mm (4.5in) gun
1

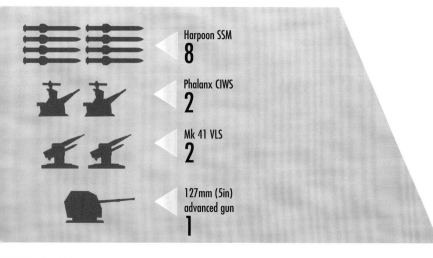

Harpoon SSM
8

Phalanx CIWS
2

Mk 41 VLS
2

127mm (5in) advanced gun
1

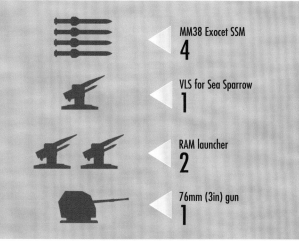

MM38 Exocet SSM
4

VLS for Sea Sparrow
1

RAM launcher
2

76mm (3in) gun
1

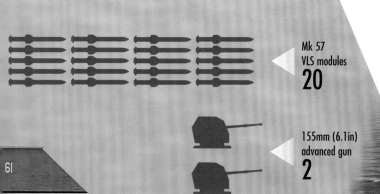

Mk 57 VLS modules
20

155mm (6.1in) advanced gun
2

Guided Missile Destroyers

Armament

▶ **HMS Edinburgh (Type 42)**
▶ **Murasame**
▶ **Brandenburg**
▶ **Zumwalt Class**

Destroyers were originally developed to protect the battle line from torpedo boats (hence their original name of 'torpedo-boat destroyers'). They soon developed into general-purpose light warships equipped with guns and torpedoes, capable of undertaking offensive and defensive operations. Over time, as the battleship has passed away, destroyers have gone from being fleet escorts to the primary warships fielded by many nations. Today's destroyers are primarily concerned with surface action, air defence and attacks against shore targets, using a mix of guns and missiles.

The guns shipped by modern destroyers are usually similar in calibre to those traditionally carried, but most ships have just one or two rather than mounting several turrets as was common in World War II designs. There has recently been a move towards larger and more powerful guns, largely for shore bombardment. Thus the recent Zumwalt class carries much more powerful guns than the earlier Type 42 class such as *Edinburgh*.

BELOW: The hull form of the US Zumwalt-class destroyer is optimized for stealth. By using vertical-launch missile systems, its designers reduced the number of corners and projections above the decks, which in turn reduced radar return, making the vessel hard to detect.

Destroyers

Speed and Range

▶ **HMS Daring (Type 45)**
▶ **Kongo**
▶ **Udaloy Class**

The line between different classes of warship has become increasingly blurred in recent years. Displacement is no longer the defining factor; some vessels designated as frigates are larger than certain destroyer classes. There is also a significant overlap in terms of role – specialist vessels optimized for anti-submarine and anti-aircraft work exist in both the frigate and destroyer classes. The issue is further confused when one navy assigns a designation to a class that has a different name in its parent navy. The Udaloy class was termed a 'large anti-submarine ship' by its Russian designers, which exactly described its designed role. Western observers designated it a destroyer, based mainly on its size.

As a general rule, destroyers are larger, more capable and more expensive than frigates, and tend to operate as part of a task force rather than independently. They also tend to have more extensive anti-air and anti-surface armament, though this depends greatly upon the operating navy. Few navies have any larger surface combatants, other than aircraft carriers, so the guided missile destroyer has stepped into the role of a capital ship in many areas.

As a significant naval asset, a destroyer requires a large operational radius and must be capable of high speed in order to pursue or evade hostile vessels. Although missiles do have a long range, the sensors that locate targets for them are often more limited and must be brought within range of an enemy force. High speed enables a destroyer to comply with the most basic of naval strategies – to attack effectively first.

HMS Daring Range
12,600km
(7000nm)

BELOW: Aircraft are one of the primary threats to modern naval forces, and the Kongo class destroyer is designed to protect itself and other vessels from attack. It can track large numbers of airborne targets simultaneously, engaging them with medium-range and short-range missiles as necessary.

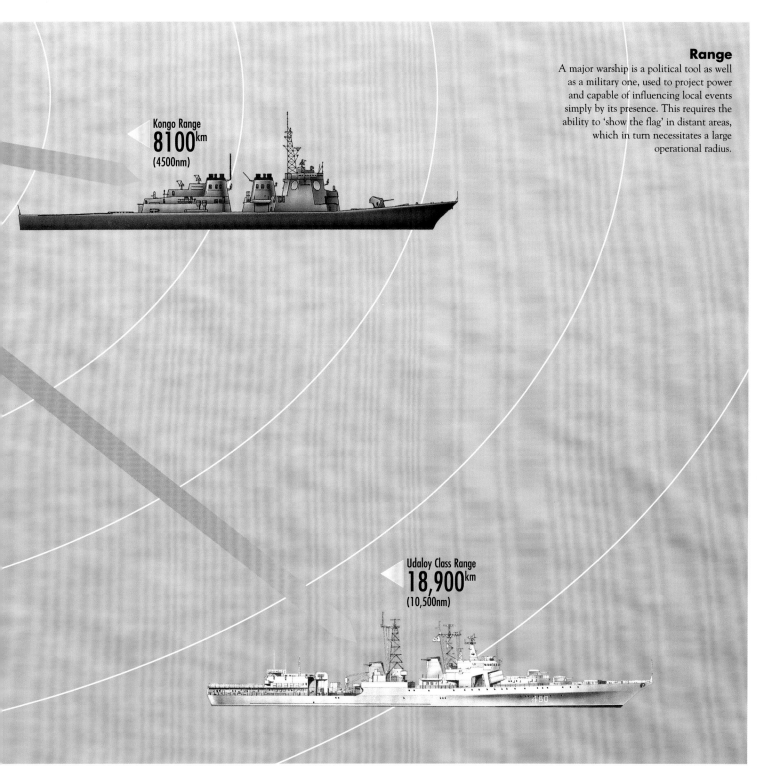

Range

A major warship is a political tool as well as a military one, used to project power and capable of influencing local events simply by its presence. This requires the ability to 'show the flag' in distant areas, which in turn necessitates a large operational radius.

Kongo Range
8100 km
(4500nm)

Udaloy Class Range
18,900 km
(10,500nm)

Speed

It was once considered that 'speed is armour' but in an age of guided missiles this is no longer the case. However, high speed does enable a warship to rapidly close to optimum firing range for its weapons, hopefully breaking the 'kill chain' by disabling enemy vessels before they attack.

HMS Daring Speed
29 knots
(52.2km/h)

Kongo Speed
30 knots
(54km/h)

Udaloy Class Speed
35 knots
(63km/h)

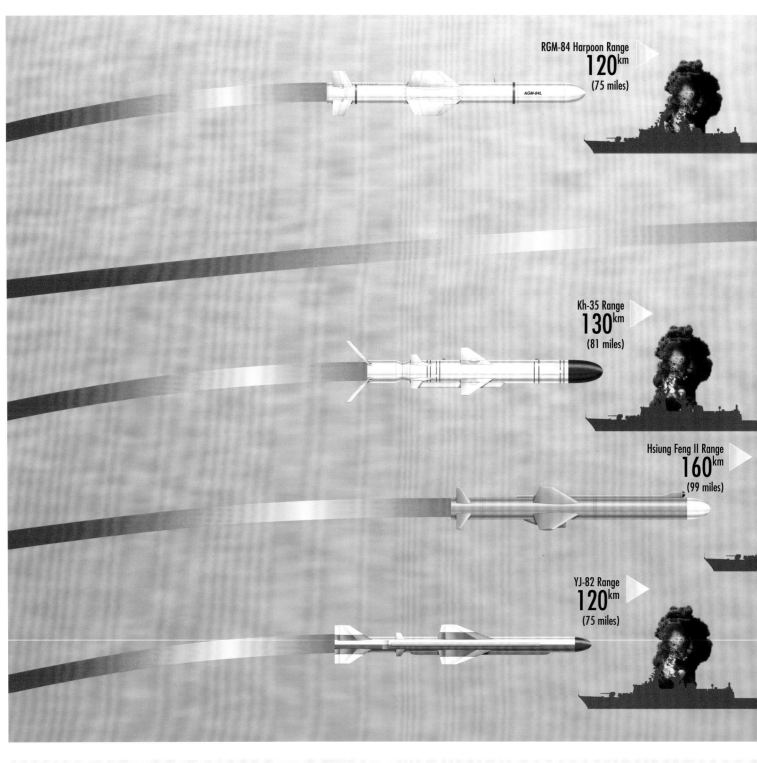

RGM-84 Harpoon Range
120km
(75 miles)

Kh-35 Range
130km
(81 miles)

Hsiung Feng II Range
160km
(99 miles)

YJ-82 Range
120km
(75 miles)

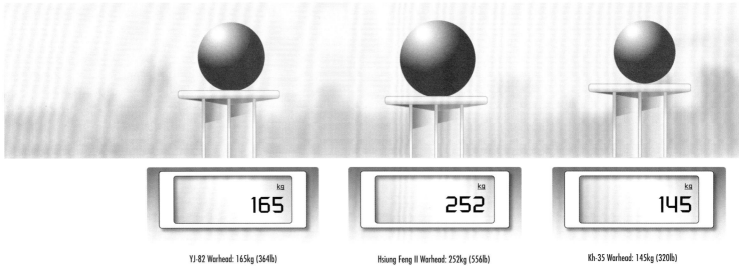

kg	kg	kg
165	**252**	**145**

YJ-82 Warhead: 165kg (364lb)

Hsiung Feng II Warhead: 252kg (556lb)

Kh-35 Warhead: 145kg (320lb)

Range

Missile ranges often greatly exceed the range of radar systems carried aboard warships. Targeting information can be obtained from other platforms such as helicopters, reconnaissance aircraft or other ships. Targeting data plus effective missiles is a winning formula; lack of either makes the other useless.

RSB-15F Range
250 km
(155 miles)

RB 15F 101
BLIND

TRYCK EJ HÄR

kg
200

RSB-15F Warhead: 200kg (441lb)

kg
221

RGM-84 Harpoon Warhead: 221kg (487lb)

Ship-to-Ship Missiles

Range and Warhead Weight

▶ **RGM-84 Harpoon**
▶ **RSB-15F**
▶ **Kh-35**
▶ **Hsiung Feng II**
▶ **YJ-82**

Long-range missiles are the primary surface-action weapons carried by warships, with guns and shorter-range missiles available as a back-up. A force that lacks long-range capability may not survive long enough to make an attack; in modern naval combat, victory usually goes to the side that can attack effectively first. This means detecting the enemy force, reaching a suitable firing position and delivering a missile strike before the enemy can launch his own weapons.

Most missiles use either thermal homing or radar guidance for terminal guidance, and are thus vulnerable to electronic countermeasures or decoys. Missiles can also be shot down by anti-aircraft missiles or close-in weapons systems (CIWS), which are designed to deal with small, fast-moving targets. If a hit is achieved, the missile will detonate after penetrating the target, to ensure that maximum damage is caused. Even so, a single hit is not guaranteed to sink a warship. Ships are very resilient even when hit in a vital area, and a missile might detonate in a non-critical part of the vessel.

Warhead size is important for ensuring that enough damage is done, but there is a trade-off between the weight and size of the warhead and the amount of propellant carried by the missile. A larger warhead means a shorter range, giving the advantage to an enemy whose missiles have a longer reach. A larger missile may be an option, but space is limited aboard a warship. Bigger missiles may mean less of them, which reduces the chances of getting through the target's defences.

Warhead Weight

Although missile waheads do not need to penetrate the thick armour of previous generations of warships, they need to be powerful enough to do serious damage to the target. Warships are designed to withstand shock and are heavily compartmentalised to contain damage. Ideally, a warhead will breach as many compartments as possible, which requires a large amopunt of explosive.

Full-load Displacement

The United States is the only nation to operate huge 'supercarriers' capable of operating a very large air group. Greater displacement equates to a longer flight deck, enabling heavier aircraft to be deployed.

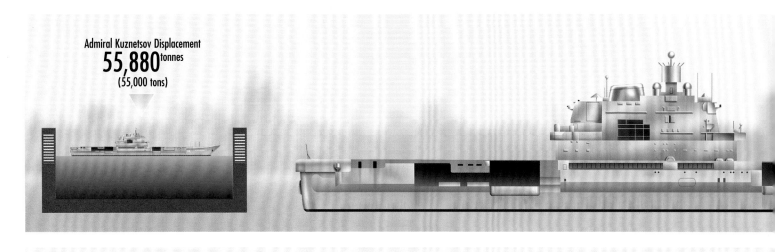

Admiral Kuznetsov Displacement
55,880 tonnes
(55,000 tons)

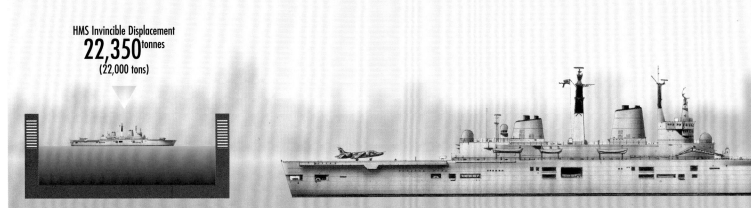

HMS Invincible Displacement
22,350 tonnes
(22,000 tons)

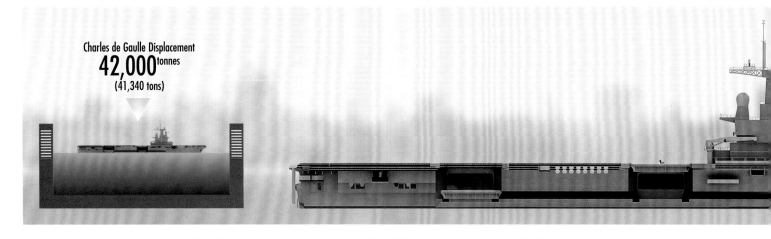

Charles de Gaulle Displacement
42,000 tonnes
(41,340 tons)

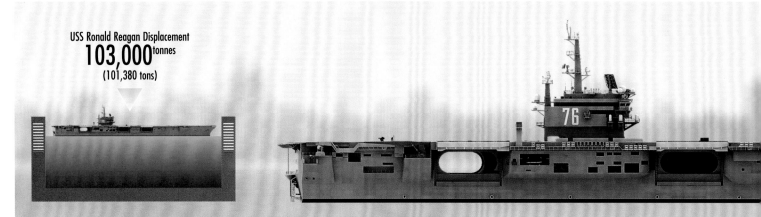

USS Ronald Reagan Displacement
103,000 tonnes
(101,380 tons)

Armament

An aircraft carrier should never need to engage any threat directly. Anti-aircraft armament is carried in case the unexpected happens, or in case the escorts are swamped by a saturation missile or air attack.

▶ **Admiral Kuznetsov**
▶ **HMS Invincible**
▶ **Charles de Gaulle**
▶ **USS Ronald Reagan**

Admiral Kuznetsov

8

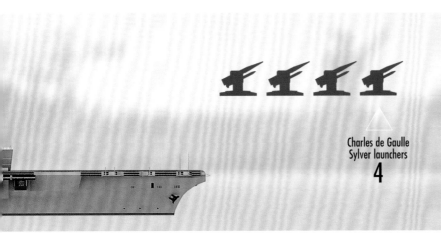

Invincible
Goalkeeper CIWS

3

Charles de Gaulle
Sylver launchers

4

USS Ronald Reagan
2 x Mk 29 ESSM launchers;
2 x RIM-116 RAM launchers

4

Aircraft carriers exist to provide a mobile base for their air group, and are optimized for that purpose alone. Aircraft carriers are the modern 'capital ship', and are as much a status symbol as they are a military asset. A navy with air power, however minor, is a major player in world events and has a significant advantage over a force that must rely on surface vessels and shore-based aircraft.

A carrier relies on its aircraft to deal with submarines and surface craft. It is unlikely that a carrier would be unescorted, and normally the escorts would deal with any threat that slipped past the carrier's air patrols. In the event of an air attack getting right through, the carrier itself relies on decoys and electronic countermeasures to defend against missiles, and can engage aircraft with its own weapons. Typically these are short- to medium-range missiles and a CIWS, which is usually a rapid-fire gun in the 20–30mm (0.79–1.2in) range, although the US RIM-116 Rolling Airframe Missile system fulfils the same function.

RIGHT: Aircraft carriers are to an extent the standard by which a navy is judged. Those that can deploy carriers have a higher status than those that do not. This can have far-reaching implications; a navy is a political tool in peacetime as well as a warfighting asset.

Aircraft Carriers 2

Number of Aircraft

▶ **Admiral Kuznetsov**
▶ **HMS Invincible**
▶ **Charles de Gaulle**
▶ **USS Ronald Reagan**

A carrier's effectiveness is judged to a great extent by the size of its air group. More aircraft mean more sorties can be generated, and operations can be sustained despite losses. However, the size of the air group is not the only factor. The efficiency with which it is operated is important; it is worth sacrificing a few aircraft for space to maintain and rearm the air group more efficiently.

The type of aircraft operated is also important. Many small carriers can employ only light aircraft, which lack the range and payload of more powerful planes. The Harrier and its derivatives make ideal aircraft for smaller carriers, as their vectored thrust allows a short take-off and a vertical landing, which does away with the need for catapults and arrester gear. A new generation of vectored-thrust aircraft is beginning to appear, ensuring that the small carrier remains viable.

A large carrier can carry a wide range of planes. A US supercarrier can deploy airborne early warning (AEW) aircraft plus strike and anti-submarine platforms, and retain a powerful fighter force. Smaller carriers must either carry a few aircraft for each mission or swap between roles by replacing part of their air group. The use of multi-role jets does offset this problem to an extent, but a large carrier's air group remains more efficient in its specialist areas as well as being more numerous.

BELOW: US supercarriers each carry an air group equivalent to some nations' air forces, and can operate more or less indefinitely, limited only by aviation fuel and munitions, and by the crew's endurance.

USS Ronald Reagan
90 aircraft

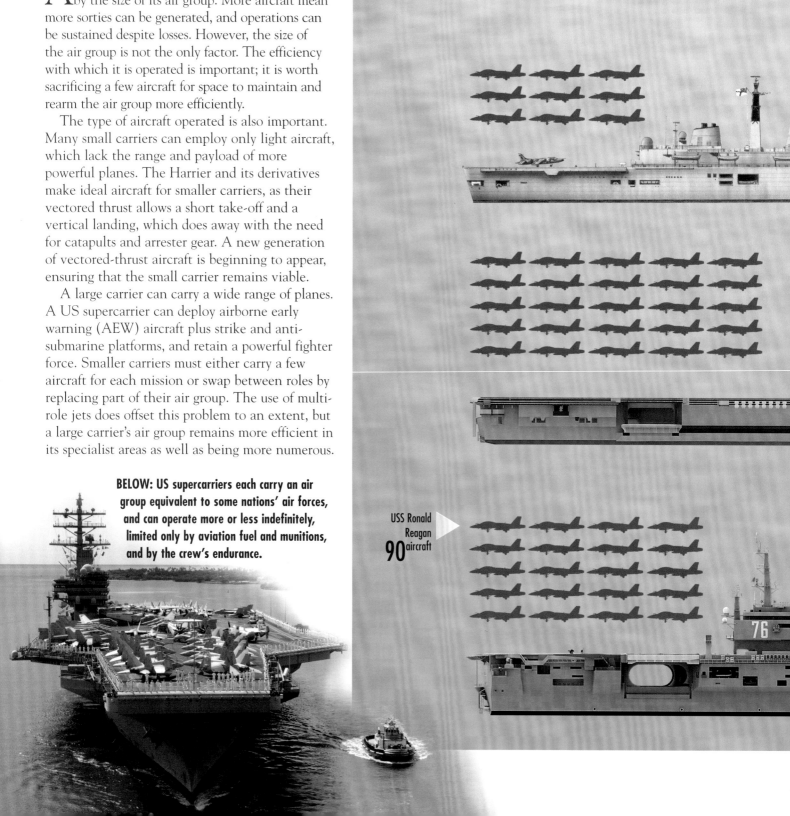

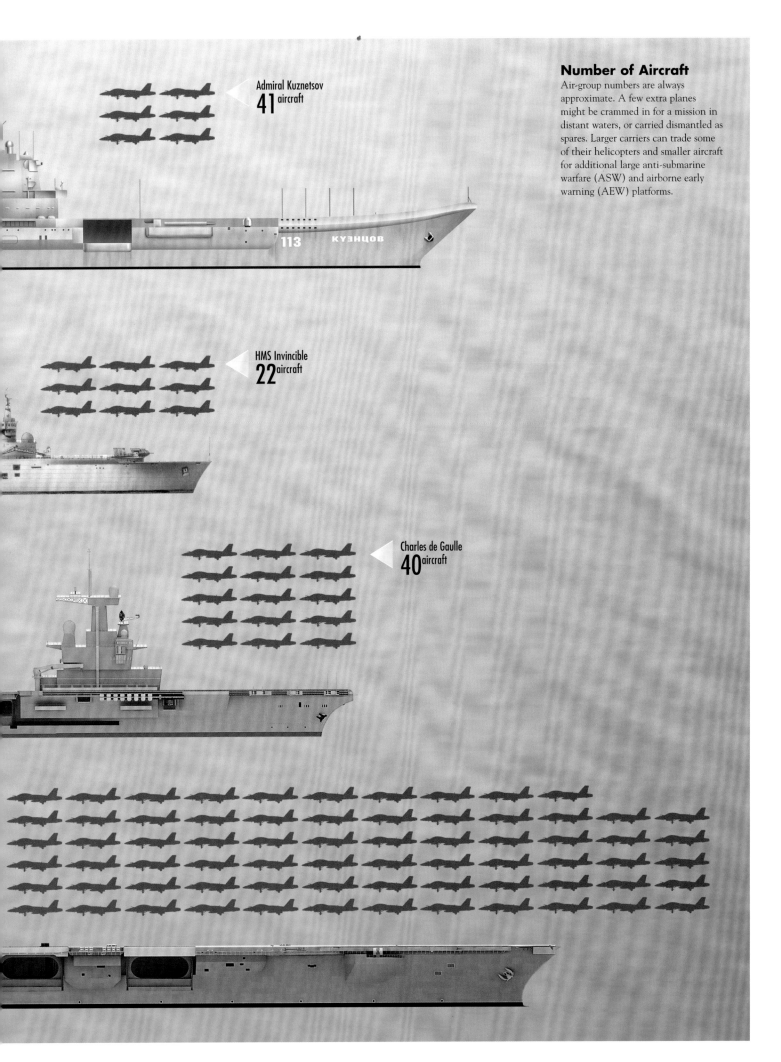

Admiral Kuznetsov
41 aircraft

113 КУЗНЦОВ

Number of Aircraft

Air-group numbers are always approximate. A few extra planes might be crammed in for a mission in distant waters, or carried dismantled as spares. Larger carriers can trade some of their helicopters and smaller aircraft for additional large anti-submarine warfare (ASW) and airborne early warning (AEW) platforms.

HMS Invincible
22 aircraft

Charles de Gaulle
40 aircraft

Littoral Operations Vessels

Complement, Speed and Displacement

▶ **USS Independence**
▶ **USS Freedom**
▶ **HDMS Esbern Snare (Absalon Class)**

For much of the twentieth century, the navies of the major world powers were primarily concerned with 'blue-water' operations, i.e. in the open seas. However, there has been a shift towards littoral, or 'brown-water', operations in recent years. This requires a different approach to ship design as vessels must operate in relatively shallow and restricted waters close to the sea/land interface and thus within reach of land-based weapons. A blue-water task force has a lot of ocean to move around in, creating ambiguity about its location, but a vessel close inshore is much easier to locate – and what can be located, can be attacked.

Blue-water vessels are primarily concerned with threats from other ships, submarines and aircraft, but the range of threats in the littoral is much greater. So is the range of missions that must be carried out: littoral operations may include bombardment of shore targets or the projection of power inland. To meet these new requirements the US Navy has created two new designs of warship optimized for brown-water operations. The Freedom class is fairly conventional, while the Independence class uses an advanced trimaran design.

The Danish Absalon class flexible support ships are larger vessels, of conventional hull design, which includes a modular section to allow them to be tailored to different missions. The vessels can act as small landing ships (each can carry a force of 200 troops) or as task-force command vessels. They can also act as support ships, carrying cargo or supplies.

Displacement

In order to achieve maximum flexibility on a limited displacement, vessels of this type often use a modular system which allows unnecessary systems to be replaced with those optimized for the current mission. However, the vessel itself remains a fast and well-armed platform capable of dealing with the whole range of threats that might be encountered in the littoral.

Complement

Vessels of this type have a core crew that is required to operate the vessel, plus a variable number of additional personnel depending on the mission. These can include troops, humanitarian-aid workers or aircrews. The vessel can be quickly retasked by changing these personnel and their equipment, with the core crew remaining constant.

USS Independence Complement
40men

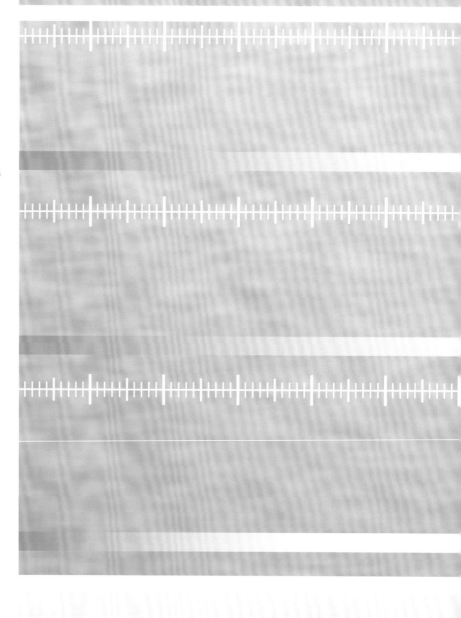

USS Independence Displacement
2829tonnes
(2784 tons)

USS Freedom Complement
50men

HDMS Esbern Snare
100men

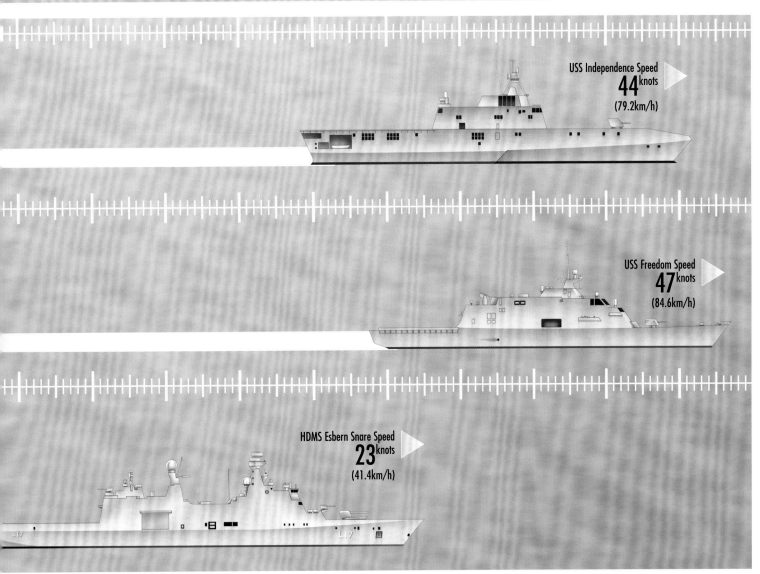

USS Independence Speed
44knots
(79.2km/h)

USS Freedom Speed
47knots
(84.6km/h)

HDMS Esbern Snare Speed
23knots
(41.4km/h)

USS Freedom Displacement
2908tonnes
(2862 tons)

HDMS Esbern Snare Displacement
6300tonnes
(6200 tons)

Number of Aircraft

Vessels of this type are sometimes mistaken for aircraft carriers, but their role is quite different. Some classes can and do operate fixed-wing aircraft, notably the AV-8B Harrier, but it is helicopters that provide the vessels' main power-projection capability.

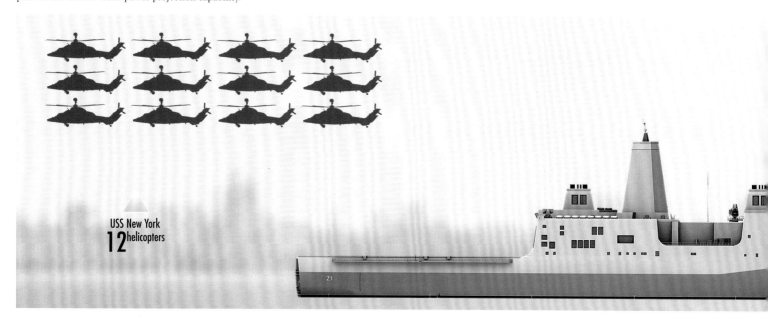

USS New York
12 helicopters

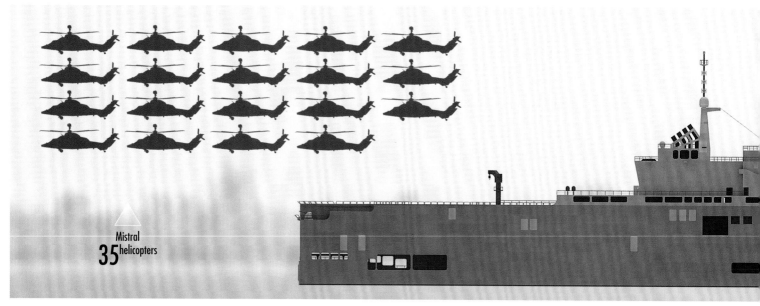

Mistral
35 helicopters

USS Tarawa
35 helicopters

Landing Ships and Support Ships

Number of Helicopters

▶ **USS New York**
▶ **Mistral**
▶ **USS Tarawa**

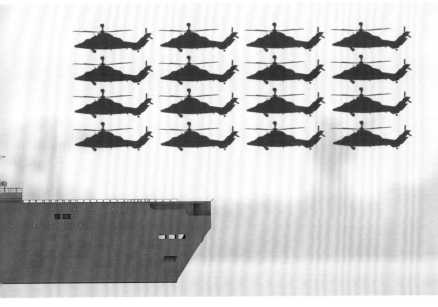

The ability to project power ashore is a vital part of maritime strategy. For centuries this meant landing troops onto a beach, which might be heavily defended, and then pushing inland towards the final objective. Helicopter-carrying landing ships make it possible to strike directly at inland targets, bypassing beach defences and other obstacles, though assault craft can also be used where it is desirable to establish a presence ashore. One advantage to using landing ships in this way is the ability to move up and down an enemy coast, striking where necessary from the safety of a task force held offshore and out of reach of retaliation by enemy ground forces.

Helicopters are the critical component of such operations. They are the link between the landing ship and the troops ashore, ferrying combat and support personnel, casualties, supplies and ammunition to and from the area of operations, and in many cases act as mobile fire support as well. Thus although landing ships are armed for self-defence, it is their troops and helicopters which are their primary combat system.

BELOW: The French Mistral class was designed as an 'intervention ship', capable of dealing with situations ranging from a war to a natural disaster. The ship provides a mobile but secure base from which to stage operations ashore, and is equipped to carry out a range of humanitarian and military missions.

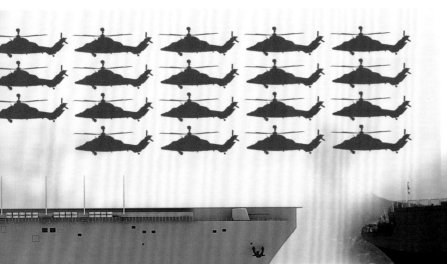

Nuclear Attack Subs

Speed and Number of Torpedo Tubes

▶ 'Granei' Class
▶ Barracuda Class
▶ Seawolf Class
▶ 'Shang' Class
▶ Virginia Class

Nuclear propulsion enabled the submarine to become a true underwater vessel, capable of remaining submerged for weeks at a time. Previously, submarines functioned more as surface vessels that could submerge for a time, using battery power to move relatively slowly underwater and returning to the surface to recharge the batteries using air-dependent diesel engines. The hull form of these early boats reflects their essentially surface-craft nature, while that of the modern submarine is optimized for underwater operations.

Early submarines needed large numbers of tubes to launch a spread of unguided torpedoes. This made hits more likely, and ensured that if one torpedo malfunctioned, the attack would not necessarily be wasted. Modern boats, using guided torpedoes, do not need so many tubes. However, a certain degree of redundancy is important in a combat vessel, and the ability to simultaneously attack more than one target requires multiple tubes. This also allows the boat to hold some tubes ready to fire in self-defence while others are being reloaded.

BELOW: The Astute class is the latest Royal Navy attack-submarine design. In addition to advanced torpedoes, the Astute class can carry Tomahawk cruise missiles, which enable it to project power far inland. However, submarines remain primarily maritime-warfare platforms.

Speed

Speed is important to an attack submarine, both in terms of covering the great distances between home port and patrol area and when in contact with the enemy. High speed produces a lot of noise, largely from cavitation – i.e. bubbles are caused by the propeller's motion through the water; they then collapse, making noise that can betray the submarine's position. The deeper a submarine dives, the faster it can go without cavitating, so fast transits are usually made at great depth.

Torpedo Tubes

Torpedo tubes are used by some boats to deliver underwater-launched missiles, not to mention divers, as well as torpedoes. Missile capability allows an attack submarine to make stand-off strikes on shipping and to attack targets far inshore, often with complete surprise.

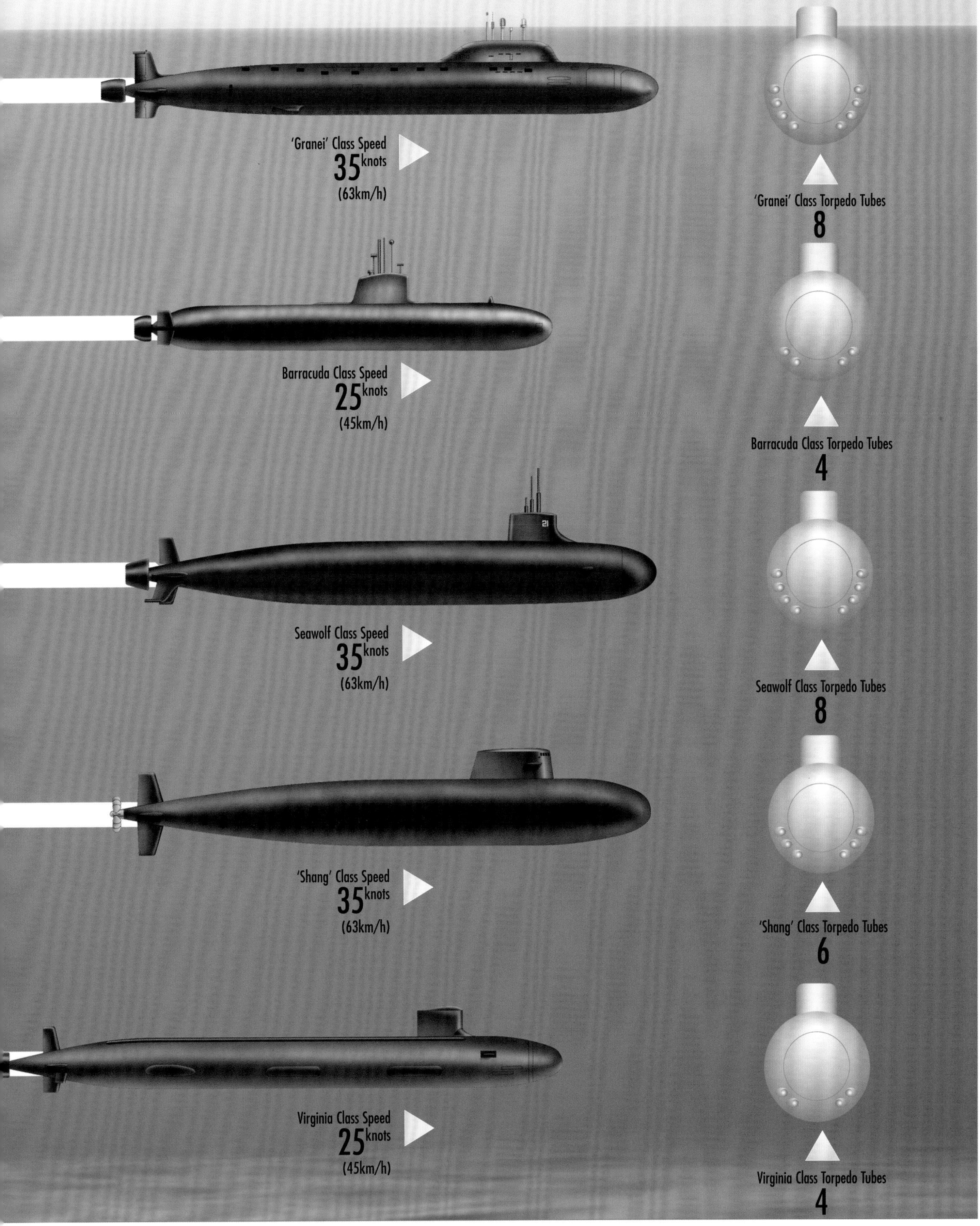

'Granei' Class Speed
35knots
(63km/h)

'Granei' Class Torpedo Tubes
8

Barracuda Class Speed
25knots
(45km/h)

Barracuda Class Torpedo Tubes
4

Seawolf Class Speed
35knots
(63km/h)

Seawolf Class Torpedo Tubes
8

'Shang' Class Speed
35knots
(63km/h)

'Shang' Class Torpedo Tubes
6

Virginia Class Speed
25knots
(45km/h)

Virginia Class Torpedo Tubes
4

Fourth-generation Nuclear Submarines

Speed and Depth

▶ 'Granei' Class
▶ Seawolf Class
▶ Virginia Class

Seawolf Class Depth
610ᵐ
(2001ft)

Attack submarines have matured from purely anti-shipping vessels into multi-role platforms that can engage targets above or below the surface, or even on land. In turn, they can be attacked by surface vessels, submarines and aircraft as well as passive weapons such as mines. In order to make a successful attack and withdraw afterwards, the boat needs to make as little noise as possible. A deep-diving sub is more difficult to detect with sonar due to temperature layers in the water.

High underwater speeds can cause a great deal of noise due to water turbulence around the boat and cavitation caused by the propeller blades. The extreme water pressures at great depths enable a boat to run faster without cavitating, so the ability to dive deep allows a higher speed to be maintained without compromising stealth. Another way to reduce propeller noise is to use pump-jet propulsion, such as is employed in the Virginia class.

The Russian 'Granei' class and the US Virginia class have vertical-launch tubes for their cruise missiles, enabling a full missile load to be carried without reducing the available torpedo armament. Conversely, the Seawolf class can carry a mix of up to 50 cruise missiles, anti-ship missiles and torpedoes, varying the loadout according to the needs of the mission. The Seawolf class was developed during the Cold War as a top-end weapons system intended to gain supremacy at sea. In the post-Cold War environment its cost was seen as excessive, and the cheaper Virginia class was put into production instead.

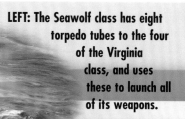

LEFT: The Seawolf class has eight torpedo tubes to the four of the Virginia class, and uses these to launch all of its weapons.

Depth

Although the depths that a modern attack sub can dive to are impressive,
it is only possible to reach the bottom in relatively shallow water such as around
the continental shelf. A boat that goes too deep will suffer structural failure and be lost.

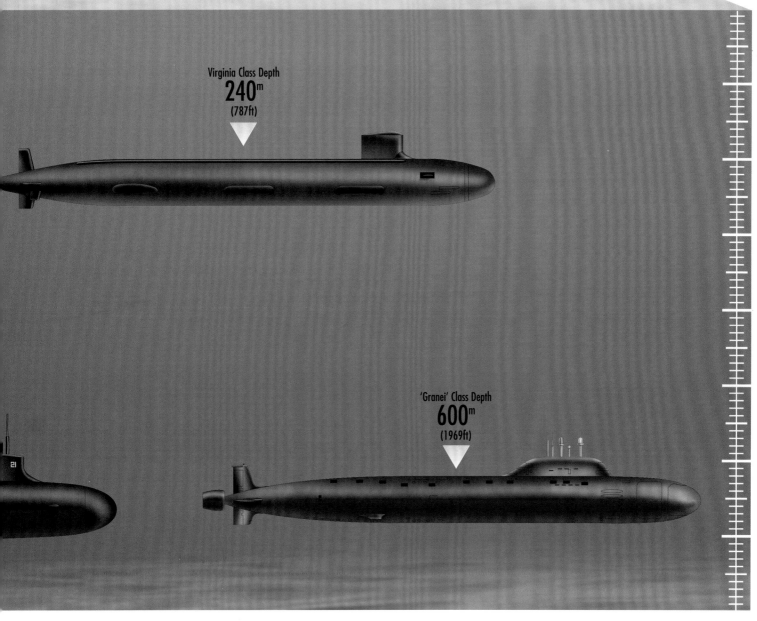

Virginia Class Depth
240^m
(787ft)

'Granei' Class Depth
600^m
(1969ft)

Speed

Extremes of speed are only used in an emergency, and then generally when running at great depth. Although
a 35-knot (63km/h) submarine may be able to stay ahead of pursuing surface ships, it cannot outrun
helicopters and aircraft. At some point the boat must slow down and hope its pursuers lose the contact.

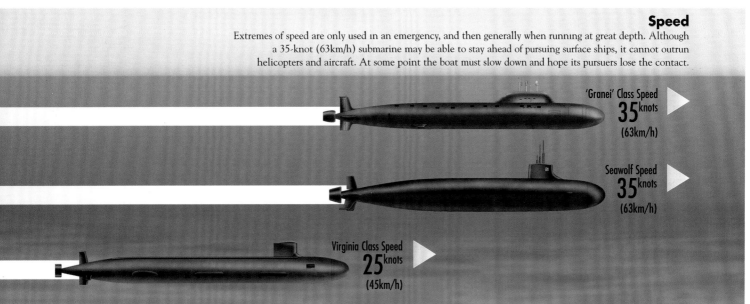

'Granei' Class Speed
35^{knots}
(63km/h)

Seawolf Speed
35^{knots}
(63km/h)

Virginia Class Speed
25^{knots}
(45km/h)

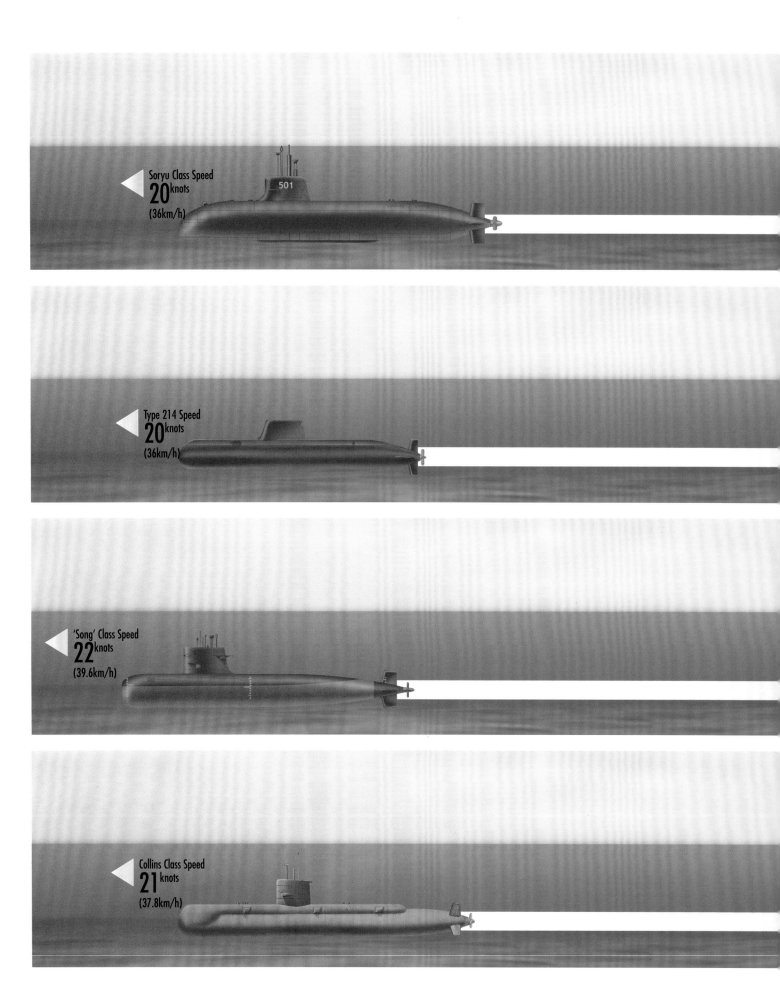

Soryu Class Speed
20 knots
(36km/h)

Type 214 Speed
20 knots
(36km/h)

'Song' Class Speed
22 knots
(39.6km/h)

Collins Class Speed
21 knots
(37.8km/h)

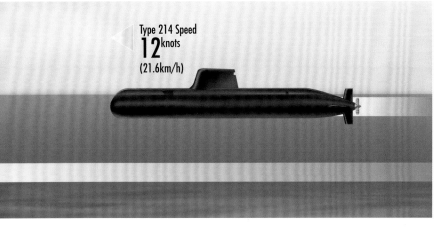

Soryu Class Speed
13 knots
(23.4km/h)

Type 214 Speed
12 knots
(21.6km/h)

'Song' Class Speed
15 knots
(27km/h)

Collins Class Speed
10.5 knots
(18.9km/h)

Conventional Attack Submarines 1

Surface and Submerged Speed

▶ **Soryu Class**
▶ **Type 214**
▶ **'Song' Class**
▶ **Collins Class**

Early submersibles used a boat-shaped hull and were significantly faster on the surface than underwater. This was a key factor in the convoy battles of World War II. A submarine that was forced down by escorts, even if it was not critically damaged or sunk, could not keep up with a convoy and would lose touch. However, modern submarines are designed primarily for underwater operations and are much faster when fully submerged.

Whereas a nuclear-powered boat can maintain high speed for as long as its reactor is functioning, a conventional vessel must conserve fuel even when on the surface or using a snorkel. Modern air-independent propulsion systems greatly increase the underwater endurance of a boat; even so, high speed can only be maintained for a finite period.

Modern boats typically use a whale-shaped or teardrop-shaped hull, which gives good resistance to water pressure as well as improving the flow of water over the hull. Streamlining is also important for noise reduction. A hull with many angles and projections creates eddies which will slow the boat down and produce underwater noise which becomes much more pronounced when the boat is moving fast.

Noise is the submarine's worst enemy, as it allows a hostile vessel to detect and track the boat, and also interferes with its own passive sensors. A submarine transiting fast underwater can become 'blind and deaf' due to self-noise, and at the same time advertises its presence to any vessel using passive sonar detection.

Speed

Conventional attack submarines are sufficiently desirable that they are a viable export item. The Scorpène class and Type 214 designs have achieved considerable overseas sales success, while the 'Song' class (Type 039) has been offered to Thailand and Pakistan. The Collins class was custom designed for a single operator and has not been offered for export.

Conventional Attack Submarines 2

Number of Torpedo Tubes

▶ **Soryu Class**
▶ **Type 214**
▶ **'Song' Class**
▶ **Collins Class**

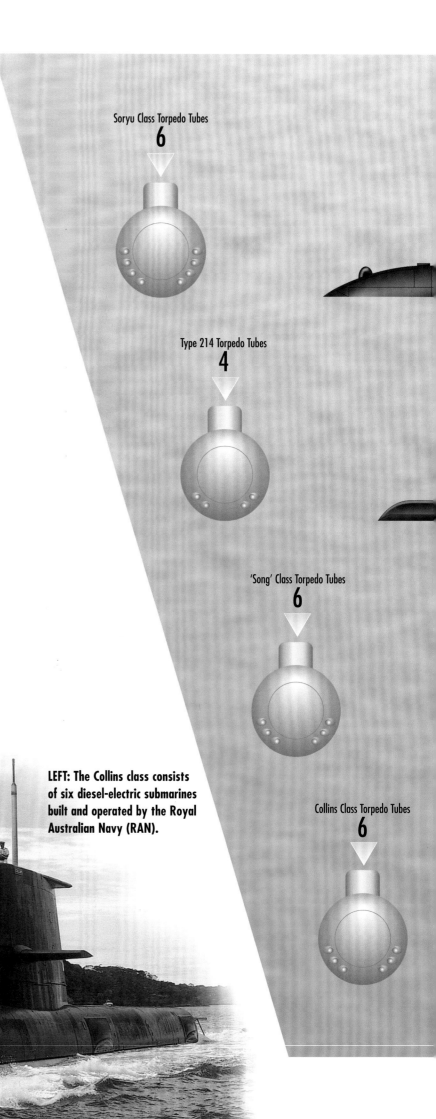

Soryu Class Torpedo Tubes
6

Type 214 Torpedo Tubes
4

'Song' Class Torpedo Tubes
6

Collins Class Torpedo Tubes
6

Not all navies have the capability, or the desire, to operate nuclear attack submarines. Some prefer to have nothing to do with nuclear energy, some lack the technical ability to maintain and operate a reactor, and others simply prefer to rely on conventional vessels. Although modern diesel-electric submarines are still dependent on air from the atmosphere, the invention of the snorkel in World War II enabled a conventional boat to stay down for an extended period, drawing in air whilst remaining submerged. Recent advances in air-independent propulsion (AIP) have also increased the viability of non-nuclear submarines.

Although their diesel-electric propulsion systems are not very different from those of previous generations, today's conventional attack submarines are vastly more capable than their predecessors. Their torpedo tubes can be used to deliver torpedoes and missiles, and many classes of boat can also lay mines. The main advantage of submarine-laid mines is stealth. Minefields can be laid defensively, to protect friendly installations, or as part of sea-denial operations. It is even possible to lay a minefield offensively, close to an enemy port or in an area that hostiles are likely to pass through or operate in.

The exact mix of weapons carried by a given boat depends upon the mission at hand. With a full load of torpedoes, the Chinese 'Song' class can carry 18 weapons, though some would probably be swapped for missiles under most circumstances, granting the capability to attack a variety of targets.

LEFT: The Collins class consists of six diesel-electric submarines built and operated by the Royal Australian Navy (RAN).

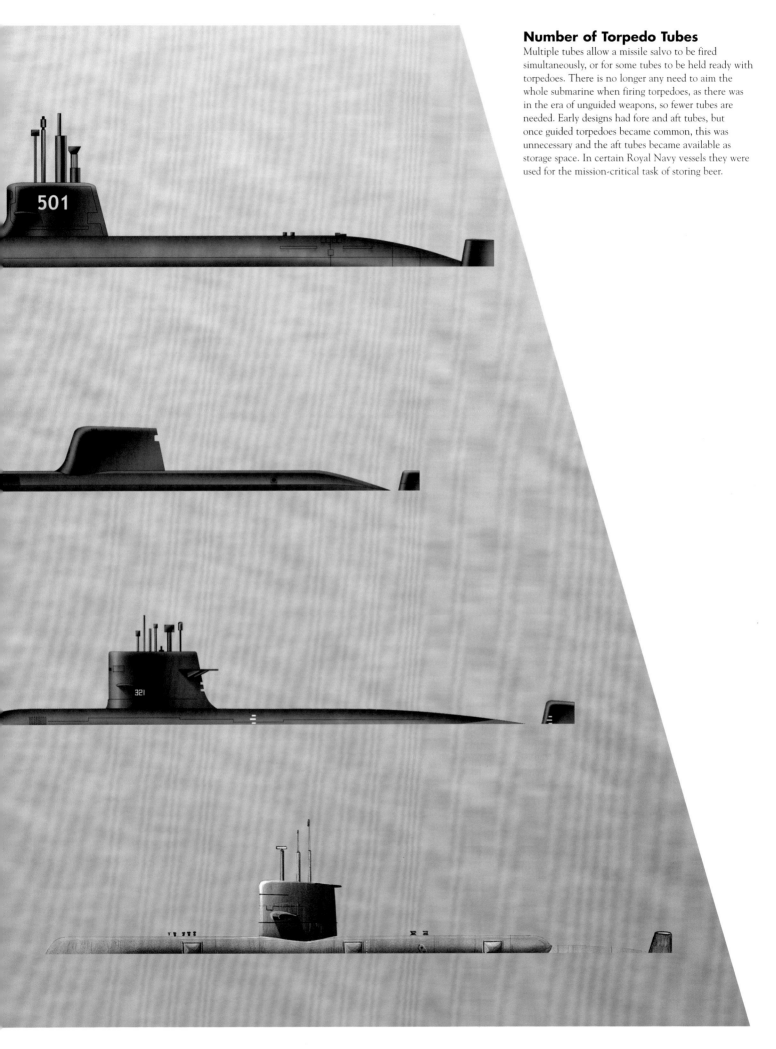

Multiple tubes allow a missile salvo to be fired simultaneously, or for some tubes to be held ready with torpedoes. There is no longer any need to aim the whole submarine when firing torpedoes, as there was in the era of unguided weapons, so fewer tubes are needed. Early designs had fore and aft tubes, but once guided torpedoes became common, this was unnecessary and the aft tubes became available as storage space. In certain Royal Navy vessels they were used for the mission-critical task of storing beer.

Patrol Submarines Head to Head

Submerged Speed, Number of Torpedo Tubes, Surface Range

▶ **Walrus Class**
▶ **Scorpène Class**

Conventional (i.e. non-nuclear-powered) attack submarines are an important part of many national navies, and can be highly effective in the hands of a well-trained crew. Conventional attack submarines lack the all-but-unlimited range of nuclear boats but are still capable of extended patrols. Underwater endurance is limited, but air-independent propulsion (AIP) systems and advanced battery technology permit modern boats to operate underwater for far longer than previous generations. In addition to endurance, the primary difference between nuclear and non-nuclear boats is sustained underwater speed. A nuclear boat can maintain a higher speed than one that must depend on batteries.

Nuclear power was originally considered for the Dutch Walrus class, but conventional diesel-electric propulsion was finally settled upon for technical as well as financial reasons. The resulting vessel is very quiet underwater and can deliver a range of weapons. The Walrus class is equipped for a torpedo or missile attack against a variety of targets, using guided 533mm (21in) torpedoes or Sub-Harpoon missiles.

The Scorpène class was a joint French–Spanish project that has thus far achieved sales to Chile, India and Brazil. Primary armament is guided torpedoes, launched from six tubes, compared with four in the Walrus class. The Scorpène can launch Exocet missiles, which have a shorter effective range than Harpoon, but is also equipped for minelaying operations. Flexibility is important to many potential operators, as a relatively small naval budget does not permit several specialist vessels to be purchased.

Submarines are effective ship-killers, but they can carry out a number of other roles, including reconnaissance and intelligence-gathering. The possession of a credible submarine force is seen in some quarters as a symbol of a 'serious navy' that can exert significant influence over the waters to which it is deployed.

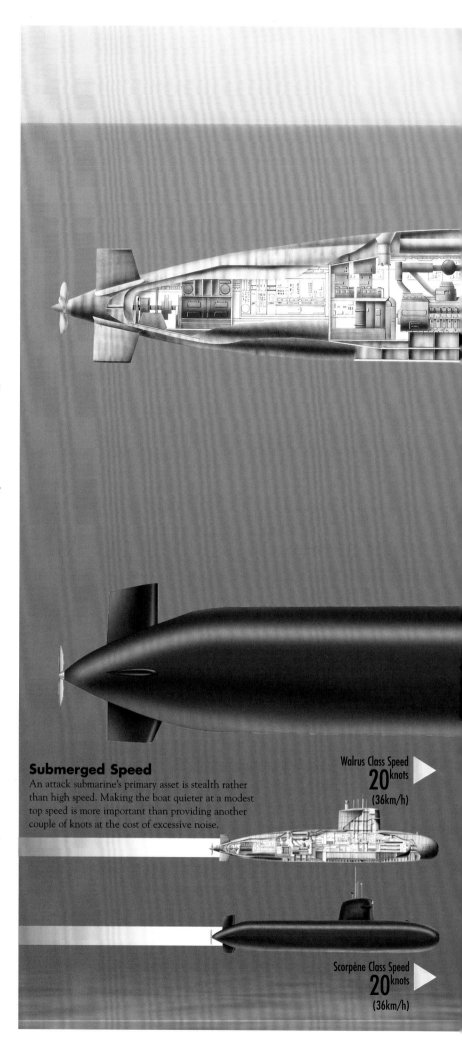

Submerged Speed
An attack submarine's primary asset is stealth rather than high speed. Making the boat quieter at a modest top speed is more important than providing another couple of knots at the cost of excessive noise.

Walrus Class Speed
20knots
(36km/h)

Scorpène Class Speed
20knots
(36km/h)

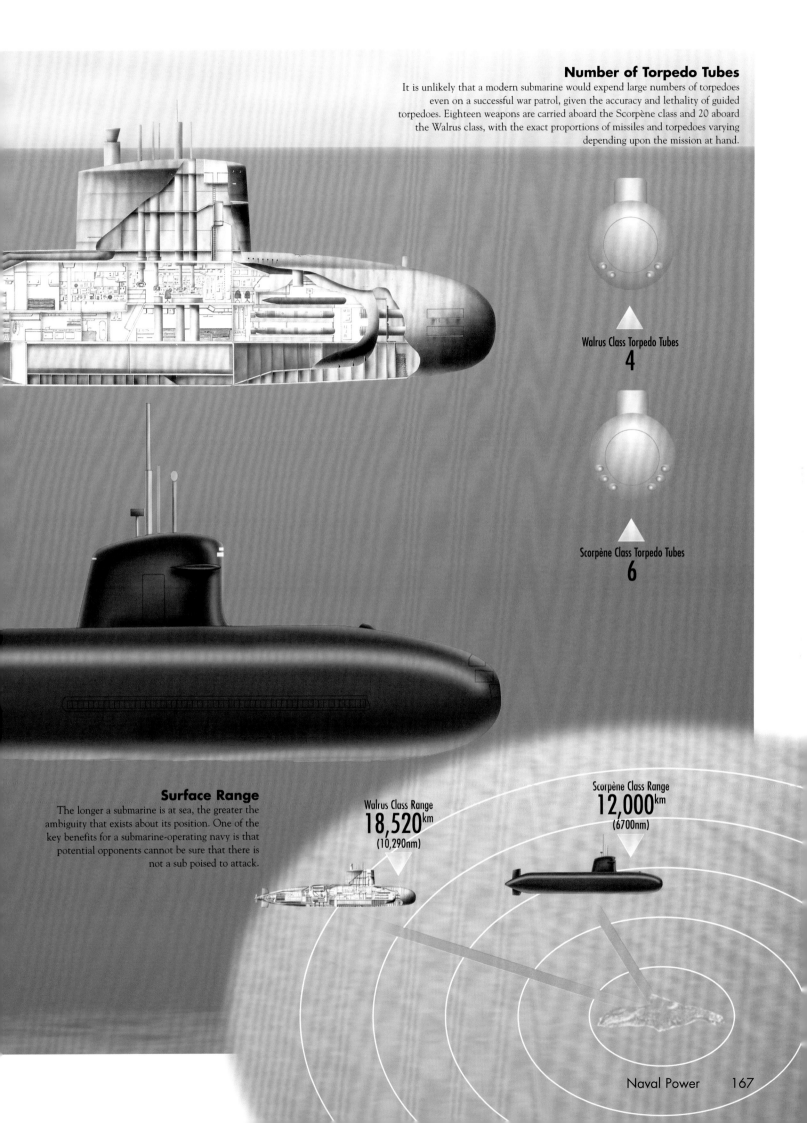

Number of Torpedo Tubes

It is unlikely that a modern submarine would expend large numbers of torpedoes even on a successful war patrol, given the accuracy and lethality of guided torpedoes. Eighteen weapons are carried aboard the Scorpène class and 20 aboard the Walrus class, with the exact proportions of missiles and torpedoes varying depending upon the mission at hand.

Walrus Class Torpedo Tubes
4

Scorpène Class Torpedo Tubes
6

Surface Range

The longer a submarine is at sea, the greater the ambiguity that exists about its position. One of the key benefits for a submarine-operating navy is that potential opponents cannot be sure that there is not a sub poised to attack.

Scorpène Class Range
12,000km
(6700nm)

Walrus Class Range
18,520km
(10,290nm)

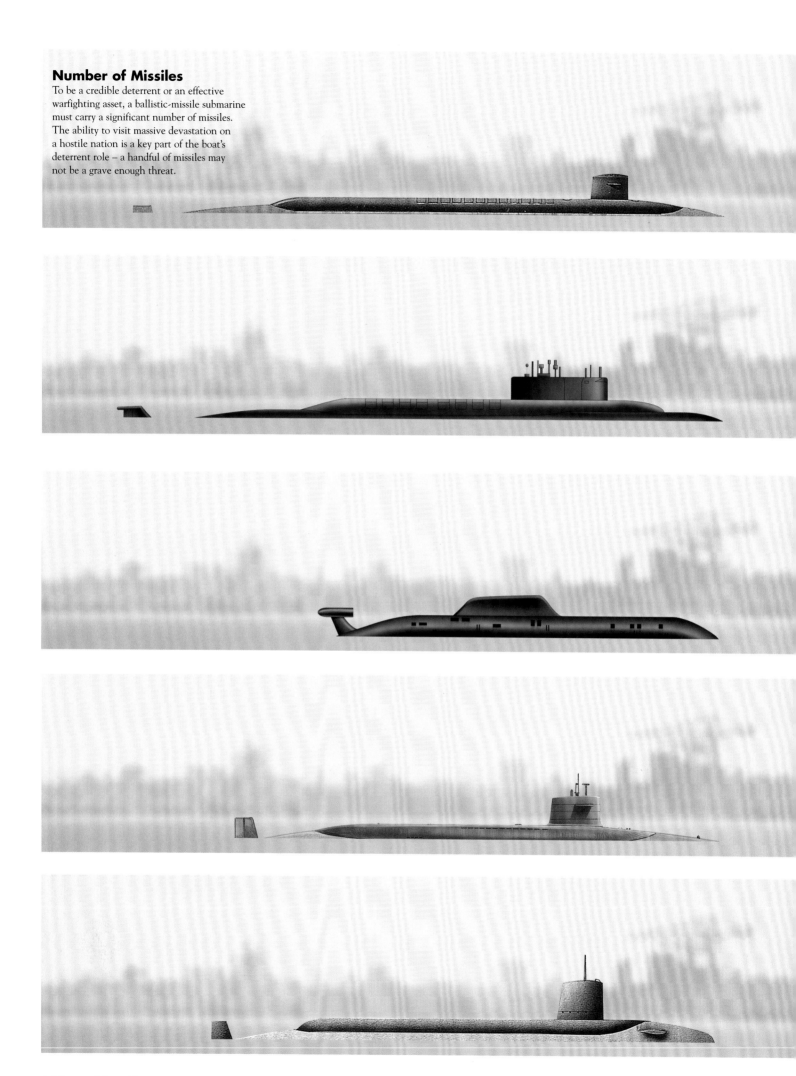

Number of Missiles

To be a credible deterrent or an effective warfighting asset, a ballistic-missile submarine must carry a significant number of missiles. The ability to visit massive devastation on a hostile nation is a key part of the boat's deterrent role – a handful of missiles may not be a grave enough threat.

Ohio Class
24 missiles

Borei Class
16 missiles

INS Arihant
12 missiles

Triomphant Class
16 missiles

Vanguard Class
16 missiles

RIGHT: Submariners on watch in the control area of a nuclear submarine.

Missile Submarines

Number of Missiles

▶ **Ohio Class**
▶ **'Borei' Class**
▶ **INS Arihant**
▶ **Triomphant Class**
▶ **Vanguard Class**

Traditionally, all submarines are 'boats' and not 'ships'; even those with the power to sink any vessel and destroy whole cities with a missile strike. However, these boats are a critical component in both peacetime and wartime strategy. To some extent their existence is a factor in preventing conflicts 'going nuclear', making them a powerful force for peace and stability.

If the worst happens and an all-out nuclear exchange begins, missile-submarine bases are a key target and in any case the matter will be decided long before a distant boat can return to port to rearm. Thus in a nuclear conflict, 'boomers', as ballistic-missile boats are popularly tagged, will fight with what they have. Once a boat's strategic missiles are expended it might be able to contribute as a reconnaissance or anti-shipping platform, but a second salvo of ballistic missiles is not likely to be an option.

Some ballistic-missile submarines can launch cruise missiles in addition to their ballistic weapons, or can be converted to carry them instead. The Ohio class has been modified to carry large numbers of vertically launched cruise missiles in place of its strategic missiles, enabling it to carry out a conventional stand-off anti-shipping or land-attack mission.

Submarine-launched Torpedoes

Range and Warhead Weight

▶ **DTCN L5**
▶ **DTCN F17**
▶ **FFV Tp42 Series**
▶ **Spearfish**

Torpedoes come in two general types, known as heavy and light. Both are guided, but differ in their mode of attack. Lightweight torpedoes carry a relatively small warhead, and are designed to impact a target directly, detonating on contact. They are usually self-guided, using acoustic homing, and are primarily anti-submarine weapons. Lightweight torpedoes are generally deployed by surface vessels, helicopters and aircraft as well as submarines, whereas heavyweight torpedoes are primarily submarine-launched weapons. Only a few nations use heavyweight torpedoes from any platform other than submarines.

The heavyweight torpedo has a much larger warhead than lightweight versions, and ideally is detonated directly beneath the keel of a target vessel. The exploding warhead creates a bubble of gas, which lifts up the central section of the ship. The target vessel's own weight places incredible strain on its structure as this occurs, possibly resulting in a 'broken back' and rapid sinking. Even a more distant detonation can cause severe damage due to underwater shock.

Heavyweight torpedoes frequently use wire-guidance, receiving signals from the launching submarine for the approach to the target and switching to active sonar for terminal guidance. Attacks can be made from very long ranges using guided weapons, which greatly improves a sub's survivability. However, a long-range attack means that the torpedo will be in the water for an extended period, during which the target could move out of range. High speed and long-duration propulsion are important if a fast-moving target is to be caught and successfully attacked.

Lightweight torpedoes are standardized in many countries at a diameter of 324mm (12.8in), and heavyweight torpedoes at 533mm (21in). Russia uses 650mm (25.6in) torpedoes for some tasks, while Sweden has 400mm (15.7in) weapons which represent a compromise between heavy and light torpedoes, and are capable of a range of missions.

DTCN L5 Range
9.25 km
(5.7 miles)

Range

Although torpedoes have a long maximum range, launching from close to the target reduces the chance of successful evasion or other countermeasures. Spearfish and some other torpedoes can be used in short-range mode, trading stand-off capability for very high underwater speed by burning rapidly through the available propellant.

Warhead Weight

Torpedoes intended for direct impact tend to use a small shaped-charge warhead focused into the target. Heavyweight torpedoes have traditionally relied on the gas-bubble effect, but future weapons may use multi-mode warheads capable of directional detonation when necessary.

kg
150

DTCN L5 Warhead Weight: 150kg (331lb)

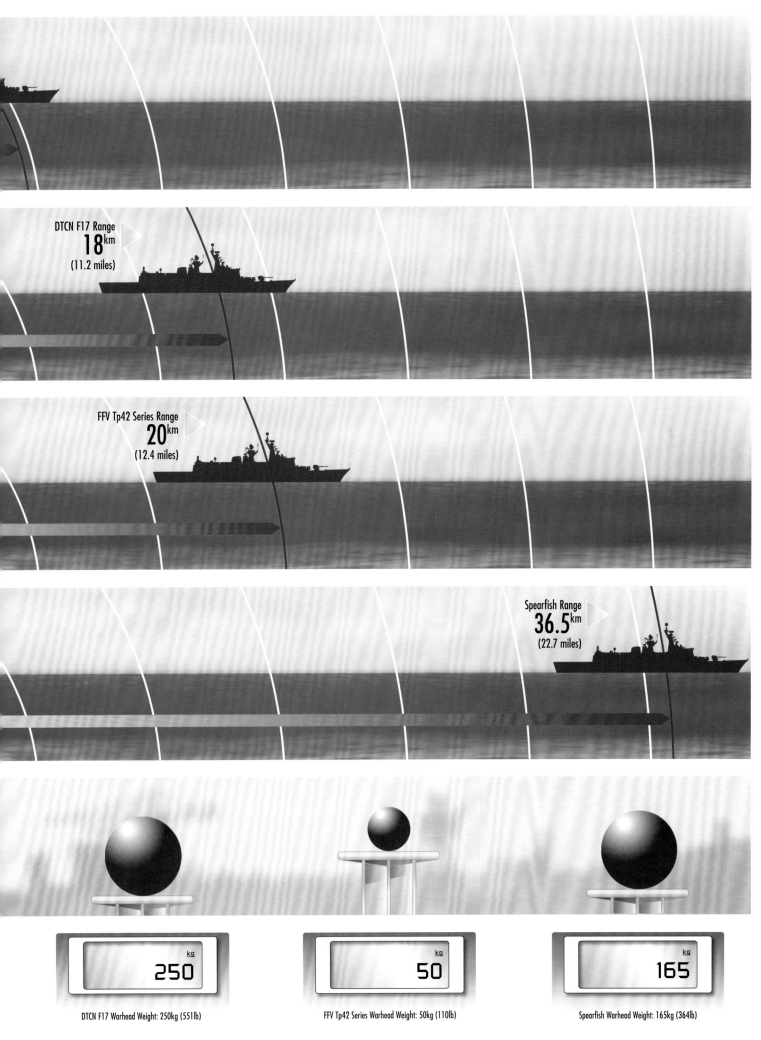

DTCN F17 Range
18km
(11.2 miles)

FFV Tp42 Series Range
20km
(12.4 miles)

Spearfish Range
36.5km
(22.7 miles)

kg	kg	kg
250	**50**	**165**

DTCN F17 Warhead Weight: 250kg (551lb)

FFV Tp42 Series Warhead Weight: 50kg (110lb)

Spearfish Warhead Weight: 165kg (364lb)

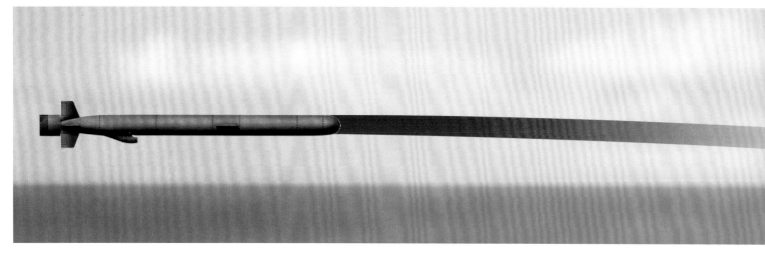

RGM-84H SLAM-ER
250km
(155 miles)

BrahMos
250km
(155 miles)

RGM-84 Harpoon SLAM
124km
(77 miles)

Land Attack Missiles

Range

▶ **RGM-84 Harpoon SLAM**
▶ **RGM-84H SLAM-ER**
▶ **BrahMos**
▶ **Tomahawk**

Tomahawk
1700km
(1056 miles)

Range

The key to effective land attack missiles is a combination of long range and good guidance systems. GPS or inertial guidance can be used. Terrain-mapping radar is also an option, though there are not many terrain features in the sea to provide guidance updates, so this is primarily useful once the coast has been crossed. Terminal guidance may use thermal, radar or optical systems to seek a specific target, or rely on GPS to hit a pre-programmed area.

Shore bombardment has always been an important naval mission, but until quite recently most targets were out of range of naval weapons. The advent of the long-range missile changed that, and in recent conflicts it has been possible to attack targets far inland using missiles launched from ships and submarines. A surface task force located offshore may be beyond the range of effective retaliation, or could move into range, attack and then retire to a safe distance. Submarine-launched land attack missiles take this one stage further; the target nation might not even be aware that a threat is present until the missiles strike.

The Tomahawk missile was developed as a nuclear delivery system, but has matured into an extremely long-range conventional missile that uses GPS, terrain-matching and inertial guidance. The recent Tactical Tomahawk variant has been redesigned to take targeting updates from sensors mounted on other platforms such as aircraft, UAVs (unmanned aerial vehicles) and personnel on the ground. The Indian BrahMos missile has a vastly shorter range but is much faster, improving the missile's ability to penetrate enemy defences.

LEFT: The Harpoon anti-ship missile was developed Into Harpoon SLAM (Standoff Land Attack Missile) by incorporating a GPS guidance unit plus systems from the Walleye and Maverick missiles. Further upgrades created SLAM-ER (Expanded Response).

Submarine-launched ICBMs

Range and Warhead Weight

▶ **Polaris A3**
▶ **SS-N-18 'Stingray' (RSM-50)**
▶ **SS-N-20 'Sturgeon' (RSM-52)**

In the early days of ballistic-missile technology, weapons had a very short range and had to be carried close to the target country. A submarine provided an effective means of doing so, provoking extensive efforts to counter the threat with anti-submarine aircraft and surface patrols. As missile ranges have increased, it has become possible to attack targets deep within a continent from distant reaches of the ocean, enormously complicating the problem of preventing an attack.

Nuclear missiles carried aboard a 'boomer' which could be literally anywhere in the world's oceans provide an effective deterrent to nuclear attack. A hostile nation might conceivably get lucky and locate a boomer with an attack submarine, but the probability is vanishingly small. Thus the submarine-borne missiles are almost certain to survive a first strike intended to wipe out land-based missile and bomber bases. Even if such a strike succeeded, which is by no means guaranteed, retaliation would be inevitable.

Most nations that operate nuclear missile submarines defend them by sending the vessels on long patrols into remote areas, relying on concealment to protect the boats. The Russian approach was rather different: missile submarines were assigned to 'bastions', which were sea areas protected by air, surface and submarine patrols. Although the general location of the boats was obvious, attack by ballistic missile remained impractical and the bastions were very heavily defended against incursion by attack submarines. Both methods served the same purpose: to ensure that a first strike by the enemy was pointless and therefore unlikely to be considered.

Range

Modern sea-launched strategic missiles have an extremely long range, greatly reducing the time required to redeploy boats against a new threat. The very fact that a boomer could be, and probably is, in range is a powerful deterrent to any nation considering the use of nuclear weapons.

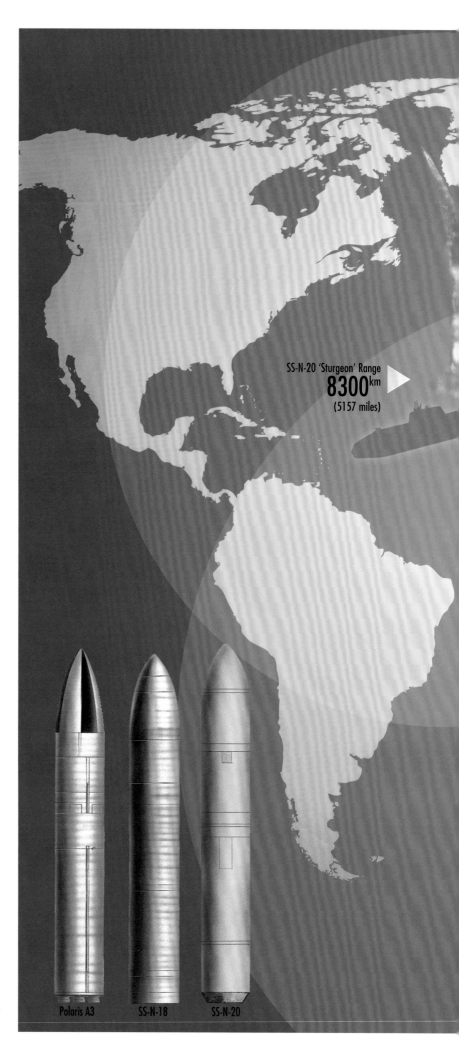

SS-N-20 'Sturgeon' Range
8300km
(5157 miles)

Polaris A3   SS-N-18   SS-N-20

Polaris A3 Range
4748km
(2950 miles)

Warhead Weight
Multiple warheads enable a single missile to attack more than one target, or to cause more damage to a single dispersed target, such as a city, than a single, larger, explosion. A pattern of shockwaves is far more effective at cracking hardened targets, like missile silos, than a single detonation.

SS-N-18 'Stingray' Range
8000km
(4971 miles)

KT
1000 100kT x10

KT
1400 200kT x7

KT
180 60kT x3

SS_N-20 Sturgeon

SS_N-18 (RSM-50) Stingray

Polaris A3

Small Arms

Despite all the air power, armoured vehicles and artillery support that can be brought to bear, it is the infantry that must take and hold ground, and for this task they need a variety of weapons. The term 'small arms' originally referred to any firearms that were smaller than a cannon, but today it applies to individual weapons and some light support systems. The term is sometimes loosely used to include all the weapons systems carried and employed by infantry, including anti-armour and anti-aircraft weapons.

The assault rifle is the principal small arm on the modern battlefield, but an infantry force also needs support weapons and specialist systems such as long-range sniper rifles. For certain tasks, such as close-assault operations, security and urban combat, other weapons such as combat shotguns or submachine guns are a solid choice. A properly equipped force will be armed with a mix of all-round weapons systems to deal with most situations that might arise, supplemented by specialist weapons in the hands of suitably trained personnel.

LEFT: A British Army sniper team carry out overwatch duties somewhere in Afghanistan, 2009. The sniper is armed with an Accuracy International L96 rifle, which has been covered with non-reflective material to stop the barrel and other surfaces giving away their position.

Side Arms

Calibre and Magazine Capacity

▶ **SIG P226**

▶ **Browning 9mm L9A1**

▶ **PMM**

▶ **Heckler & Koch USP**

▶ **FN Five-Seven**

Handguns are issued in the military as back-up weapons, or where a measure of self-defence capability might be necessary but there is no space for a larger and more effective weapon. They are carried by officers, pilots, vehicle crews and other specialists who will only have to use their weapons when something has gone badly wrong.

Military semiautomatic pistols normally have a high magazine capacity. Handgun ammunition lacks stopping power and the weapon itself is far from accurate, so volume of fire can be critical. Early semiautomatics such as the Browning L9A1 and Makarov (PM/PMM), with a modest magazine capacity by today's standards, still offered an immense increase in firepower over revolvers.

Since the introduction of these weapons, handgun technology has steadily improved. The high-capacity SIG P226 is prized for its accuracy and reliability, whilst the USP returned to a traditional 11.4mm (0.45in) cartridge for improved stopping power, though at the price of reduced capacity. The Five-Seven uses a revolutionary small-calibre round with similar ballistics but improved penetrating power compared with the 9mm (0.35in) round. This gives even a handgun some chance to penetrate body armour or light cover.

Calibre

The stopping power of a handgun round depends on its mass and velocity. As a rule, a big round will put the target down more reliably than a smaller one. Many handgun users still swear by the 11.4mm (0.45in) round.

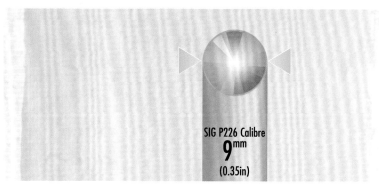

SIG P226 Calibre
9mm
(0.35in)

Browning 9mm L9A1 Calibre
9mm
(0.35in)

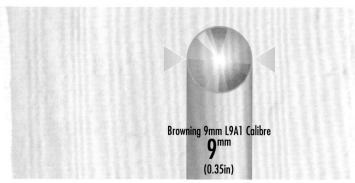

BELOW: The Sig Sauer P226 is a classic service pistol produced in Switzerland and used by numerous army and police forces throughout the world. The handgun chambers the powerful 9mm Parabellum round.

PMM Calibre
9mm
(0.35in)

H&K USP Calibre
11.4mm
(0.45in)

FN Five-Seven Calibre
5.7mm
(0.224in)

Magazine Capacity

Magazine capacity is determined by the size of the magazine and the calibre of the rounds that go in it. Many modern handguns use a double-stacking system that increases capacity at the cost of a chunkier weapon. There is a limit to how wide a handgun grip can be before it becomes unusable.

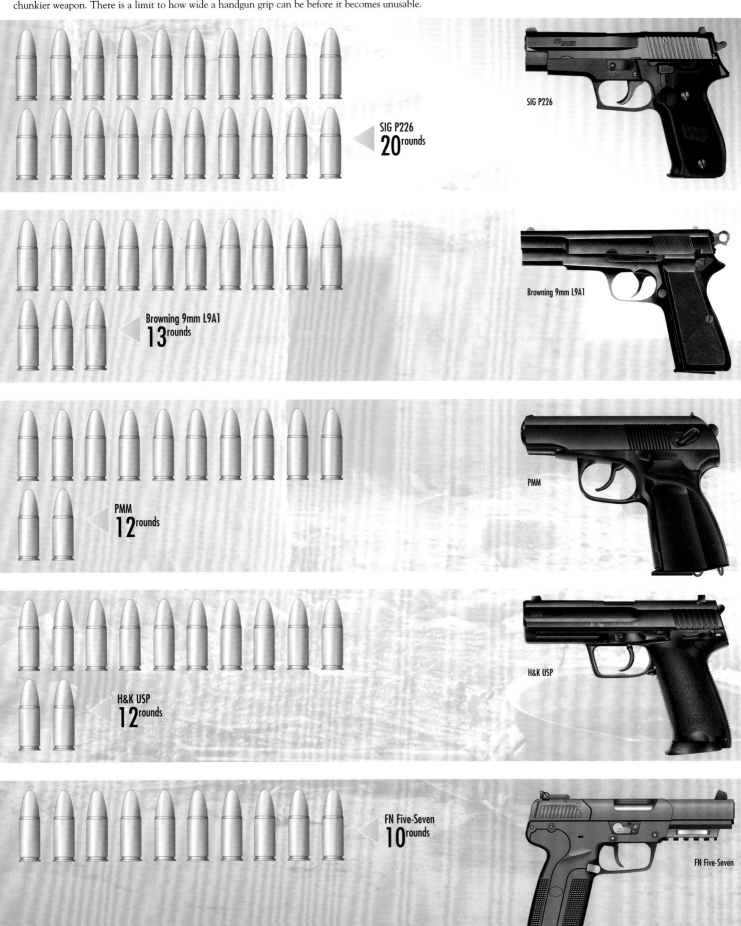

SIG P226
20 rounds

SIG P226

Browning 9mm L9A1
13 rounds

Browning 9mm L9A1

PMM
12 rounds

PMM

H&K USP
12 rounds

H&K USP

FN Five-Seven
10 rounds

FN Five-Seven

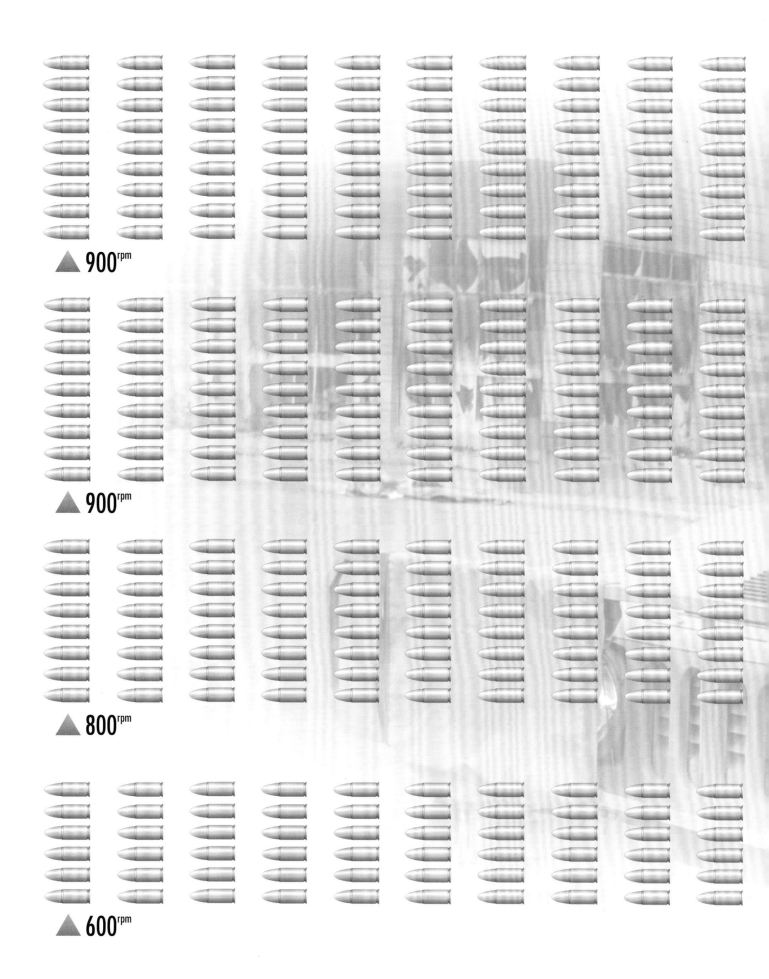

▲ 900^{rpm}

▲ 900^{rpm}

▲ 800^{rpm}

▲ 600^{rpm}

Steyr TMP

H&K MP5K

Agram 2000

Ruger MP-9

Personal Defence Weapons 1

Rate of Fire

▶ **Heckler & Koch MP5K**
▶ **Agram 2000**
▶ **Ruger MP-9**
▶ **Steyr TMP**

The concept of a personal defence weapon is not new. Traditionally, artillery and vehicle crews, engineers and other personnel whose duties do not normally involve direct combat with the enemy were issued a carbine, submachine gun or handgun for self-defence. The modern personal defence weapon (PDW) has the same characteristics as these weapons, i.e. small size and light weight compared with a rifle, but is custom designed to offer an excellent combination of firepower and compactness.

Many PDWs are essentially small submachine guns, and fire handgun-calibre ammunition. The 'industry standard' for most PDWs is 9mm (0.35in) Parabellum, offering a reasonable compromise between stopping power and capacity. Although a PDW's effective range is longer than that of a handgun, it is still short. This is perfectly acceptable – PDWs are intended for self-defence in an emergency, not as standard-issue combat weapons. Intense close-range firepower enables the user to deal with the immediate problem and then seek reinforcements or withdraw from the threat, so rate of fire and magazine capacity are more important than long-range accuracy.

A common feature on many PDWs is some kind of foregrip, which makes a weapon far more controllable in automatic-fire mode. The greater the distance between the user's hands, the more stable the weapon will be, even if it is being used without a shoulder stock. Although most PDWs can be fired one-handed, recoil tends to spray bullets around without a solid two-handed grip, and with a high rate of fire the weapon can be out of ammunition before the user brings it back on target.

Rate of Fire

In most situations where a PDW becomes necessary, the most effective course of action is to pour fire into the threat and withdraw rapidly. Close-range firefights tend to be brutally short, and victory will often go to whoever can get the most rounds downrange the fastest.

Personal Defence Weapons 2

Effective Range

▶ **Heckler & Koch MP7**
▶ **Heckler & Koch UMP**
▶ **Steyr TMP**
▶ **Kinetics CPW**
▶ **FN P90**

H&K MP7

H&K UMP

Steyr TMP

Kinetics CPW

FN P90

The term 'personal defence weapon' describes a role rather than a precise weapon design, and approaches to the concept vary considerably. Many PDWs are very small submachine guns, incorporating heavy firepower into a package little larger than a handgun. Others are larger, up to the size of a traditional submachine gun, and generally have a longer effective range. These types to some extent define the two main PDW concepts – either more potent but not much bigger than a handgun, or somewhat smaller but not hugely less effective (at least at short range) than a rifle.

Effective range is the product of various complex factors including muzzle velocity and barrel length. These largely determine the inherent accuracy of the weapon, but ergonomic factors are arguably more important. It does not matter so much how accurate a PDW is as how reliably its user can get it on target. A shoulder stock aids considerably in longer-range shooting, as does a longer barrel. The general layout of the weapon is also a critical factor: a well-designed weapon is instinctive to aim, which greatly improves effectiveness in short-range point-and-shoot engagements.

The smaller PDWs have a fairly short effective range, not least because they lack the mass to absorb recoil and thus suffer from muzzle climb under automatic fire. The MP7 suffers less from recoil effects due to its specialist 4.6x30mm (0.18x1.2in) ammunition, which produces relatively little recoil and offers both improved penetration and a much higher muzzle velocity than the standard pistol rounds used by many PDWs.

A handgun is better than nothing if a sudden threat emerges, whereas a PDW is much better than nothing. It is still not a battlefield weapon, however, and cannot replace an assault rifle except in security-related tasks and perhaps urban combat.

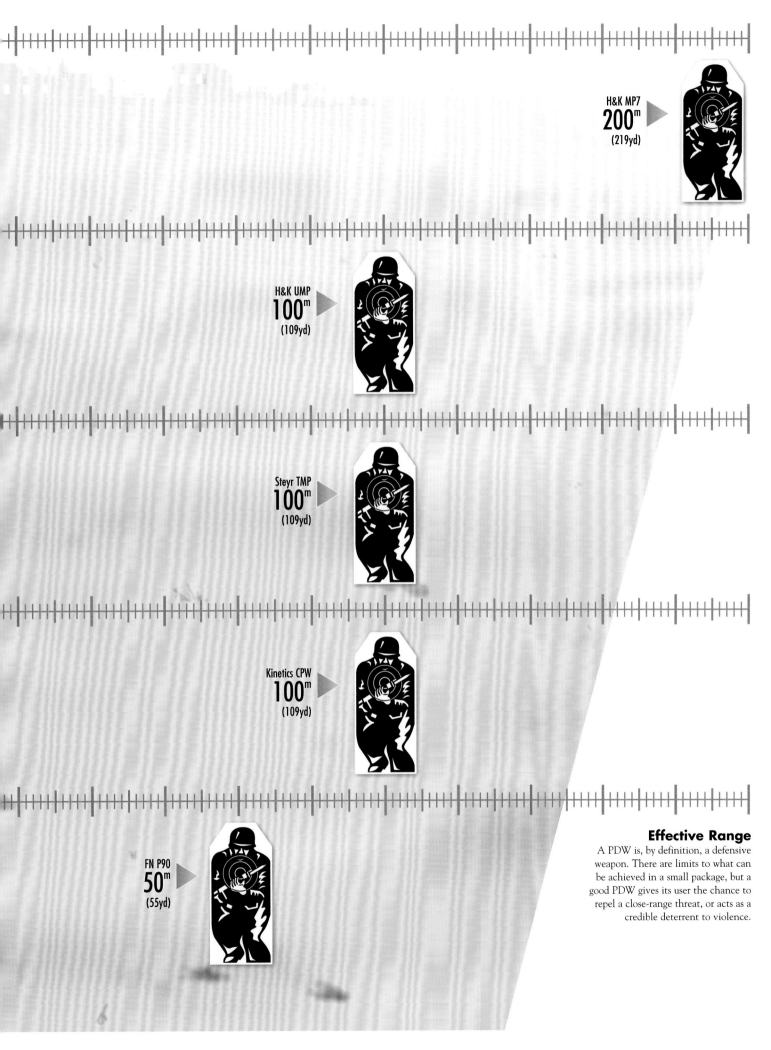

H&K MP7
200ᵐ
(219yd)

H&K UMP
100ᵐ
(109yd)

Steyr TMP
100ᵐ
(109yd)

Kinetics CPW
100ᵐ
(109yd)

FN P90
50ᵐ
(55yd)

Effective Range

A PDW is, by definition, a defensive weapon. There are limits to what can be achieved in a small package, but a good PDW gives its user the chance to repel a close-range threat, or acts as a credible deterrent to violence.

Close Assault Weapons 1

Effective Range and Magazine Capacity

▶ **Heckler & Koch MP5**
▶ **CZW 438 M9**
▶ **USAS-12**
▶ **Benelli M4/M1014**

For the close assault role, the weapons of choice are shotguns and light automatic weapons such as submachine guns. An assault weapon needs to be easily manoeuvred in tight spaces and must be able to lay down heavy firepower to disable any threat quickly. At such a close range, an enemy that manages to shoot back has a good chance of inflicting casualties, so all hostiles need to be taken out of the fight quickly. A burst of pistol-calibre rounds or a shell filled with heavy buckshot will accomplish the task with great effectiveness.

Shotguns such as the semiautomatic M1014 are capable of fairly rapid fire, and each shell has good knockdown power against unarmoured opponents. Shotguns are also useful for breaching doors, but they lack effectiveness against body armour and may not be able to engage multiple targets. Fully automatic shotguns, such as the USAS-12, can do so, and have a large magazine capacity to facilitate automatic fire.

Even so, drums are bulky and more traditional shotguns must be reloaded one shell at a time. Great precision is not necessary using standard shotgun ammunition, and the spread of shot does mean that a hit is likely even with a very hasty attempt. However, shot loses energy fast and becomes ineffective at ranges where a bullet would still be highly lethal.

Submachine guns and fully automatic personal defence weapons offer good firepower and can engage at somewhat longer ranges than shotguns. This is not significant when fighting through a building, but can be critical in a more open environment. Traditional submachine guns typically use 9mm (0.35in) ammunition, against which most body armour is effective.

OPPOSITE, TOP: US Navy SEALs train using H&K MP5 light assault weapons. The H&K MP5 is popular with special forces and police units.

Effective Range

Close combat requires light, short, handy weapons with high firepower, allowing a rapid and devastating response to any threat. An engagement at over 50m (55yd) is unlikely under most circumstances, making both shotguns and light automatic weapons good choices.

H&K MP5 Range **200**ᵐ (219yd)

CZW 438 M9 Range **200**ᵐ (219yd)

H&K MP5

CZW 438 M9

32 rounds

30 rounds

USAS-12 Range
200^m
(219yd)

Benelli M4/M1014 Range
100^m
(109yd)

USAS-12

20 rounds

Benelli M4/M1014

6 rounds

Magazine Capacity

The larger magazine capacity of the light automatic weapons is offset by their greater rate of fire and the fact that it may take several bullets to achieve the same effect as a single shotgun shell. However, changing a detachable magazine is much quicker than reloading the internal tube magazine of a traditional shotgun.

Close Assault Weapons 2

Weight

▶ **Heckler & Koch MP5**
▶ **CZW 438 M9**
▶ **USAS-12**
▶ **Benelli M4/M1014**
▶ **FN P90**

Close assault weapons are normally used by specialist assault units, and by security forces optimized for short-range combat in an urban area. In both cases, personnel need to be able to move quickly, and must be as little encumbered as possible by their equipment.

Heavy weapons are tiring to use, especially when making rapid movements between the rooms of a building and constantly changing the weapon's position. They are also slow to come onto target, which can be a crippling deficiency in a situation where a threat may suddenly appear at close range, from an unexpected angle or from cover.

Submachine guns and personal defence weapons, firing small-calibre ammunition, tend to be very light but may require several rounds to put down a target that might be instantly disabled by a shotgun shell. Conversely, shotguns must, of necessity, be robust, which requires a fairly heavy construction. To this must be added the weight of ammunition – shotshells weigh much more than pistol cartridges, and while this is offset by a smaller capacity in traditional shotguns, weapons such as the USAS-12 carry a lot of weight in their drum magazines.

Spare drums are also bulky to carry and heavy, limiting the amount of ammunition that can be carried into action. Given the lethality of a fully automatic shotgun, this may not be too much of a drawback. Indeed, though ammunition capacity may be an issue for any close assault weapon, the question of how much can be carried by the user is less of a problem.

Protracted firefights are uncommon in a close-assault situation: fighting is intense and lethal, and tends to be over very quickly. How much ammunition is in the weapon is more of a consideration than how many spare magazines are carried.

FN P90
2.8kg
(6.2lb)

CZW 438 M9
2.7kg
(6lb)

kg
2.80

FN P90

kg
2.70

CZW 438 M9

H&K MP5
3.08kg
(6.8lb)

Benelli M4/M1014
3.8kg
(8.4lb)

USAS-12
5.5kg
(12.1lb)

Weight

Modern lightweight materials have made it possible to create lighter weapons than previously, but there are some components such as the barrel and firing mechanism that still have to be made from high-quality steel. There is thus a practical limit to how light a weapon can be made.

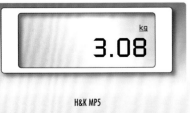

kg
3.08

H&K MP5

kg
3.80

Benelli M4/M1014

kg
5.50

USAS-12

Muzzle Velocity

The amount of harm done by a bullet depends on its kinetic energy, which is determined by its mass and the square of its velocity. High velocity is thus a critical factor, but a certain amount of mass is needed for a round to remain effective.

948m/sec
(3110ft/sec)

940m/sec
(3084ft/sec)

930m/sec
(3051ft/sec)

900m/sec
(2953ft/sec)

884m/sec
(2900ft/sec)

Assault Rifles 1

Muzzle Velocity

▶ **M16A4**
▶ **L85A2**
▶ **QBZ-03**
▶ **AK-107/108**
▶ **Colt M4 Carbine**

M16A4

L85A2

QBZ-03

AK-107/108

Colt M4 Carbine

Assault rifles fire an intermediate cartridge, which is smaller than a battle-rifle round and therefore has a lower mass with which to damage the target. This is compensated for by a high muzzle velocity, which not only increases the round's hitting power but also accuracy, range and penetration of body armour or cover.

A high muzzle velocity allows the weapon to be fired in a very flat trajectory, enabling the user to point-and-shoot at ranges where accuracy with some weapons would require using and adjusting the sights. A high-velocity round also reduces the distance a moving target can travel between trigger pull and impact, which further contributes to the likelihood of a hit.

Assault-rifle ammunition tends to be similar the world over. The M16A4, M4 carbine and L85A2 all fire the standard NATO 5.56x45mm (0.219x1.8in) cartridge, while the Chinese QBZ-03 uses a marginally larger and heavier 5.8x42mm (0.228x1.65in) round. The AK-107 uses a lighter 5.45x39mm (0.215x1.54in) round, while the AK-108 variant uses NATO-compatible ammunition. The performance of these various rounds is remarkably similar in a combat scenario.

The muzzle velocity achieved by a weapon is determined by the amount of propellant in the cartridge, the weight of the bullet and the length of the barrel it is fired through. A light bullet accelerates faster than a heavy one, and a long barrel increases the time during which the bullet is being pushed by expanding propellant gases, i.e., the time during which it accelerates. Thus the M16A4 and the M4, which fire the same round, achieve a significantly different muzzle velocity.

OPPOSITE: This US infantryman is armed with an M4 carbine, which has replaced the M16 as the standard US longarm in recent years. The M4 has an effective range of 400m (437yd) and is fitted with a 30-round box magazine.

Assault Rifles 2

Rate of Fire

▶ **M16A4**
▶ **L85A2**
▶ **QBZ-03**
▶ **AK-107/108**
▶ **Colt M4 Carbine**

The assault rifle emerged as a result of experience in World War II, when urban and mechanized combat became increasingly prevalent. Troops moving in and out of vehicles need a light, short weapon that requires less room to manoeuvre. The same applies to personnel engaged in urban operations. Long-range accuracy is less useful than the ability to lay down withering firepower in response to a threat that emerges suddenly at close range. A lightweight weapon can be brought into action quickly and need only be accurate out to 300–400m (328–437yd). Combat beyond this range is unlikely.

Rate of fire is extremely important in this sort of combat, as it increases the chance of hitting a hostile with enough rounds to put him down before he can shoot back. A burst can be 'walked' onto a target and multiple hits are far more likely to stop an opponent than a single one. Conversely, automatic fire can result in a prodigious expenditure of ammunition, and troops that spray bullets all over the countryside risk running short when it really counts.

Automatic fire is hard to control, resulting in a lot of misses. The main problem is 'muzzle climb', where recoil pushes the barrel up and away from the target. However, controlled, aimed bursts of automatic fire are extremely effective when limited to a particular target. A high rate of fire can be an advantage when attempting accurate burst fire, as it ensures that the whole burst leaves the weapon before it moves too far off target.

OPPOSITE: A US Marine aims an M16A4 fitted with an M203 grenade launcher. The modern assault rifle is a mature weapons system which can be integrated with a range of accessories. Advanced sighting systems give the individual soldier a significant advantage at longer ranges, while an underbarrel grenade launcher gives the squad some indirect fire-support capability against well-dug-in targets.

The assault rifle permits entire squads to lay down suppressing fire, where previously this was a job for support weapons. This makes fire-and-movement tactics more effective and less hazardous for the personnel involved.

100 rpm

60 rpm

45 rpm

40 rpm

40 rpm

Rate of Fire

The theoretical rate of fire for a weapon is based on its cyclic rate – the speed with which it can chamber and fire rounds from its magazine. This takes no account of the time required to reload the magazine. The M16A4 has a cyclic rate of more than 700 rounds per minute, but on a semiautomatic setting it is more likely to achieve around 60 rounds per minute. A trained rifleman using the Garand can fire 16–24 aimed rounds per minute.

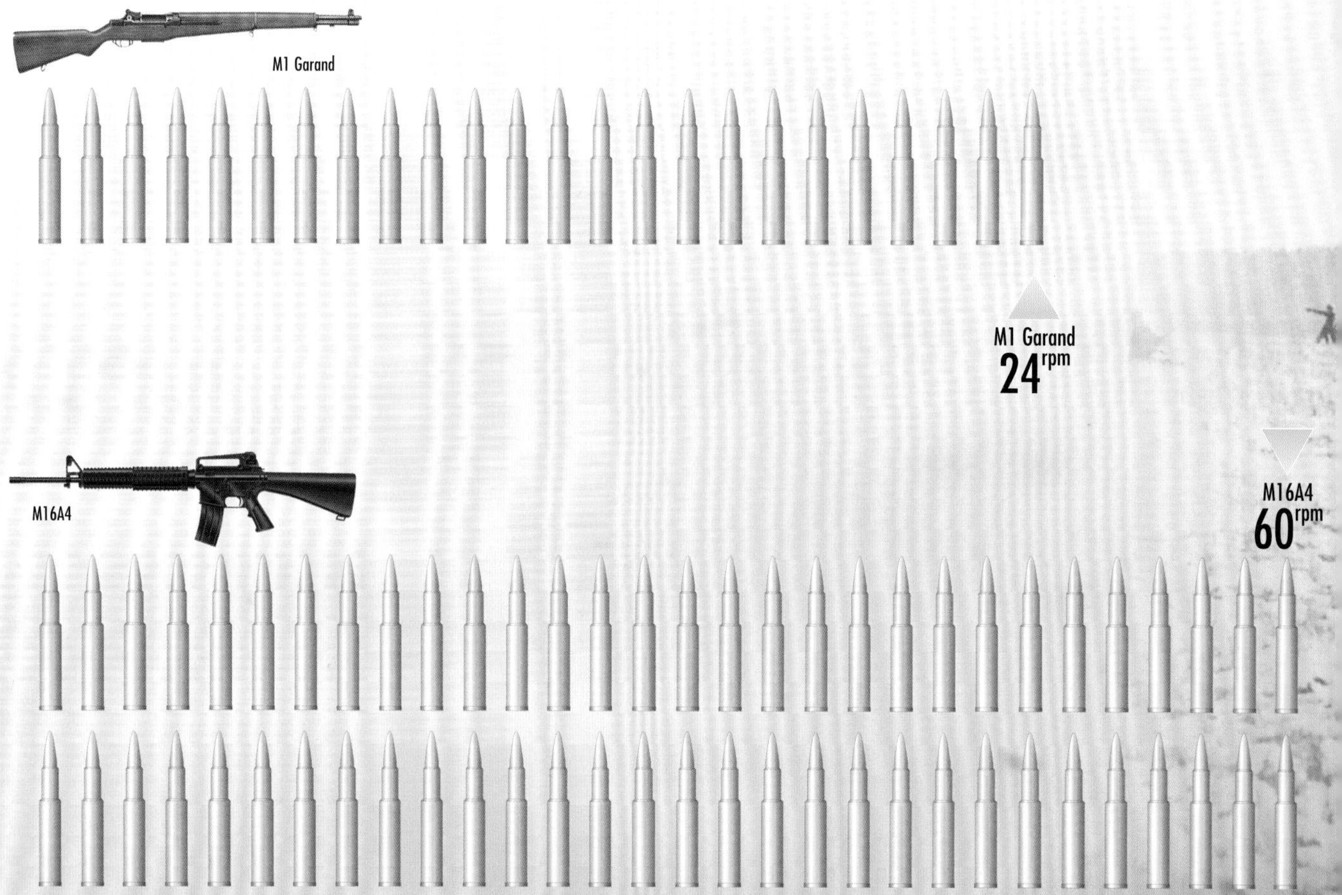

M1 Garand

M1 Garand
24^{rpm}

M16A4

M16A4
60^{rpm}

Effective Range

The M1 Garand is theoretically capable of shooting out to 3200m (3500yd) according to some sources. Its effective range is more realistically stated as 400m (437yd), which is much further than most soldiers can shoot accurately with iron sights.

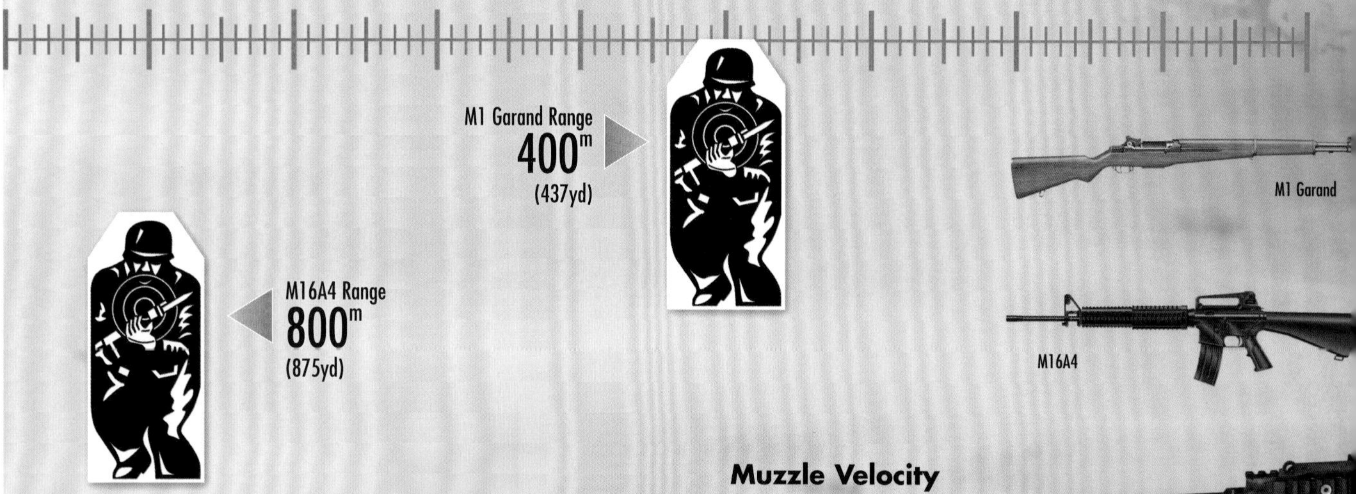

M1 Garand Range
400^m
(437yd)

M16A4 Range
800^m
(875yd)

M1 Garand

M16A4

Muzzle Velocity

The high muzzle velocity of the M16A4's 5.56x45mm (0.219x1.8in) round is offset by its tendency to lose energy more quickly than the heavier 7.62x51mm (0.3x2in) round fired by the Garand.

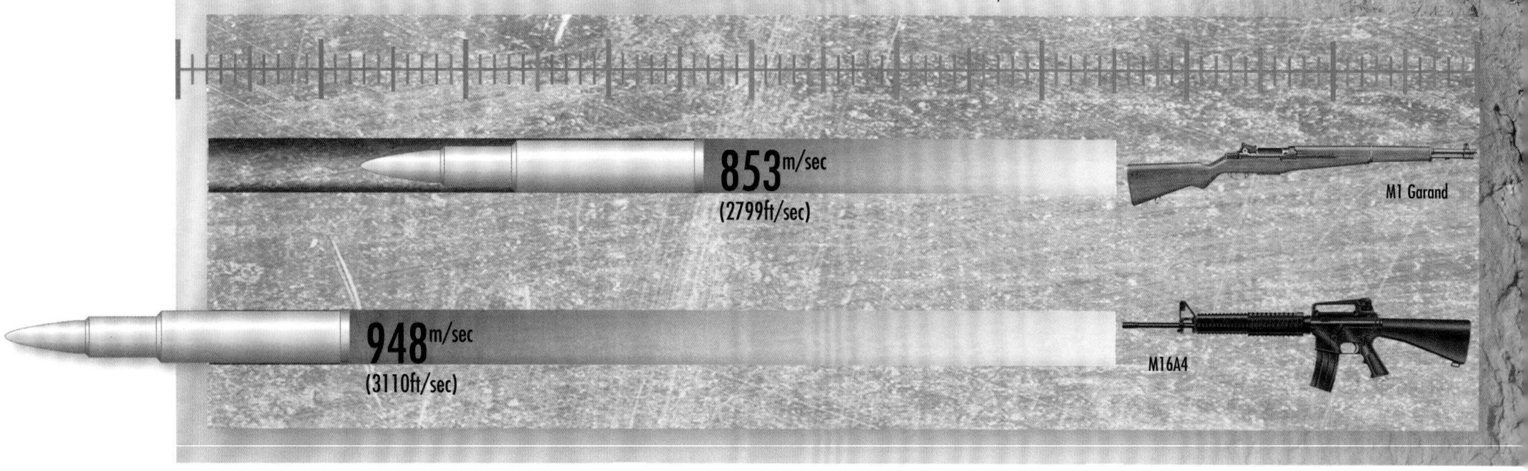

853^{m/sec}
(2799ft/sec)

M1 Garand

948^{m/sec}
(3110ft/sec)

M16A4

WWII versus Modern Infantry Rifles

Rate of Fire, Effective Range and Muzzle Velocity

▶ **M1 Garand**
▶ **M16A4**

In the early years of the twentieth century, the standard infantry weapon was a bolt-action rifle accurate out to several hundred metres. Individual marksmanship and large numbers of riflemen offset a low rate of fire. The M1 Garand was the first semiautomatic rifle to be adopted by the US armed forces, and provided each infantryman with an enormous superiority over personnel armed with bolt-action weapons. Every bit as rugged and accurate as the standard rifles of the day, the Garand could shoot more rapidly and be quickly reloaded with a new en bloc clip of ammunition.

However, even semiautomatic weapons were at a disadvantage in urban terrain when they came up against hostiles armed with submachine guns. An intermediate-calibre weapon was needed, capable of engaging accurately at a respectable range but offering fully-automatic firepower for a close-quarters engagement. The assault rifle came to dominate the battlefield, and led to today's M16A4 rifle.

In addition to fully automatic fire when needed, the M16A4 also has a vastly greater ammunition capacity than the M1, and its detachable magazine offers quicker reloading than the Garand's clip-loading system. Its chief advantage, perhaps, is its adaptability. The M16A4 can be quickly and easily fitted with a range of accessories, including advanced optical sights, a vertical foregrip, a grenade launcher, a tactical light or even a laser sight. Although not intrinsically part of the rifle, these accessories enable the user to tailor it to a variety of specialist applications, improving effectiveness in the chosen role whilst retaining all-round capability.

LEFT: At about 90 per cent of the length and 80 per cent of the weight of an M1 Garand (see above left), the M16A4 is handier and less tiring to carry. However, once accessories such as a telescopic sight are considered, the infantryman's load has not changed much in the decades since the M1 was phased out.

Bullpup Assault Rifles 1

Effective Range and Magazine Capacity

▶ **FAMAS F1**
▶ **QBZ-95**
▶ **SAR-21**
▶ **FN F2000**
▶ **IMI Tavor TAR21**

A 'bullpup' rifle has the feed mechanism behind the trigger group rather than in front of it as a conventional rifle does. The magazine well and part of the action are located in the stock, making a folding stock impossible but greatly reducing the overall length of the weapon. This permits troops to carry a weapon which has the same accuracy as a full-sized rifle yet is short and handy. This is an advantage in urban combat or for mechanized troops who must mount and dismount from vehicles. The term 'bullpup' may have been adopted from the name of an experimental post-World War II weapon, but whatever its origins it has come to apply to all weapons of this type.

The bullpup design did not become common until the late twentieth century, and has not supplanted the conventional rifle, as there are advantages to both traditional and bullpup configurations. The primary drawback with bullpup weapons is that they can only be fired from one shoulder (usually the right), due to the location of the ejection port. Certain designs, such as the FAMAS assault rifle and the Israeli Tavor TAR-21, overcome this by allowing the bolt and ejection port cover to be swapped, turning the weapon into a left-handed version.

The bullpup design is an evolution of the factors that gave rise to the assault rifle. Most combat takes place at ranges of less than 300m (328yd), so although long-range accuracy is useful at times, it is not the primary factor in assault-rifle design. For the typical infantry soldier, heavy firepower at a modest range is the most important feature of an assault rifle, backed up by reliability, ease of handling and lightness.

Magazine Capacity

A magazine capacity of about 30 rounds is the 'industry standard' for most assault rifles. Indeed, many use standardized magazines based on those developed for the M16 family of rifles.

300m

FAMAS F1 Range
300ᵐ
(328yd)

25 x 5.56mm (0.219in) rounds

400m

QBZ-95 Range
400ᵐ
(437yd)

30 x 5.8mm (0.228in) rounds

SAR-21 Range
460ᵐ
(503yd)

30 x 5.56mm (0.219in) rounds

FN F2000 Range
500ᵐ
(547yd)

30 x 5.56mm (0.219in) rounds

IMI Tavor TAR21 Range
550ᵐ
(601yd)

30 x 5.56mm (0.219in) rounds

Effective Range

Although most combat is a matter of suppressive automatic fire or short-range point-and-shoot, the ability to accurately hit a target at several hundred metres remains a desirable feature in an infantry weapon.

L85A2

Muzzle Velocity

Minor differences in the construction of an assault rifle can cause variations in muzzle velocity. Chief among these is the length of the barrel. Within normal limits, a variation of a few metres per second will not greatly affect the accuracy or hitting power of a bullet.

940m/sec
(3084ft/sec)

IMI Tavor TAR21

910m/sec
(2986ft/sec)

FN F2000

900m/sec
(2953ft/sec)

L85A2 Weight: 4.13kg (9.1lb)

IMI Tavor TAR21 Weight: 3.27kg (7.2lb)

FN F2000 Weight: 3.6kg (7.9lb)

Bullpup Assault Rifles 2

Muzzle Velocity and Weight

▶ **L85A2**
▶ **FN F2000**
▶ **IMI Tavor TAR21**

The modern bullpup assault rifle, despite its futuristic appearance, represents an evolution rather than a revolution in weapon design. Plastic and lightweight alloys began to replace traditional steel and wood as early as the 1960s, though early attempts at plastic components could be brittle in cold conditions. The earliest bullpup assault rifle to be widely adopted, the Steyr AUG, entered service in 1979 and rapidly proved itself as a reliable and robust infantry weapon. With the concept proven, further development was assured and led to today's advanced rifles.

These weapons differ from previous generations of infantry rifles in more ways than their configuration. Construction uses advanced, strong but weight-saving materials which create a robust but lightweight weapon, and many rifles are designed either with a built-in optical sight or the capacity to fit one easily.

Such devices permit faster target acquisition and more accurate shooting than traditional iron sights. The design process uses modern ergonomic research, resulting in a weapon that is well balanced and easy to use under the stress of combat.

However, no weapon is better than its ammunition permits it to be, and most bullpup rifles are built around cartridges that have been in service for decades. This is largely dictated by logistical considerations: a change to a new ammunition type would be expensive and wasteful of existing stockpiles. There are weapons that use new cartridges, some with an extremely high muzzle velocity, but most mainstream rifles are built around existing ammunition such as the NATO standard 5.56x45mm (0.219x1.8in) round.

Weight

An assault rifle is inevitably going to be a fairly heavy piece of kit, especially once the weight of ammunition is considered. Modern weapons are constructed of lightweight materials to reduce weight, but one of the chief advantages of a bullpup weapon is the balance point, lying close to the user's body, which makes the weapon feel lighter than it actually is.

Conventional Assault Rifles 1

Effective Range and Calibre

▶ **AN-94**
▶ **INSAS**
▶ **FX-05 Xiuhcoatl**
▶ **Heckler & Koch G36**

The conventional assault rifle was not displaced by bullpup weapons. Indeed, many users find that a conventional layout offers more advantages than a bullpup, and have retained an existing design. In some cases, this is due to the evolution of an existing weapons system. For example, the US armed forces use variants of the M16 family, and the M4 carbine which is derived from it, and prefer to create ever more advanced variants of a proven weapons system than to replace it with an entirely new weapon.

The Heckler & Koch G36 and the visually similar FX-05 Xiuhcoatl drew on concepts used in previous generations of assault rifles, combining proven systems with new materials to create an advanced version of the traditional rifle. The INSAS was derived from the immensely successful Russian AK series of weapons, and incorporated concepts from other weapons including the FN FAL, which it replaced in service. It is chambered for NATO standard 5.56x45mm (0.219x1.8in) ammunition, which has become the standard assault-rifle cartridge in much of the world.

Conversely the AN-94, which was intended to become the new Russian service weapon, was built around the 5.45x39mm (0.215x1.54in) round and magazines used by the existing AK-74 but is a highly innovative design. Among its features is the ability to deliver a two-round 'burst' at an incredibly high cyclic rate, effectively putting out two bullets instead of one. This is intended to aid penetration and stopping power without affecting accuracy. The weapon is also capable of more conventional automatic fire.

Effective Range

Effective range is, to a great extent, a theoretical concept. The weapon itself might be able to put a bullet where it is aimed at several hundred metres, but other than in the hands of a highly trained marksman this will not be achieved. It is a very rare soldier who can shoot accurately at his weapon's theoretical maximum range.

AN-94 Calibre
5.45mm
(0.215in)

Calibre

The traditional 5.56x45mm (0.219x1.8in) and 5.45x39mm (0.215x1.54in) rounds have proved themselves a satisfactory balance of lightness, accuracy and stopping power at the ranges where an assault rifle is effective. Heavier and lighter rounds have been put forward, but have never achieved widespread popularity.

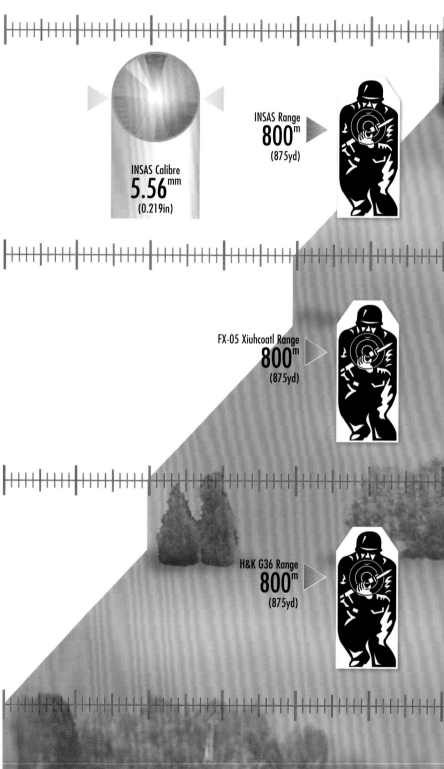

INSAS Calibre
5.56mm
(0.219in)

INSAS Range
800m
(875yd)

FX-05 Xiuhcoatl Range
800m
(875yd)

H&K G36 Range
800m
(875yd)

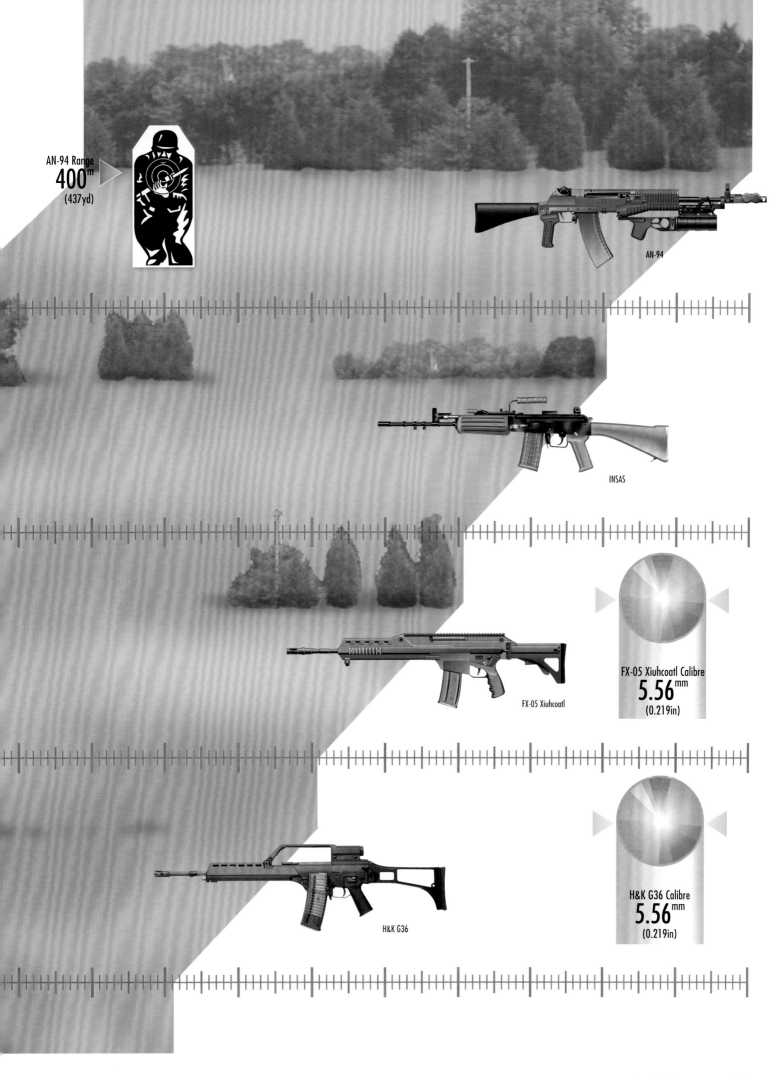

AN-94 Range
400m
(437yd)

AN-94

INSAS

FX-05 Xiuhcoatl Calibre
5.56mm
(0.219in)

FX-05 Xiuhcoatl

H&K G36 Calibre
5.56mm
(0.219in)

H&K G36

Heckler & Koch G36

H&K G36 Range
800^m
(875yd)

AN-94

AN-94 Range
400^m
(437yd)

Beretta SC70/90

Effective Range

The ability to put bursts of automatic fire into a reasonably tight area at long range is an important factor in assault-rifle design, as it allows the whole squad to lay down suppressive fire rather than leaving this task to a support weapon. In this role, a balance between accuracy and volume of fire is more important than long-range precision.

Beretta SC70/90 Range
400^m
(437yd)

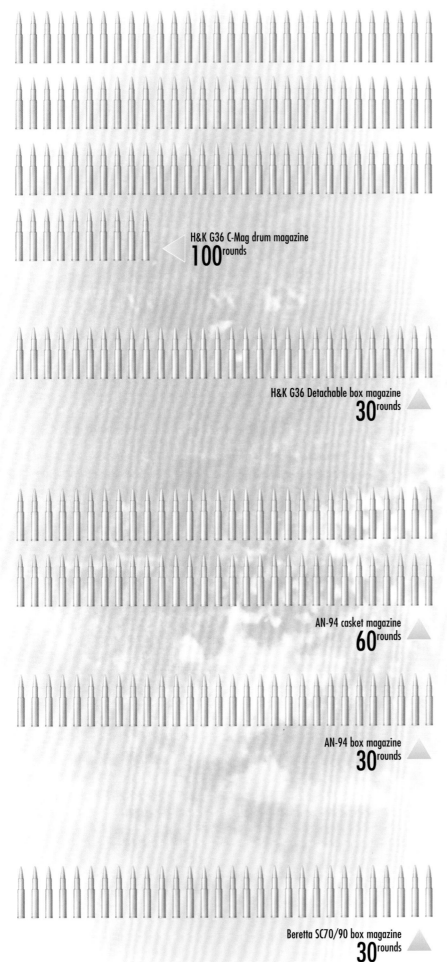

H&K G36 C-Mag drum magazine
100rounds

H&K G36 Detachable box magazine
30rounds

AN-94 casket magazine
60rounds

AN-94 box magazine
30rounds

Beretta SC70/90 box magazine
30rounds

Conventional Assault Rifles 2

Effective Range and Magazine Capacity

▶ **Heckler & Koch G36**
▶ **AN-94**
▶ **Beretta SC70/90**

Automatic fire eats up a lot of ammunition. When conducting suppressive fire at medium to long range, it is usually possible to take cover and reload, though this reduces the amount of fire going downrange at any given moment. In a closer-range engagement, the number of rounds remaining in a magazine can be a matter of life and death. One way to ensure a suitable amount of ready ammunition is tactical loading, whereby the soldier reloads his weapon with a fresh magazine at every opportunity, even if he has only fired a few shots.

An alternative is to use high-capacity magazines that hold far more than the standard 30 rounds. There are two general types of large-capacity assault-rifle magazines. One is the 'casket' type, which is wider than a standard box magazine at the bottom. This allows far more ammunition to be carried in a magazine of the same length, by stacking the rounds so that they overlap. This gives a 'quad-stack' at the base, tapering to a dual-stack similar to some pistol magazines and finally to a single round presented at the magazine lips.

A drum-type magazine does not overlap rounds as much, though many use a double column. A drum magazine simply fits more length into the same volume by curling the feed mechanism around, and a C-Mag-type drum takes this one step further by using paired drums on opposite sides of the weapon, feeding into a common column that fits into the weapon's magazine well. The Heckler & Koch G36 can carry up to 100 rounds with the C-Mag-type drum configuration, while the AN-94 can also fit a 60-round casket magazine, as well as the more conventional 30-round box magazine.

Magazine Capacity

High-capacity magazines increase the individual soldier's firepower, but they are heavy and can make the weapon clumsy compared with one using a conventional box magazine. Stoppages can also be an issue with complex feed devices – if your life depends on your weapon functioning when you need it, then you may be better off with half as many rounds but solid reliability.

Effective Range

As a general rule, effective range is greater with larger-calibre weapons, though other factors such as the length of the weapon's barrel also affect performance over long distances.

5 4 3 2 2 3 4 5

AK-103 Range
300ᵐ
(328yd)

5 4 3 2 2 3 4 5

AICW Range
500ᵐ
(547yd)

5 4 3 2 2 3 4 5

SIG 716 Range
600ᵐ
(656yd)

Magazine Capacity

The downside of using larger-calibre ammunition is additional weight and size, which may lead to a reduced ammunition capacity.

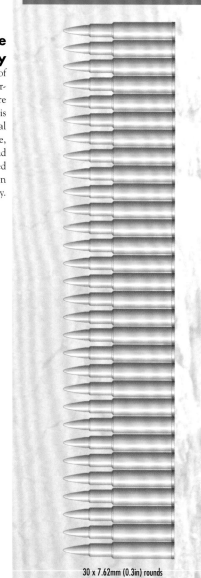

30 x 7.62mm (0.3in) rounds

30 x 5.56mm (0.219in) rounds

20 x 7.62mm (0.3in) rounds

Conventional Assault Rifles 3

Effective Range and Magazine Capacity

► **AK-103**
► **AICW**
► **SIG 716**
► **FN SCAR-H**
► **SR88A**

FN SCAR-H Range
600ᵐ
(656yd)

SR88A Range
800ᵐ
(875yd)

20 x 7.62mm (0.3in) rounds

30 x 5.56mm (0.219in) rounds

The requirements of modern infantry and special-operations units are always changing, and weapons developed to meet the needs of a previous generation may not always be appropriate to the current situation. Experience during and since World War II showed that an intermediate-calibre assault rifle was ideal for most combat situations, and that most combat troops did not need to engage at long range other than with suppressing fire. Recent experience in Afghanistan and other theatres has challenged this, and there is a current need for accurate fire at longer ranges.

Thus there has been a move back towards the heavier 'battle-rifle' cartridge, which retains its energy and resists wind effects better than an intermediate-calibre round at longer ranges. The AK-103 returns to the original 7.62x39mm (0.3x1.54in) round used by its ancestor, the AK-47, while advanced Western rifles such as the SIG 716 and SCAR-H use the 7.62x51mm (0.3x2in) round favoured for general-purpose machine guns and many sniper rifles.

This move is by no means universal. Advanced weapons such as the Australian Advanced Infantry Combat Weapon use the intermediate 5.56mm (0.219in) round, not least to reduce the weight of a weapons system that has two barrels, firing mechanisms and feed devices. Many armed forces continue to make exclusive use of 5.56mm (0.219in) weapons for their infantry, though environmental factors make it highly unlikely that a typical solider can shoot accurately at even half of the weapon's theoretical effective range.

OPPOSITE: A US Navy SEAL aims an FN SCAR-H assault rifle somewhere in Afghanistan, 2010. Introduced in 2009, the Special Operations Combat Assault Rifle (SCAR) is a modular system that includes a sniper rifle, close-quarters-battle rifle and grenade launcher. It has been adopted by many special forces, including those of the US military.

Effective Range

Sniping weapons have a lot in common with top-end hunting rifles, but hunters rarely shoot at the extremely long distances expected of a military sniper. Achieving a single-shot kill at several hundred metres requires a specialist weapon and an equally rare marksman.

Sako TRG22 Range
1100ᵐ
(1203yd)

SIG SSG3000 Range
1000ᵐ
(1094yd)

L96A1 Range
1000ᵐ
(1094yd)

SIG SSG3000

L96A1

Sako TRG22

5 x 7.62mm (0.3in) rounds

10 x 7.62mm (0.3in) rounds

10 x 7.62mm (0.3in) rounds

Bolt-action Sniper Rifles

Effective Range and Magazine Capacity

- ▶ **SIG SSG3000**
- ▶ **L96A1**
- ▶ **Sako TRG22**
- ▶ **Steyr HS .50**
- ▶ **L115A3**

Opinion is divided on the relative merits of bolt-action and semiautomatic sniper rifles. Although semiautomatics offer faster follow-up shots and are more useful if the sniper team becomes involved in a close-range contact, bolt-action weapons have the advantage that they do not eject brass until the action is worked, which aids concealment. Bolt-action weapons are also slightly more accurate at long range, as there is no movement of internal parts until the bullet is long gone.

Sniping weapons are made to an extremely high standard and are accurate out to far greater ranges than ordinary rifles. They will send a bullet further than their listed effective range, but at such great distances there will be considerable variation in the point of impact even if the weapon is kept perfectly steady, so sniping beyond the weapon's effective range is a matter of luck as well as skill. Very large-calibre weapons such as the HS .50 and L115A3 can achieve a greater effective range by a combination of heavy bullet and high velocity, but there is an upper limit to how powerful a rifle can be and remain portable by a sniper team.

For most applications, a 7.62x51mm (0.3x2in) round is entirely adequate, though specialist 'match-grade' ammunition is preferred as it has the least variation between individual cartridges. A miniscule imperfection may not be very relevant at 100m (109yd), but in a 1000m (1094yd) shot it can cause significant deviation from the expected flight path and therefore a miss. The flight time of a bullet at long range is sufficiently long that many targets will be out of sight before a second shot can be taken.

Steyr HS .50 Range
1500ᵐ
(1640yd)

L115A3 Range
1500ᵐ
(1640yd)

Magazine Capacity

Bolt-action sniper rifles tend not to have a large magazine capacity, and in general one is not needed. A sniper will generally take at most three or four extremely precise shots before his target takes cover or is downed. In any situation where the sniper needs a greater ammunition capacity, he is using the wrong weapon entirely and is probably in serious danger.

Steyr HS .50

L115A3

1 x 12.7mm (0.5in) round

5 x 8.58mm (0.338in) rounds

OPPOSITE, TOP: Wearing the standard desert combat-dress uniform, a British infantryman aims an L96A1 sniper rifle.

Semi-automatic Sniper Rifles

Weight

▶ **L129A1**
▶ **Dragunov SVD**
▶ **Stoner SR-25**
▶ **M14 Enhanced Battle Rifle**
▶ **M110**

Modern semiautomatic weapons are only slightly less intrinsically accurate than bolt-action equivalents, and at medium ranges this may not affect the shot significantly. There are times when a sniper may have the opportunity to engage several targets in rapid succession, and for such situations a semiautomatic weapon with a high magazine capacity offers very significant advantages. Semiautomatic weapons of this sort are often issued to designated marksmen, who are not fully trained snipers but infantrymen trained and equipped for long-range shooting. The presence of a specialist marksman and his weapon provides an infantry unit with the means to hit back at distant hostiles.

L129A1
4.5kg
(9.9lb)

Dragunov SVD
4.68kg
(10.3lb)

kg
4.50

L129A1

kg
4.68

Dragunov SVD

Stoner SR-25
4.88kg
(10.8lb)

M14 Enhanced
Battle Rifle
5.1kg
(11.2lb)

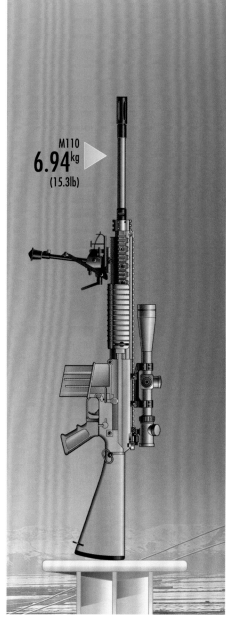

M110
6.94kg
(15.3lb)

Weight

A sniping weapon must be robust enough to retain its accuracy despite the inevitable knocks it will receive while in the field. This requires a fairly heavy weapon to start with, on top of which the sniper must also carry a range of specialist equipment including camouflage and vision devices.

4.88 kg

Stoner SR-25

5.10 kg

M14 Enhanced Battle Rifle

6.94 kg

M110

OPPOSITE: Two US soldiers carry out overwatch duties somewhere in Afghanistan. It is not uncommon for the primary sniper of a team to carry a bolt-action rifle, as here, while his observer (in the foreground) is armed with a semiautomatic weapon that can be used for both sniping and short-range firepower.

1 An Afghan Army marksman aims a Dragunov SVD rifle.

Anti-materiel Rifles

Effective Range and Magazine Capacity

▶ **McMillan TAC-50**
▶ **Accuracy International AS-50**
▶ **Barrett M82A1**
▶ **Harris M87R**
▶ **Gerard M6**

The original anti-materiel rifles were created in World War I as a response to tanks, and though advances in armour protection soon rendered them ineffective, the concept of a powerful rifle capable of destroying hard targets remained viable. Today's anti-materiel rifles are sophisticated long-range weapons which can, in many cases, deliver specialist ammunitions such as explosive or armour-piercing rounds.

Anti-materiel weapons are intended for use on high-value equipment such as radar and communications sets, and are used by some law-enforcement agencies to disable fleeing vehicles. The US Coast Guard uses powerful 12.7mm (0.5in) rifles to cripple the engines of suspected drug-running boats that refuse to stop.

BELOW: A US Army sniper team uses an M82A1 anti-materiel rifle. Large-calibre weapons can be used for extremely long-range sniping and counter-sniping operations, or to eliminate key enemy personnel such as artillery observers and commanders who venture a little too close to the battle area.

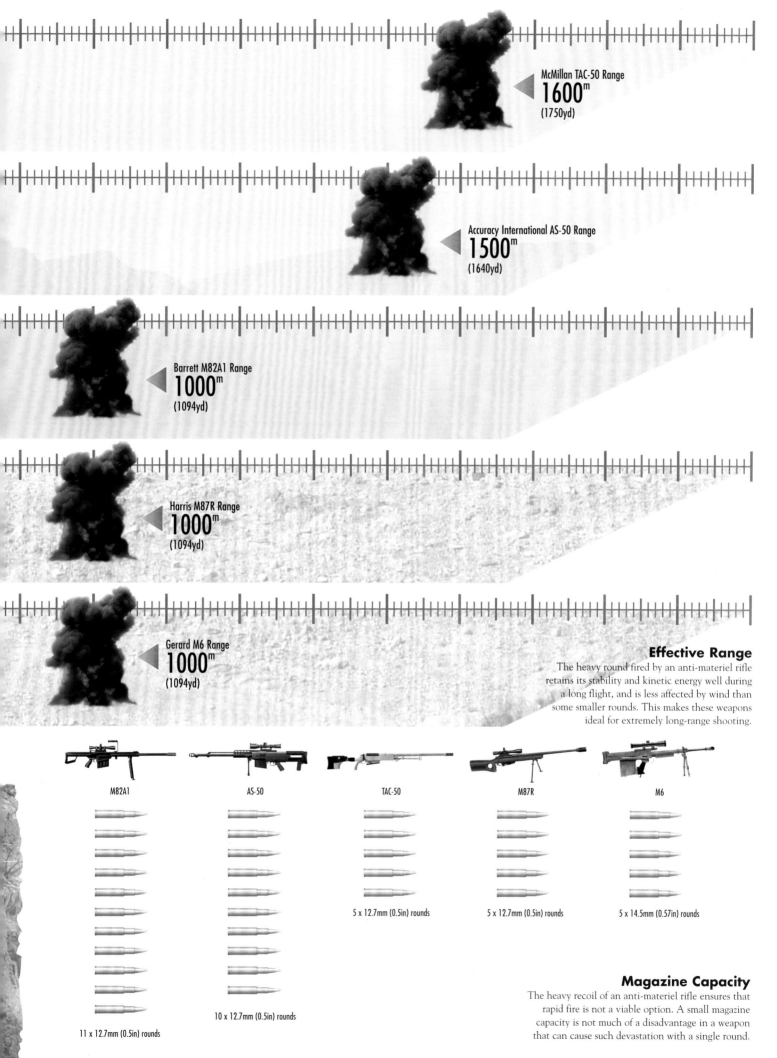

McMillan TAC-50 Range
1600^m
(1750yd)

Accuracy International AS-50 Range
1500^m
(1640yd)

Barrett M82A1 Range
1000^m
(1094yd)

Harris M87R Range
1000^m
(1094yd)

Gerard M6 Range
1000^m
(1094yd)

Effective Range

The heavy round fired by an anti-materiel rifle retains its stability and kinetic energy well during a long flight, and is less affected by wind than some smaller rounds. This makes these weapons ideal for extremely long-range shooting.

M82A1	AS-50	TAC-50	M87R	M6

5 x 12.7mm (0.5in) rounds

5 x 12.7mm (0.5in) rounds

5 x 14.5mm (0.57in) rounds

10 x 12.7mm (0.5in) rounds

11 x 12.7mm (0.5in) rounds

Magazine Capacity

The heavy recoil of an anti-materiel rifle ensures that rapid fire is not a viable option. A small magazine capacity is not much of a disadvantage in a weapon that can cause such devastation with a single round.

One-second Burst Weight of Fire

A light support weapon allows an infantry squad to bring intense firepower to bear when it is needed.
In a close-range engagement, the ability to get a lot of lead moving downrange fast is often more important
than sustained-fire capability.

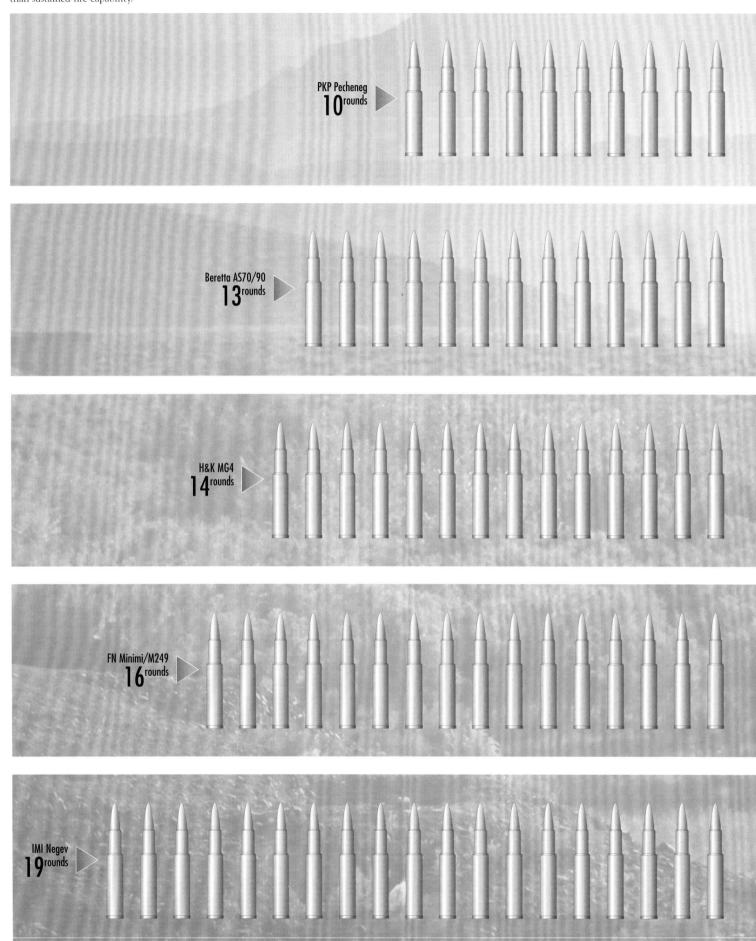

PKP Pecheneg
10 rounds

Beretta AS70/90
13 rounds

H&K MG4
14 rounds

FN Minimi/M249
16 rounds

IMI Negev
19 rounds

PKP Pecheneg

Beretta AS70/90

H&K MG4

FN Minimi/M249

IMI Negev

Light Support Weapons 1

One-second Burst Weight of Fire

▶ **PKP Pecheneg**
▶ **Beretta AS70/90**
▶ **Heckler & Koch MG4**
▶ **FN Minimi/M249**
▶ **IMI Negev**

Light support weapons are intended to increase an infantry squad's firepower without reducing its mobility. Some are effectively overgrown assault rifles, while others are true machine guns with a quick-change barrel and large-capacity feed device. Light support weapons often lack the sustained firepower of a general-purpose machine gun, but they have the advantage of being integral to a squad and thus always available. Light support weapons are normally chambered for the same ammunition used by the rest of an infantry squad, and many can share magazines with riflemen if larger-capacity feed devices are not available. This creates an effective but lightweight weapons system that augments the squad's capabilities without imposing an increased logistics burden.

BELOW: The RPK-74 is simply an AK-74 rifle with a heavier barrel and larger magazine. It has served in the light-support role for decades but is being supplanted by more modern weapons, such as the PKP Pecheneg.

Light Support Weapons 2

Effective Range

▶ **PKP Pecheneg**

▶ **Beretta AS70/90**

▶ **Heckler & Koch MG4**

▶ **FN Minimi/M249**

▶ **IMI Negev**

It is often possible to tell at a glance which design philosophy drove a given light support weapon's development. Those that were developed from general-purpose machine guns are usually belt-fed (though the belt may be carried in a box or drum) and have a quick-change barrel. These two factors greatly increase sustained-fire capability, as an overheated barrel can be changed and allowed to cool, and the weapon itself has the ammunition capacity to cause such overheating.

Light support weapons derived from assault-rifle designs have the advantage of commonality with the infantry squad's individual weapons. They are generally little more than an assault rifle with a heavier barrel to dissipate heat better, plus other accessories tailored to the machine-gun role. This simplifies logistics and maintenance, and permits any soldier to take over the weapon if its user is disabled. Another key advantage is the ability to share ammunition. Even if the light support weapon normally uses a drum or large-capacity box magazine, if it can take the same magazines as the rifle it was derived from, it can stay in action when its own ammunition supply is exhausted.

However, light support weapons tend to sacrifice range and sustained firepower for lightness and mobility. Assault-rifle-calibre light support weapons have an effective range that is little longer than that of a standard rifle.

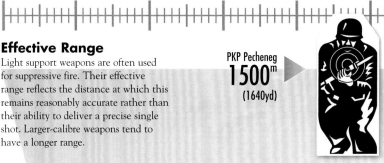

Effective Range

Light support weapons are often used for suppressive fire. Their effective range reflects the distance at which this remains reasonably accurate rather than their ability to deliver a precise single shot. Larger-calibre weapons tend to have a longer range.

PKP Pecheneg
1500ᵐ
(1640yd)

BELOW: The M249 is clearly a machine gun rather than an overgrown rifle but remains light enough to move with an infantry squad. It is normally fed from a 200-round belt carried in a box.

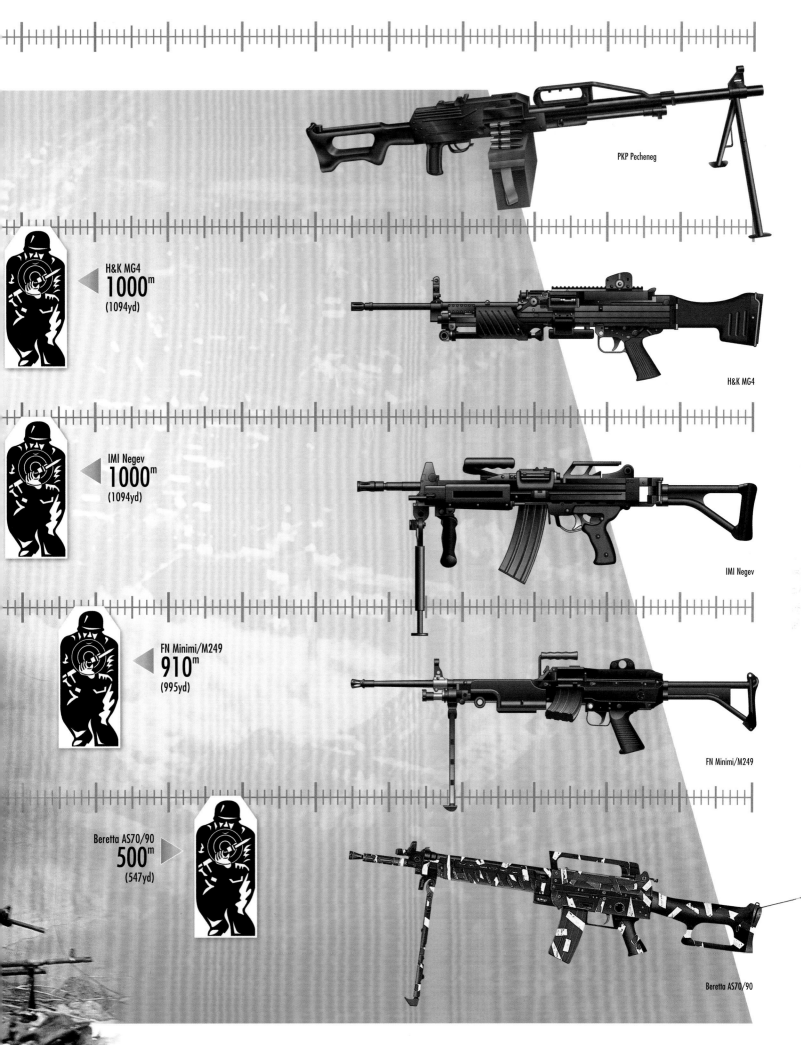

PKP Pecheneg

H&K MG4
1000^m
(1094yd)

H&K MG4

IMI Negev
1000^m
(1094yd)

IMI Negev

FN Minimi/M249
910^m
(995yd)

FN Minimi/M249

Beretta AS70/90
500^m
(547yd)

Beretta AS70/90

Effective Range

Most soldiers cannot shoot accurately at long distances under the stress of combat, so extremes of accuracy are wasted except in weapons intended for use by highly trained specialists.

McMillan TAC-50
1600^m
(1750yd)

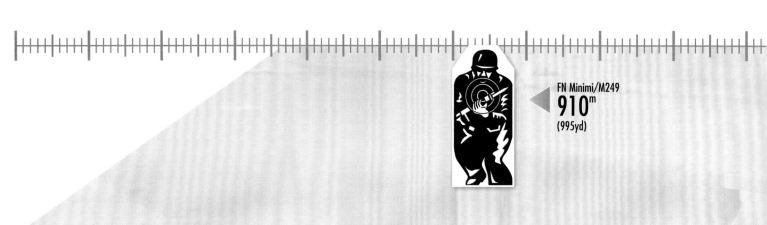

FN Minimi/M249
910^m
(995yd)

Colt M4 Carbine
600^m
(437yd)

LEFT: A US soldier practises on the firing range with an M4 carbine.

Weapons Types Compared

Effective Range

▶ **McMillan TAC-50**
▶ **FN Minimi/M249**
▶ **Colt M4 Carbine**
▶ **Browning 9mm L9A1**

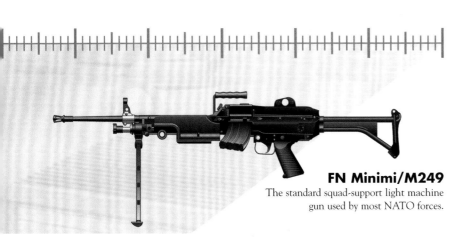

McMillan TAC-50
Used as a long-range sniper weapon
and anti-materiel rifle.

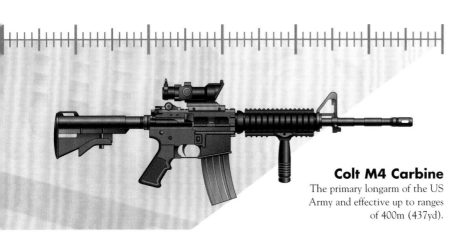

FN Minimi/M249
The standard squad-support light machine
gun used by most NATO forces.

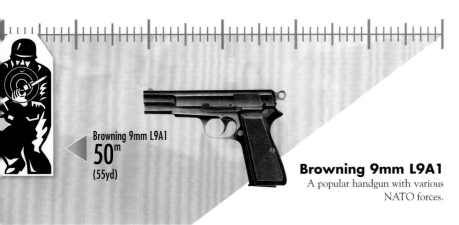

Colt M4 Carbine
The primary longarm of the US
Army and effective up to ranges
of 400m (437yd).

Browning 9mm L9A1
50ᵐ
(55yd)

Browning 9mm L9A1
A popular handgun with various
NATO forces.

There is no such thing as a 'best weapon'; each has a role to play and offers its user significant advantages in the right situation. A side arm such as the Browning L9A1 is useless at even fairly modest ranges, but there are circumstances where it is the only weapon that can be carried. A handgun leaves one hand free to open doors and undertake other tasks during room-clearance operations, and can be brought to bear in tight spaces. However, it is normally carried as a back-up or by personnel who do not expect to encounter the enemy directly.

The assault rifle and the squad automatic weapon (SAW) are the workhorse tools of the infantry soldier, offering a good balance of firepower and mobility. Their performance at all ranges is respectable, stopping power is acceptable and they will not slow down a squad's movement too much. The M4 carbine is a lightened and shortened assault rifle optimized for fairly close-range combat, in much the same way as the FN Minimi/M249 serves as a light fire-support platform. There are weapons with more hitting power or accuracy available, but these tend to be heavier, which may be a disadvantage in a combat environment where mobility and a rapid response time is critical.

Specialist tools such as anti-materiel rifles – for example the TAC-50 – are sometimes the only ones that can get a certain job done. However, they are bulky and heavy, and while the stopping power of a squad armed with 12.7mm (0.5in) rifles would be incredible, these weapons are simply not suited to highly fluid combat conditions.

Weapons Types

Infantry weaponry has evolved to suit the needs of modern combat, which typically takes place at ranges of at most 300m (328yd). The average infantry soldier needs a weapon that is most effective at this distance or less, where a few seconds of intense combat can be decisive. Long-range engagement is a task for specialists with precision weapons, or for an entire squad using automatic fire.

Infantry Soldiers Compared

Weapons and Effective Range

▶ **US Infantryman**
▶ **Taliban Insurgent**

The equipment of combat personnel – be they highly trained regular soldiers or insurgent gunmen – tends to be surprisingly similar the world over. The assault rifle, in some form or another, has become the standard all-round infantry weapon. It offers a good balance of weight against firepower, effective range and ease of use. Assault rifles are also relatively cheap and easy to obtain, an important consideration when arming a large number of troops or militia fighters.

Taliban insurgents tend to be armed with weapons from the Soviet era, not least because large numbers of these weapons were obtained as a result of the Soviet involvement in Afghanistan in the 1980s. AK assault rifles in particular are very common on the international market – legally and otherwise – and are built under licence or copied in small workshops worldwide.

The typical Taliban insurgent is lightly equipped other than his personal weapon, but stocks of support weapons such as RPD machine guns, SVD marksman rifles and the infamous RPG-7 are available.

Where support weapons are patchily available to some Taliban militia groups, the US military has a formal policy of ensuring that infantry are properly supported with squad automatic weapons, general-purpose machine guns and other heavy weapons, with additional support on call. In addition, the US infantryman's personal equipment includes vision aids, body armour and an array of useful tools. This level of support is a powerful force-multiplier that can enable US forces to defeat large numbers of gunmen whose weapons are, at first glance, apparently equivalent.

Effective Range

The capabilities of a weapon are less important than what a soldier can do with it. Properly supported by suppressing fire, an infantryman can move to a good position or take a carefully aimed shot, making best use of his weapon's capabilities, where an individual gunman may be forced to merely 'spray and pray'.

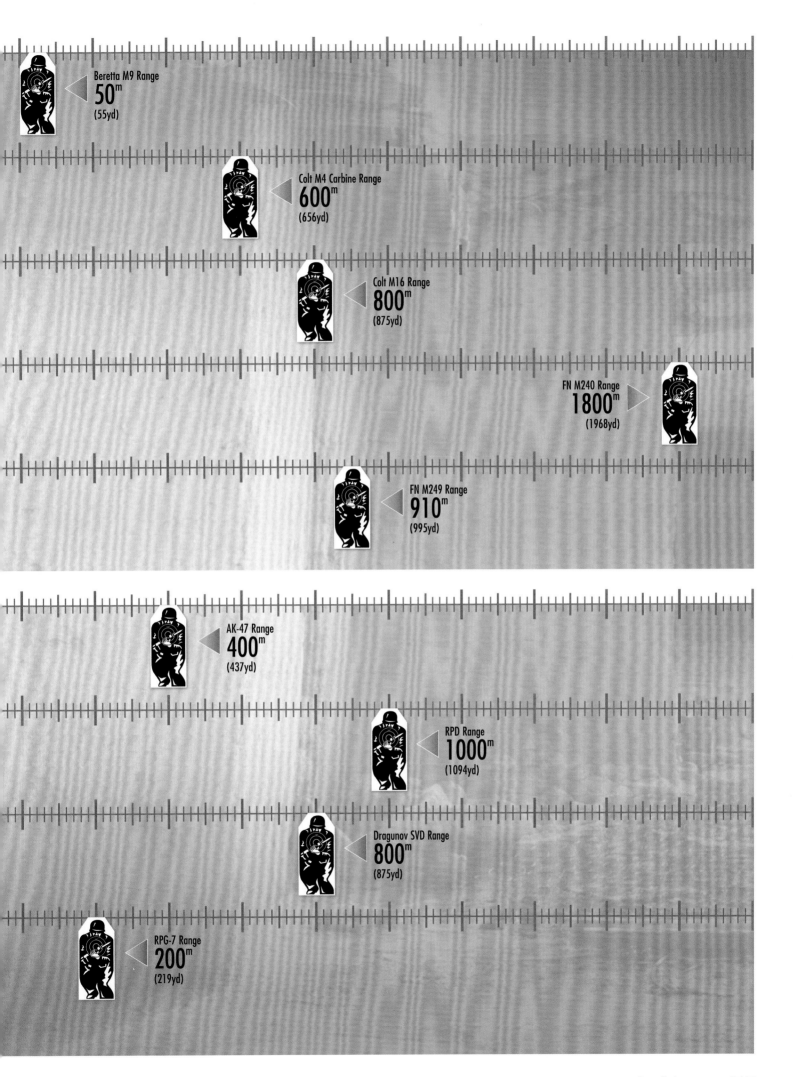

Beretta M9 Range
50^m
(55yd)

Colt M4 Carbine Range
600^m
(656yd)

Colt M16 Range
800^m
(875yd)

FN M240 Range
1800^m
(1968yd)

FN M249 Range
910^m
(995yd)

AK-47 Range
400^m
(437yd)

RPD Range
1000^m
(1094yd)

Dragunov SVD Range
800^m
(875yd)

RPG-7 Range
200^m
(219yd)

Glossary

Air Superiority: A situation whereby enemy air forces can only operate at a significant disadvantage. This may be a local and temporary situation, or may be a more widespread advantage.

Airborne Early Warning (AEW): An aircraft mission using specialist platforms equipped with powerful radar to detect air threats as early as possible and to direct the response.

Anti-Materiel Rifle: A powerful rifle intended for attacking enemy equipment rather than personnel, such as radar or radio systems, vehicles and other military hardware.

Anti-Submarine: Any vessel, aircraft or weapons system intended primarily for use against enemy submarines. Also, the missions carried out by these platforms, which can include detection and tracking without making an attack.

Armoured Fighting Vehicle (AFV): A heavily armoured combat vehicle designed to directly engage the enemy with a powerful weapon; i.e., a tank.

Artillery: Heavy support weapons, normally firing in a high ballistic arc. Artillery may be of the gun (tube) type or launch rockets. Some guided-missile launchers are considered to be artillery weapons.

Automatic, Fully Automatic: A weapon that will continue to load and fire as long as the trigger is held and ammunition is available, using the energy of firing each round to load the next.

Ballistic Missile: A missile that follows a ballistic arc. Ballistic missiles are unpowered for much of their flight, relying on velocity gained while their motor is running.

Ballistics: A body of science connected with the behaviour of projectiles. **Internal Ballistics** is concerned with conditions inside the weapon as it is fired; **External Ballistics** is concerned with the projectile in free flight; **Terminal Ballistics** deals with the behaviour of the projectile once it has struck the target.

Bolt-Action: A bolt-action weapon may be a single-shot design, loaded directly into the chamber, or fed from a magazine. Either way, the spent case is not ejected until the bolt is manually worked. This makes it easy to collect spent cartridge cases but does not allow very rapid shooting.

Bullet Drop: The effect of gravity on a bullet in flight will cause it to drop. Over a short distance this is insignificant but on a long shot, bullet drop must be compensated for or the round will fall short.

Burst Fire: Firing an automatic weapon in controlled 'bursts' of a few rounds is termed 'burst fire'. Some weapons are designed to be capable of firing a burst (usually three rounds) per pull of the trigger in the manner of an automatic weapon, then cutting off the burst until the trigger is released and pulled again.

Cannon: Traditionally, a smoothbore artillery piece used for more or less direct fire. The term 'cannon' is today applied to large-calibre tank guns as well as lighter direct-fire guns. Many such lighter weapons – in the 20–50mm (0.79–2in) range – are capable of automatic fire and are referred to as automatic cannon.

Close-In Weapons System (CIWS): A last-ditch defensive weapon fitted to warships. A CIWS is intended to shoot down missiles and aircraft that have evaded other defences. Most are rapid-fire gun systems, but short-range missile systems do exist.

Cluster Bombs: Small explosive/fragmentation devices carried by a larger warhead, often dispersed by an airburst over the target area.

Concealment: Concealment is any obstacle or object that will obscure sight but provides little protection from a bullet or shell fragment to anyone concealed behind it.

Cover: Cover, or 'hard cover', is any obstacle or object that will protect someone behind it from a bullet or shell fragment.

Cruise Missile: A large missile designed to fly much like an aircraft, rather than following a ballistic trajectory.

Designated Marksman: An infantry soldier trained to a high standard of accurate shooting and equipped with a precision rifle, but who lacks the advanced stealth and concealment skills of a fully trained sniper. Designated Marksmen generally operate with and as part of an infantry force.

Electronic Countermeasures (ECM): Defensive measures intended to prevent enemy missiles from being successfully guided to the target. ECM attempts to confuse the missiles' guidance systems using electronic emissions. Also known as 'jamming'.

Flash Hider: A short extension to the barrel of a weapon which conceals the 'flash' of burning muzzle gases as they leave the barrel. A flash hider makes it much harder for hostiles to visually pinpoint a sniper's location by observing his muzzle flash, and also aids in night shooting by preserving the sniper's night vision.

Guided Missile: A self-propelled munition with a guidance system. This may be internal, such as GPS guidance or thermal seeing, or can be external such as a manually guided system using a camera aboard the missile.

Hard Point: A station on the wing or fuselage of an aircraft where munitions, fuel tanks or equipment pods can be carried.

High Explosive (HE): A warhead intended to cause damage by exploding. This results in blast damage and secondary fragmentation from objects destroyed in the explosion.

Incendiary: A weapon designed to cause damage by burning at high temperatures.

Infantry Fighting Vehicle (IFV): An armoured vehicle designed to transport infantry personnel and to support them with machine guns, automatic cannon and/or missiles.

Lead: It is necessary to 'lead' a moving target, to compensate for the time taken for the bullet to reach it. Greater lead is required for a fast-moving or distant target.

Lock Time: The delay between squeezing the trigger and the weapon actually discharging, a term derived from the firing mechanism of early firearms, known as a 'lock'; e.g. flintlock, matchlock.

Marksman: A skilled and accurate shooter, or a holder of a formal shooting qualification at that level. Many police snipers could perhaps be more correctly termed marksmen as they lack the stealth and concealment skills of a military sniper, but by convention they are usually termed snipers.

Munitions: A general term for bombs, rockets, missiles, shells and other weapons that are expended in use.

Muzzle Brake: A device by which some of the muzzle gases generated by firing a weapon are redirected in a direction which counteracts recoil and the tendency of the muzzle to rise. A muzzle brake makes a powerful weapon much more controllable.

Muzzle Energy: The kinetic energy of a bullet as it leaves the weapon. Kinetic energy is a function of the velocity and mass of the bullet; greater muzzle energy equates to a shorter flight time, a flatter ballistic trajectory and greater wounding potential.

Payload: The part of a bomb, missile or rocket that carries out the task assigned to it. Payloads can be destructive, such as explosives or incendiary materials, or can be non-lethal, such as smoke or propaganda leaflets.

Rifling: Spiral grooves cut into the barrel of a weapon to spin the bullet as it passes. A spun bullet is gyroscopically stabilized and therefore much more accurate than otherwise. Any longarm which possesses a rifled barrel is technically a 'rifle'.

Rocket Artillery: A long-range bombardment system using self-propelled rockets. Conventionally, rockets are unguided, but some systems now use GPS guidance, which arguably makes them guided missiles instead.

Semi-automatic: Also referred to as 'self-loading', a semiautomatic weapon uses the energy of firing a round to eject the spent case and chamber the next. This may not always be desirable for a sniper, as spent cases may land outside his cover or attract attention as they reflect light. The internal workings of the weapon can also disrupt the aim point.

Small Arms: Firearms light enough to be carried by infantry soldiers. The term is sometimes also loosely applied to support weapons such as man-portable anti-tank-missile launchers and machine guns, though this is technically incorrect.

Smoothbore: A non-rifled weapon such as a musket or shotgun, which fires a ball or group of pellets without imparting spin stabilization. Smoothbore weapons are inherently inaccurate and generally unsuitable for sniping, though a long barrel can somewhat compensate.

Sniper: The leader and main shooter of a sniper team, or a graduate of a formal sniper-training school. Also, a military marksman trained to observe and shoot from a concealed position. In popular usage, any person who uses a rifle from a concealed position.

Submunitions: A group of smaller payloads carried in a missile, rocket or shell. Commonly submunitions are lethal, such as mines, cluster bombs and the like.

Support Weapons: Relatively light weapons intended to support infantry from fairly close range. Support weapons include grenade launchers, machine guns and anti-tank weapons.

Suppressing Fire: High-intensity fire from small arms or support weapons aimed at the general area of the target. Suppressing fire is mainly intended to force the enemy to seek cover instead of shooting back, though it can cause casualties.

Suppressor: A device designed to reduce the noise of a weapon being fired by trapping some of the muzzle gases. It is not possible to completely 'silence' a weapon; there will always be some sound upon firing. A more popular term is a 'silencer'.

Tube Artillery: Traditional gun and howitzer systems, firing a heavy shell. Conventionally, howitzers have a short barrel and fire in a high arc, while guns have a longer barrel, higher muzzle velocity and fire in a flatter arc. Modern guns generally blur the line between these distinctions.

Trajectory: The path followed by a bullet in flight, which will be a ballistic arc caused by the interaction of the projectile's muzzle energy, gravity and air resistance.

Unitary Warhead: A single warhead; e.g., an explosive device, rather than a number of submunitions.

Vulcan: A multiple-barrel weapon in which the barrels are rotated to the firing position in turn, then cool and are reloaded as they move around. Also referred to as 'Gatling' or 'rotary' weapons.

Warhead: The destructive payload of a weapon such as a bomb, missile or rocket.

Index

Page numbers in *italic* indicate a photo.